CONVERSE IN THE SPIRIT

CONVERSE IN THE SPIRIT

William Blake, Jacob Boehme, and the Creative Spirit

KEVIN FISCHER

Madison • Teaneck
Fairleigh Dickinson University Press

Associated University Presses
2010 Eastpark Boulevard
Cranbury, NJ 08512

The paper used in this publication meets the requirements of the American National Standard for Permanence of Paper for Printed Library Materials
Z39.48-1984.

Library of Congress Cataloging-in-Publication Data

Fischer, Kevin, 1963-
Converse in the spirit : William Blake, Jacob Boehme, and the creative spirit /Kevin Fischer.
p. cm.
Includes bibliographical references and index.
ISBN 0-8386-4006-0 (alk. paper)
1. Blake, William, 1757–1827—Philosophy. 2. Böhme, Jakob, 1575–1624—Influence. 3. English poetry—German influences. 4. Creation (Literary, artistic, etc.) 5. Philosophy in literature. 6. Mysticism in literature. 7. Visions in literature. 8. Philosophy, German. I. Title.
PR4148.P5F57 2004
821'.7—dc22

2003015336

PRINTED IN THE UNITED STATES OF AMERICA

For Kerry

In my Brain are studies and Chambers filld with books and
pictures of old which I wrote and painted in ages of Eternity.
before my mortal life and whose works are the delight
and Study of Archangels.

—Blake

Contents

Acknowledgments

I wish to thank Routledge and Princeton University Press for permission to use material from Coleridge, Samuel Taylor, *Biographia Literaria: or Biographical Sketches of my Literary Life and Options*, edited by James Engell and W. Jackson Bate, 2 bks., vol. 7 of *The Collected Works of Samuel Taylor Coleridge,* London: Routledge and Kegan Paul, 1983.

I wish to thank Constable and Robinson Ltd. for permission to use material from Boehme, Jacob, *De Electione Gratiae and Quaestiones Theosophicae,* translated by John Rolleston Earle, London: Constable, 1930.

Every effort has been made to locate all persons having any rights in the material appearing in this book, and to secure permission from the holders of such rights. Any queries regarding the use of material should be addressed to the author c/o the publishers.

Introduction

There are many notable similarities between William Blake and Jacob Boehme, affinities that in many ways mark them out as peculiarly kindred spirits. *Converse in the Spirit* explores the relationships and correspondences between their writings. While suggesting in detail the extent of Boehme's influence on the poet, this book intends to breathe life into the dynamic spiritual interplay between their writings, and through this realize the value of studying such individuals in the light of one another. In so doing, it gives a glimpse of the vital importance of a living tradition, of a community of vision and aspiration that provides support, guidance, and inspiration. Accordingly, I also suggest the close and necessary relationship between spiritual and artistic activity, as is conveyed, for instance, in the many correspondences drawn between Boehme's vision and the content of Blake's poetry and prose. This in turn works toward a fuller appreciation of both the spiritual and creative possibilities offered to the reader through an active engagement with Blake and Boehme, an ongoing "converse in the spirit."

It is hard to place Boehme. He was a mystic, a visionary, and a philosopher. At the same time, his thought and vision are imaginative, symbolic and mythopaeic. His work may be seen, as Waterfield proposes, as esoteric psychology or "psychology of the depths."[1] Warren Stevenson has suggested that there is an "avant-garde" aspect to him:[2] it can be argued that in his writings Boehme created his own individual art form. Boehme's and Blake's views of the spiritual are unconventional. Boehme's God, for instance, occupies no place or space, does not exist in time, cannot be thought of and is Nothing. Their mysticism is one that is opposed to a literal belief in an overseeing God in the heavens. For them, such a view reified the divine. As William Law stated, "there is nothing that is supernatural, however mysterious."[3] To regard this another way, for Blake and Boehme everything was supernatural or spiritualized. It is quite possible to have entirely rejected belief in the God of orthodox religion and nonetheless perceive the divine and sacred as Blake and Boehme apprehended it. In fact, this can be as good a point as any from which to start, to understand the living, if elusive spirit that animates their writings.

Both visionaries' works are difficult, and each illuminates the other. However, as Blake's relationship to Boehme was potent and opens up many imaginative and creative possibilities, *Converse in the Spirit* does not set out to present an exhaustive comparative discussion. It would be quite possible to devote an entire book to a single idea or perception, for instance, that appears in the writings of both. While this further suggests the relevance and significance of discussing Blake and Boehme together, it has, therefore, also made certain limitations necessary: comparison with other writers in the esoteric tradition have been kept to a minimum, it has not been possible to deal with all areas in which Blake and Boehme differ, and I have not discussed Blake's visual art or the Freher designs that appear in the "Law" edition of Boehme's works. While previous works have been helpful, I have endeavored as far as possible not to retread ground already sufficiently covered. Such works have in many respects been points of departure for a fuller, more expansive, detailed, and imaginative approach that embraces the practical realities and infinite variety of the inner life. The creative spirit that found expression through Blake and Boehme is of primary importance. All other aims, intentions, or considerations, such as proposals of Blake's "debt" to Boehme, or the significance of Boehme as measured against Blake's other sources, are by comparison and at best of secondary importance.

Abbreviations

Am	*America a Prophecy*
Ann. Bacon	*Annotations to Bacon's "Essays Moral, Economical and Political"*
Ann. Berk.	*Annotations to Berkeley's "Siris"*
Ann. Boyd	*Annotations to Boyd's "Historical Notes on Dante"*
Ann. DLDW	*Annotations to Swedenborg's "Divine Love and Divine Wisdom"*
Ann. DP	*Annotations to Swedenborg's "Divine Providence"*
Ann. HH	*Annotations to Swedenborg's "Heaven and Hell"*
Ann. Lav.	*Annotations to Lavater's "Aphorisms on Man"*
Ann. Ren.	*Annotations to "The Works of Sir Joshua Reynolds"*
Ann. Thorn.	*Annotations to Thornton's "The Lord's Prayer"*
Ann. Wat.	*Annotations to "An Apology for the Bible," by R. Watson*
AoI	*Auguries of Innocence*
ARAO	*All Religions are One*
Aur	*Aurora*
BA	*The Book of Ahania*
BL	*The Book of Los*
BU	*The [First] Book of Urizen*
Clavis	*The Clavis: or, An Explanation of Some Principle Points and Expressions in His Writings*
Conf.	*The Confessions of Jacob Boehme*
DC	*A Descriptive Catalogue of Pictures*
DLJ	*A Description of the Last Judgment*
EG	*The Everlasting Gospel*
EOG	*Of the Election of Grace*
Ep	*The Epistles of Jacob Behmen*
Eur	*Europe a Prophecy*
FQ	*Forty Questions Concerning the Soul . . . Answered*
F. Rev	*The French Revolution*

FZ — *The Four Zoas*
GA — *The Ghost of Abel*
GP — *For the Sexes: The Gates of Paradise*
Inscrip. — *Inscriptions and Notes on or for Pictures*
Jer — *Jerusalem: The Emanation of The Giant Albion*
The Key — *The Key and Other Writings*
Laocoön — *The Laocoön*
Milton — *Milton a Poem in Two Books*
MHH — *The Marriage of Heaven and Hell*
MM — *Mysterium Magnum: or, An Explanation of the First Book of Moses Called Genesis*
NNR — *There Is No Natural Religion*
OCT — *A Treatise of Christ's Testaments, Baptism, and the Supper*
OHP — *On Homer's Poetry*
PA — *Public Address*
Rem — *The Remainder of books written by Jacob Boehme*
SB — *Songs and Ballads*
SL — *The Song of Los*
SoIE — *Songs of Innocence and of Experience*
SP — *Six Theosophic Points and Other Writings*
SR — *The Signature of All Things*
Thel — *The Book of Thel*
TLM — *The Threefold Life of Man*
ToI — *Treatise of the Incarnation*
TP — *The Three Principles of the Divine Essence*
TQ — *Quaestiones Theosphicae*
VDA — *Visions of the Daughters of Albion*
VLJ — *A Vision of the Last Judgment*
WC — *The Way to Christ*

CONVERSE IN THE SPIRIT

PART I

1
Background

In 1575 Jacob Boehme was born to a relatively prosperous farming family[1] in Alt Seidenberg, a village near Görlitz in Silesia. After an elementary education at the village school, he was apprenticed to a shoemaker at the age of fourteen, traveled the country for several years as a journeyman, returned to Görlitz at the age of twenty-four, became a citizen, married, and settled into family life and business, first as a master-shoemaker and then, in later years, as a linen trader. Outwardly, he led what would appear to be a largely normal, unassuming, and unremarkable life. But he was also deeply involved in the spiritual life as a mystic, visionary, and philosopher, looking into the mysteries of God, man, and nature. During his lifetime his convictions drew to him both the attention and support of certain learned and powerful figures and, in the age of religious conflict in which he lived, the disapproval of Lutheran orthodoxy, which led to his being banned from writing, persecution at the hands of the clergy and his neighbors, and brief spells of banishment from his home town.

Since his death he has been a source of inspiration to those interested in the inner life of the spirit, to philosophers, theologians, and artists. Yeats described him as "certainly the greatest of the Christian mystics since the Middle Ages."[2] Novalis, Tieck, Emerson, Carlyle, Franz von Baader, William Law, Goethe, Coleridge, and the Schlegels are among those influenced by him. The theologian Paul Tillich, whose own thought bears the mark of Boehme's insights, suggests that through Schelling's *On Human Freedom*, which is "thoroughly dependent on Boehme's vision," Boehme's "indirect influence reaches Hegel and Schopenhauer, Nietzsche and Hartmann, Bergson and Heidegger."[3] Hegel similarly affirms Boehme's importance in his *Lectures on the History of Philosophy*, acknowledging his own debt: "It was, in fact, through him that philosophy first appeared in Germany with a character peculiar to itself: Boehme stands in exact antithesis to Bacon."[4] For Friedrich Schlegel Boehme was "without doubt . . . the most inclusive, richest, and most many sided of all mystics":

> If it should be found that imagination has far greater share than has enlightened understanding in the development of his genius, it must be con-

> fessed that it is a very poetic imagination that we discover in this strange spirit. Considering him merely as a poet and comparing him with other poets who have attempted to deal with supersensual things, with Klopstock, or Milton, or Dante, it must be admitted that he almost surpasses them in the richness of his fancy and the depth of his feeling, nor is he inferior to them in the beauty of his poetic expressions.[5]

Boehme provided German Romanticism with an antidote to the rationalism of the Enlightenment. Schelling states:

> One cannot avoid saying of Böhme that he is a miracle in the history of humanity and especially in the history of the German mind. If one could ever forget what a treasure of natural profundity of mind and heart is to be found in the German nation, one would only have to remind oneself of Böhme. He is, in his way, just as far exalted above the ordinary psychology by which one seeks to explain him and is as little explicable by it as is mythology.[6]

In England William Law (1687–1762), the great eighteenth-century religious writer whose discovery of Boehme threw him into such a "perfect sweat" that he became his disciple, wrote of the works that had so profoundly affected the latter years of his life: "the true ground of every doctrine and article of Christian faith and practice is there opened in such a ravishing, amazing depth and clearnes of truth and conviction as had never been seen or heard of in any age of the Church."[7] Although Coleridge thought that Boehme was at times subject to "the dreams of his own over excited nerves, the phantoms and witcheries from the cauldron of his own seething fancy,"[8] Boehme had made a sufficient impression upon the poet for him to say that if the German mystic had "received the discipline of education, above all a knowledge which would have guarded him against his own delusions, I scarcely know whether we should have had reason to attribute greater genius even to Plato himself."[9] He "possessed in very truth 'The Vision and the Faculty Divine!'"[10] In *Biographia Literaria* Coleridge emphasizes the impact Boehme made upon him:

> Why need I be afraid? Say rather how dare I be ashamed of the Teutonic theosophist, Jacob Behmen? . . . there exist folios on the human understanding and the nature of man which would have a far juster claim to their high rank and celebrity, if in the whole huge volume there could be found as much fulness of heart and intellect as burst forth in many a simple page of GEORGE FOX, JACOB BEHMEN, and even of Behmen's commentator, the pious and fervid WILLIAM LAW.
>
> The feeling of gratitude which I cherish toward these men, has caused me to digress further than I had foreseen or proposed: but to have passed them over in an historical sketch of my literary life and opinions, would have

> seemed to me like the denial of a debt, the concealment of a boon. For the writings of these Mystics acted in no slight degree to prevent my mind from being imprisoned within any single dogmatic system. They contributed to keep alive the heart in the head; gave me a presentiment that all the products of the mere reflective faculty partook of death, and were as rattling twigs and sprays in winter, into which a sap was yet to be propelled from some root to which I had not penetrated, if they were to afford my soul either food or shelter.[11]

However, while Boehme has inspired such minds and been described by Evelyn Underhill as "one of the most original and astonishing of the Christian mystics,"[12] his very originality and independence, his peculiar subtleties and complexities, coupled with the abstruseness and at times awkwardness of his means of expression have also been a source of confusion and miscomprehension. In *The Way to Divine Knowledge*, William Law highlights this through the character of the learned Academicus:

> though I have been reading for more than two years some one or other of his books with the utmost attention, and I everywhere find the greatest truths of the Gospel most fundamentally asserted, yet presently I am led into such depths as I know not where I am and talked to in such a new, intricate, and unintelligible language as seems quite impossible to be comprehended. Sometimes I almost suspect that the author understood not himself: For I think, if I knew any Truths, though ever so deep or uncommon; yet, if I understand then plainly myself, I could set them before others in the same Plainness, that they appeared to me.[13]

In Durant Hotham's translation (1650) of his brother Charles's pamphlet on Boehme, *Ad Philosphiam Teutonicam Manductio* (1648), he reflects the effect Boehme might have upon his reader:

> As to the . . . author of the Teutonic Philosophy, which you here abbreviate; though you know I alwaies affected it and him, yet durst never saile into the ocean of his vast conceits with my little skull, me thought the reading of him was like the standing upon a precipice or by a cannon shott off, the waft of them lickt up all my brains.[14]

Others have been merely contemptuous. Referring to the Behmenist groups in seventeenth-century England, the Puritan Richard Baxter argued that "Their doctrine is to be seen in Jacob Behmen's books, by him that has nothing else to do than to bestow a great deal of time to understand him that was not willing to be easily understood, and to know that his bombasted words do signify nothing more than before was easily known by common familiar terms."[15] Similarly, John Wesley dismissed Boehme as "sublime nonsense, inimitable bombast, fustian not to be paralleled," while Bishop William Warburton stated that "Behmen's works would disgrace Bedlam at full moon."[16]

Certain affinities may already be seen between Boehme and William Blake, as in the opposition to a fixed dogmatic system, the "poetic imagination," the unorthodoxy, and the concern with forging a vital creative spiritual life. Similar remarks to those made about Boehme may and indeed have been made about Blake. At the same time "the new, intricate, and unintelligible language" that animates Boehme's writings with depth and resonance begins to give a sense of the difficulties involved in gauging the manner and extent of Boehme's influence upon Blake. As the Behmenist Herman Vetterling has suggested, much of the potency of Boehme's vision is not immediately apparent: "The understanding of Boehme comes only by degrees. We begin to read his writings usually with the same ardor that we would begin to read a Chinese puzzle book; in the course of a few years we comprehend a little of what we read; and as we continue our interest grows, our horizon widens, slowly, very slowly, but surely."[17] This observation can also be applied to much of Blake. An adequate understanding of either visionary is only achieved by degrees. This mirrors the struggles each underwent in the creation and development of his vision. In turn, Blake's own understanding and use of Boehme was itself worked out and cultivated over many years. Boehme's presence may be felt in varying degrees throughout Blake's work, from, for instance, the tracts of 1788, *All Religions Are One* and *There is No Natural Religion*, which as Mona Wilson among others has noted "show the impress of Boehme," suggesting "how stimulating and congenial" the German mystic "must have been to the young Blake,"[18] to the refined Behmenist aspects of later writings such as *Jerusalem*. In 1825, in the poet's last few years, Blake was more able than most to appreciate and pay tribute to Boehme, as Henry Crabb Robinson records: "Jacob Boehme was spoken of as a divinely inspired man."[19] Although a brief statement and one of only three existing direct acknowledgments of Boehme's importance, this is significant praise from someone who had devoted his life to the revelation of the divine in man and who believed that "Inspiration and[20] Vision was . . . and now is and I hope will always Remain my Element my Eternal Dwelling Place" (*Ann. Ren.* 660–61).[21]

Comparison of Blake and Boehme reveals some fairly obvious similarities and very probable areas of influence.[22] However, as much of what lies in each is not easily tapped, there is a great deal in Blake's relationship to Boehme that is not readily apparent. This is in part due to the nature of influence as each understood it. As with many of the forces that play a role in forming and directing the life of anyone, its nature is in many respects complex. Often it works subtly, gradually, and at a level beyond immediate recognition, guiding, building upon, reinforcing, and at times rejecting the impact that each encounter with its source has had. Blake and Boehme's view of tradition was one that viewed living personal experience as paramount. It was something to which one contributes rather than being received superficially. Schelling speaks of this in the contrast he draws between those who breathe new life into the spiritual and those who do not:

> One must distinguish Jacob Böhme in whose works all is of the purest and most original nature from another class of mystics in whose works there is nothing living and original but where everything is already corrupted. In this class there belongs especially the well known St. Martin. In him one no longer hears, as in Böhme, the original inspiration, but only the copyist or recorder of another's ideas. . . . That which is still living in Böhme is dead in St. Martin.[23]

Blake himself was not simply a passive recipient of various strands of spiritual thought. In *The Marriage of Heaven and Hell* he makes quite clear how restrictive the approach of a "copyist or recorder" can be, stressing the need for an active and creative role in relation to tradition:

> Swedenborg boasts that what he writes is new; tho' it is only the Contents or Index of already publish'd books. . . .
>
> Now hear a plain fact: Swedenborg has not written one new truth: Now hear another: he has written all the old falsehoods. . . .
>
> Swedenborgs writings are a recapitulation of all superficial opinions, and an analysis of more sublime, but no further.
>
> Have now another plain fact: Any man of mechanical talents may from the writings of Paracelsus or Jacob Behmen, produce ten thousand volumes of equal value with Swedenborg's, and from those of Dante or Shakespear, an infinite number.
>
> But when he has done this, let him not say that he knows better than his master, for he only holds a candle in sunshine. (*MHH* 42–43, pls. 22–23)

Blake regarded Boehme as a "master." Nonetheless a sense of proportion is necessary, as he placed Dante and Shakespeare higher than him. Boehme was not Blake's only influence and quite often might not have been anything approaching a predominant one. Many of his sources offered depths and possibilities that are not readily accessible. Space does not allow for extensive commentary on the various influences that contributed to, for instance, a specific concept or symbol. All the same, this does not mean that the importance of a particular source–of Neoplatonism, Gnosticism, alchemy, Antinomianism or Kabbalism, for example–is denied. In part, each source is valuable in the manner that it relates to, questions, and sheds light on other sources. Although Blake came to view Swedenborg critically, probably at some point between his annotations to *Divine Love and Divine Wisdom* in 1788 and those of 1790 in *Divine Providence*, Swedenborg's continuing influence should not be underestimated. Blake wrote in 1809, "The works of this visionary are well worthy the attention of Painters and Poets; they are foundations for grand things" (*DC* 546). While certain critics such as F. R. Leavis[24] have dismissed the importance of Blake's more esoteric sources, part of his art lay in the way he learned from, interpreted, and created anew what lies at the core of such sources. To deny this view can be to miss the important point that certain of these sources are valuable precisely in the degree that they demand and encourage autonomy and creativity of the individual, and that in this they may illuminate rather than obscure Blake. Blake was clear about where he stood in terms of the potential of others. The "Devil in a flame of fire" states at the beginning of the "Memorable Fancy" that follows on from the naming of "Paracelsus and Jacob Behmen . . . Dante or Shakespear":

> The Worship of God is. Honouring his gifts in other men each according to his genius. and loving the greatest men best, those who envy or calumniate great men hate God, for there is no other God. (*MHH* 43 pls. 22–23)

Greatness and genius may lie in unexpected quarters, among those who are "divinely inspired" and thus able to cast light, "sunshine" on the divine in man. Aware of the possibilities that may lie in disciplines that are usually regarded as quite distinct from artistic activity, Blake's understanding of art is one that extends beyond formal limitations to include all attempts "To open the Eternal Worlds, to open the immortal Eyes / Of Man inwards into the Worlds of Thought: into Eternity" (*Jer* 147, pl. 5, ll. 18–19). He regards true art as a spiritual activity, a creative life that every individual should pursue: "The whole Business of Man Is The Arts and All Things Common." As he also writes in *The Laocoön*, "Christianity is Art": "A Poet a Painter a Musician an Architect: the Man / Or Woman who is not one of these is not a Christian." This view unites the endeavors of the truly creative with Christ, for "Jesus and his Apostles and Disciples were all Artists" (*Laocoön* 273–74). Following Boehme, Blake saw creativity and the exploration of possibility as a central part of life, as one that should be continually broadened. He did not regard the poetry that critics such as Leavis have admired as if it were an activity quite separate from and unrelated to the spiritual efforts of Christians such as Boehme, for "The bounded is loathed by its possessor" (*NNR* 2). It is therefore necessary to distinguish between any personal distaste for esoteric thought per se and the seriousness with which Blake himself regarded it. Edward Larrissy has commented on this:

> Readers do not *need* to read anything: they have always already read something and thus will arrive at some sort of understanding. But, if the question is whether Blake's work as a whole makes reference to the occult tradition, the answer must surely be that it does. Only by some very purist notion of the text can one ignore the hermeticist and neo-Platonic connections evoked by the prophetic books.[25]

In order to mirror and appreciate the spirit of both Blake's and Boehme's work a degree of flexibility and imagination is necessary. J. P. Natoli goes some way to this in his understanding of Blake's relation to tradition:

> What we desire to do is to see Blake's work as fully as possible within its historical and intellectual setting, to perceive concurrent modes of thought and expression and to finally perceive the uniqueness of Blake's own work. While rich descriptions of various analogues cause us to come to Blake with reawakened senses, pronouncements based on the establishment of supposedly unarguable sources cause us to wonder why Blake more than any other author is looked upon as needing buttressing by this or that tradition or individual.[26]

It is quite possible to read widely in Blake's esoteric sources, in the works of figures such as Cornelius Agrippa, Paracelsus, Roger Bacon, Robert Fludd, Thomas Taylor, Thomas Vaughan, or the mythical Hermes Trismegistus, and nonetheless achieve little truly valuable insight into either Blake or such kindred writers. Throughout his works Boehme voices his distaste for conventional scholarship and repeatedly stresses its limitations: "My Beloved Reader, if you would understand the High Mysteries, you need not first put an Academy on your nose, nor use any such Spectacles" (*TLM* 3.29).[27] Just as Blake encourages an approach that does not restrict one to a mere repetition of the "Contents or Index of already publish'd books," Boehme vigorously dissociates himself from any discipline that would attempt to reduce him to such a category: "I teach, write, and speak of what has been wrought in me. I have not scraped my teaching together out of histories and so made opinions. I have by God's grace obtained eyes of my own" (*Ep* 5.50). It is through such assertion of one's independence that a sense of the value of certain traditions can then become significant.

While Blake drew important distinctions between "imitation" and "invention" and wrote that "The Man Either Painter or Philosopher who Learns or Acquires all he Knows from Others. Must be full of Contradictions" (*Ann. Ren.* 639), he far from denies the importance of others. Samuel Palmer recalled that Blake was "fond of the works of St. Theresa, and often quoted them with other writers on the interior life."[28] Frederick Tatham suggests the extent of Blake's reading in a letter to the bookdealer Frances Harvey concerning *The Pickering Manuscript*:

> The MS you purchased of me was part of the possessions into which I came by legacy from Mrs Blake, the widow of that extraordinary and excellent man, William Blake, Visionary, Poet and Painter, who also had a most consummate knowledge of all the great writers in all languages. To prove that, I may say that I have possessed books well thumbed and dirted by his graving hands, in Latin, Greek, Hebrew, French, and Italian, besides a large collection of works of the mystical writers, Jacob Behmen, Swedenborg, and others. His knowledge was immense, his industry beyond parallel.[29]

All Boehme's writings had been translated into English and published between 1645 and 1662 by John Sparrow, in collaboration with John Ellistone[30] and Humphrey Blunden. Between that time and Blake's death in 1827, various criticisms and biographies of the German philosopher appeared, alongside several selections and editions of Boehme's works,[31] the most important being the four volumes commonly known as the "Law edition," published between 1764 and 1781. William Law had hoped to translate and publish all of Boehme's works himself—he had learned German expressly for this purpose—but died before he was able to undertake the task. The edition that has been attributed to him was in fact edited by two of his friends, George Ward and Thomas Langcake, contains only seventeen of Boehme's thirty-two treatises, and is in the main a reprint of Sparrow's translations.[32] The four volumes of Boehme also include "Figures, illustrating his Principles" devised toward the beginning of the eighteenth century by the German Behmenist Dionysius Andreas Freher and executed by an associate, a draughtsman named Leuchter. The Law edition of Boehme is the only one to be accompanied by these designs. In this it can quite safely be argued that Blake owned and read this version, although, as Tatham's letter would seem to imply, he might also have possessed other books by and about Boehme. As Crabb Robinson records: "Blake praised . . . the figures in Law's translation as being very beautiful. Michael Angelo could not have done better."[33]

That Blake should have expressed such enthusiasm, suggesting parity with an artist whom he held in the highest regard may appear extravagant. However, the statement has about it the provocative quality apparent in many of the remarks he made to Crabb Robinson, as if the poet were teasing and challenging his friend's preconceptions. The comment is not based on any usual conceptions of aesthetic criteria, but rather conveys Blake's appreciation of the Behmenist vision to which the designs give form. Each manifestation of independent genius was for him "the gift of God, it is inspiration and vision" (*DC* 544). As such, each may be considered as being both comparable to other manifestations and yet valid in its own right. The remarks that Boehme was a "divinely inspired man" and that "Michael Angelo could not have done better" than Freher's "figures" is in accord with Blake's view that the finest instances of the divine "gift" "cannot be surpassed":

> The human mind cannot go beyond the gift of God, the Holy Ghost. To suppose that Art can go beyond the finest specimens of Art that are now in the world, is not knowing what Art is; it is being blind to the gifts of the spirit. (*DC* 544)

Similarly,

> If Art was progressive We should have had Mich Angelo's and Raphaels to Succeed and to Improve upon each other. But it is not so. Genius dies with its Possessor and comes not again till Another is Born with it. (*Ann. Ren.* 656)

This casts light on how Blake regarded himself in relation to those before him, stressing again the absolute centrality of individual genius, while suggesting that such genius may unite one with other endeavors in that in each it is "the gift of God," that, ultimately, those such as Boehme, Michelangelo and Blake are drawing from the same core:

> As all men are alike (tho' infinitely various) So all Religions and as all similars have one source
> The true Man is the source he being the Poetic Genius. (*ARAO* 2)

To acknowledge genius in others is to recognize its possibilities in oneself.

In this spirit it is possible to appreciate a significant role that certain traditions played for Blake. As suggested, the various forces that participate in the shaping of each individual often work in a manner that is elusive. In many respects, the individual is always subject to and works and lives within some or other framework of thought and understanding. Blake, like Boehme before him, was himself acutely aware of the influences to which the individual may be subject, and of how they might work to the detriment of the "true Man," the "Poetic Genius." He also saw that there were influences that could be a source of support and wrote of

> those who tho willing were too weak to Reject Error without the Assistance and Countenance of those Already in the Truth for a Man Can only Reject Error by the Advice of a Friend or by the Immediate Inspiration of God it is for this Reason among many others that I have put the Lords Supper on the Left hand of the [*Picture*] for it appears so at the Last Judgment for a protection. (*VLJ* 563)

The Lord's Supper conveys the importance of brotherhood and community in the spiritual body of Christ. "One of the Eternals" speaks of this in *The Four Zoas*: "Man subsists by Brotherhood and Universal Love," "Man liveth not by Self alone" (402, Night 9, ll. 639, 642). "Brotherhood is Religion" (*Jer* 207, pl. 57, 1.10). Blake himself did not underestimate the power that "Error" might exert and the limitations to which everyone is subject. Talking of "Common opinion," he admits "I myself am also infected with it and my Visions is [*sic*] also infected" (*VLJ* 563). He therefore believed that "Life consists of these Two Throwing off Error <and Knaves from our company> continually and receiving Truth <or Wise Men into our Company> continually" (*VLJ* 562). Drawing upon Matthew Arnold, Morton D. Paley highlights the need for some form of intellectual communion that confronted Blake:

> Blake and some of his contemporaries faced the dilemma of the artist in what Matthew Arnold called "an epoch of concentration." In such an age society does not provide the creative power with "a current of ideas in the highest degree animating and nourishing to the creative power" characteristic of an "epoch of expansion," but "books and reading may enable a man to construct a kind of semblance of it in his own mind, a world of knowledge and intelligence in which he may live and work."[34]

In many ways Blake's needs were such that they would be at odds with the spirit of any age. T.S. Eliot has argued that "What his genius required, and what it sadly lacked, was a framework of accepted and traditional ideas which would have prevented him from indulging in a philosophy of his own, and concentrated his attention upon the problems of the poet."[35] Apart from the fact that Blake was not the unlearned person he was once thought to be, such a framework would have limited his vision. As John Howard writes in *Blake's "Milton"*:

> Let the fruit of Eden be ever so varied, there is not variety enough to satisfy the hungry spirit if there is a single caveat against newness. Men like Blake have always wished to change the concept of Eden from that of a garden to the idea of an endless universe, a limitless expanse of mental action that satisfies their yearning for more.[36]

The search for the new can lead to isolation. Blake's desire for a life of fuller possibilities placed him outside the understanding of most and thus beyond the possibility of easy communion with others. Crabb Robinson described Blake to Dorothy Wordsworth as someone "whose works have been the subject of derision to men in general . . . he has lived in obscurity and poverty, to which the constant hallucinations in which he lives have doomed him."[37]

Even Coleridge commented of Blake, naming him a "mystic," "verily I am in the very mire of common-place common-sense compared with Mr Blake."[38] Just as Boehme was subjected to scorn and has been regarded as being at the mercy of his own delusions, Blake lamented that his "lot" was "to be left and neglected" and to see his work "cried down as eccentricity and madness" (*DC* 538). His letters show that this was not a situation he bore lightly.

In this, in that Blake has written that "Rent from Eternal Brotherhood we die and are no more" (*FZ* 328, Night 3, l. 76), in that "Genius has no Error it is Ignorance that is Error" (*Ann. Ren.* 652), it may be seen that in writers such as Boehme, in whom there lies the possibility of "a limitless expanse of mental action," Blake found a source of support and encouragement, a bond and sense of community with kindred spirits throughout the centuries. In turn he was able through his art to keep alive and pass on the spirit that animated those like Boehme. The twentieth-century Russian philosopher and theologian Nicholas Berdyaev, whose own thought is thoroughly Behmenist in its outlook, observes that "the man who is seeking the spiritual life must join himself to all those who have participated in the development of the knowledge of spirit in history. That is why a philosophy of the spirit inevitably contains within itself a traditional element and presupposes fellowship with tradition."[39] Crabb Robinson recalled that Blake "is not so much a disciple of Jacob Bohmen and Swedenborg as a fellow Visionary." That he adds that "He lives as they did in a world of his own, enjoying constant intercourse with the world of spirits,"[40] does not simply show how such figures may be misunderstood, but also unwittingly points toward the subtle understanding that they are united in inhabiting the same imaginative sphere.

It is therefore not surprising that Blake wrote in his copy of Lavater's[41] *Aphorisms on Man* that

> Man is bad or good. as he unites himself with bad or good spirits . . .
>
> As we cannot experience pleasure but by means of others . . . And as all of us on earth are united in thought, for it is impossible to think without images of somewhat on earth—So it is impossible to know God or heavenly things without conjunction with those who know God and heavenly things. therefore, all who converse in the spirit, converse with spirits. (*Ann. Lav.* 660)

When Blake was preparing to move from London to Felpham, Sussex, in 1800 to work under William Hayley's patronage, he wrote to his friend John Flaxman in anticipation of a change of fortune: "the time is now arrivd when Men shall converse in Heaven and walk with Angels" (*Letters* 707-8). He then evokes those who figured significantly in his life—the letter was written in his forty-third year—suggesting a relationship between certain friends "upon Earth," namely Flaxman, Fuseli, and, he hoped, Hayley, and the "Company" of "Wise Men" (*VLJ* 562), great poets, prophets, and visionaries "in Heaven," stating that "the blessed of Heaven are my friends upon Earth," affirming the supportive role that "converse" within a community of such "spirits" might play. Heaven and Earth need not be regarded as separate from one another, as the sense of immediacy and vividness that charges Blake's account of his encounters with those in Heaven indicates:

> Now my lot in the Heavens is this; Milton lovd me in childhood and shewd me his face
> Ezra came with Isaiah the Prophet, but Shakespeare in riper years gave me his hand
> Paracelsus and Behmen appeard to me. terrors appeard in the Heavens above
> And in Hell beneath and a mighty and awful change threatened the Earth.

As Blake was to write to Hayley of his "lot" three years later, when the time spent under his patronage in Felpham had revealed that "Corporeal Friends are Spiritual Enemies" (*Milton* E98, pl. 4, l. 26), "if on Earth neglected I am in heaven a Prince among Princes" (*Letters* 736). In the letter to Flaxman Boehme is again named among those Blake held in the highest esteem. The fact that he is associated with the appearance of "terrors" and the threat of "awful changes" may seem to run contrary to the spirit of a supportive influence, particularly as these "terrors" are also associated here with the "dark horrors" of the War of Independence and the French Revolution.[42] However, as will be seen, Blake speaks here in terms pertinent to Boehme's vision, highlighting the impact made upon him by Boehme's apprehension of the interdependence of Good and Evil, Love and Wrath, and Heaven and Hell. Although a source of encouragement and inspiration may reaffirm the importance of particular beliefs and perceptions, it can be most supportive precisely in the degree that it challenges and makes demands upon those beliefs and in how far it reveals new insights, depths, and possibilities. The difficulties that surround Boehme do not merely lie in the complexity of his vision, but also, as Blake here conveys, in the experiences and insights which that vision evokes. In this light, that Boehme, along with Paracelsus, is spoken of in the context of the revolutions in America and France, of which he had voiced his approval, serves to emphasize the effect that Boehme had upon him and, more subtly, points to the poet's understanding that revolution and the life of the visionary spirit do not necessarily belong to separate worlds. Boehme cannot be encountered passively and indifferently.

2

Boehme, Blake, and Tradition

As the sense of presence, of an immediate personal interaction with Boehme and the other guiding spirits in the letter to Flaxman underlines, Blake understood that a valuable tradition is one that works actively, that lives through the creative individual. However, just as the vital "spirits" evoked in the letter cannot be apprehended by the usual literal understanding of the idea "spirit," the very fact that such a relationship is potent and living, that it is subject to the subtle movements and developments—conscious and otherwise—of a living process, emphasizes that it is a relationship that might have worked through Blake in ways and at levels that he could not always have recognized. Harold Bloom has dismissed the "hunt" for Blake's sources for being "all too successful."[1] The success is there because each stream of esoteric thought draws, according to its needs, purposes, and means of interpretation, from a common core of experience. Consequently, each manifestation of such thought does not stand apart from others, as the many resemblances, correspondences, and recurrences of, for example, themes, symbols, and ideas testify. As suggested, the echoes and reaffirmations that sound throughout the spiritual tradition often find resonance at a depth that is not easily gauged. It is not merely a matter of borrowing and adaptation. Throughout the centuries many strands of esoteric thought have to a greater or lesser degree intermingled, meeting at points in a fertile interaction that gives birth to new aspirations, new understandings, and new forms of the spiritual life. The relationship between them can therefore be complex and intricately interwoven. As a result, when dealing with Blake's own relationship to tradition it can be difficult, if not at times impossible to disentangle the network of correspondences that aided his artistic growth, to trace a particular thread back to one specific source.

Part of Boehme's significance arose from his own interaction—conscious and otherwise—with various manifestations of spiritual thought. Although he repeatedly asserts his independence in his writings, he too drew from and gave new form to such thought. Significantly, certain aspects of the mystical tradition that appear in his work also figure in Blake's, as Blake himself would very likely have recognized. It is possible that Blake learned certain of these aspects through Boehme. It is quite probable that he found in Boehme an active and guiding example of how the creative mind might feed and benefit from the spiritual endeavors and discoveries of others.

For instance, Blake would almost certainly have detected affinities with Kabbalism in Boehme's work. Gershom Scholem has suggested that in the seventeenth century Christian Kabbalism "received two great impetuses," namely Boehme's writings and, some years later, the Kabbalistic compendium *Kabbala Denundata* (1677–84).[2] As touched upon, Boehme's understanding of the nature and role of Evil made a significant impact upon Blake's thought. Scholem argues that Boehme's vision of the origin of Evil "bears all the traits of Kabbalistic thought. . . . Boehme, more than any other Christian mystic, shows the closest affinity to Kabbalism precisely where he is the most original. He has as it were discovered the world of the Sefiroth all over again."[3] While Boehme's kinship with Kabbalism should not be too greatly stressed, Scholem touches upon an important point here. Although Boehme might not have studied Kabbalism conscientiously, and although he almost certainly would not have regarded himself as a Kabbalist, his creative originality nonetheless found expression, in part, through his personal re-creation of aspects of this tradition. It cannot be known how consciously he followed Kabbalistic paths. However, Kabbalism did play some part in his work, whether directly, or indirectly through other streams of thought; or rather, as suggested, in a subtle interplay between the two. A. E. Waite suggests that

> A comparison between Böhme's MYSTERIUM MAGNUM, which is a commentary on Genesis, and the ZOHAR in the same text would bring out some extraordinary parallels and would increase the zeal of speculation concerning the glass of vision into which the German mystic looked. It was assuredly a glass which was common in several respects to other seers beside himself. His intimations on the first estate of man, on the making of woman, on Paradise and the Mystery of the Fall offer recurring analogies with Jewish Theosophy.[4]

Blake would have found embodied in Boehme the insight that it is independent inspiration which is most able to penetrate and keep alive the truths enshrined at the core of such spiritual approaches as Kabbalism. It is the very distinctness of Boehme's vision which, akin as it is to Blake's work in its creative singularity, suggests just how congenial the German mystic's endeavors would have been to the poet's. As such, it is quite possible that through Boehme's writings Blake approached a greater appreciation of the possibilities and limitations of wisdom such as that of the Kabbalah. Scholem has suggested that students (as well as opponents) of Jacob Boehme had discovered the strong affinity between his own theosophical system and that of the Kabbalah, though there would seem to be no historical connection between them. In certain circles, particularly in Germany, Holland and England, Christian Kabbalah henceforward assumed a Boehmian guise.[5]

It may be that Scholem underestimates Boehme's learning here, as others have done. Boehme's repeated portrayal of himself as a "poor despised" and uneducated man (*Aur* 9. 2–13) springs from the significance he attributed to humility and from his distrust of predominantly rational thought and scholasticism. Like Blake, he drew upon less orthodox schools of knowledge. There were historical connections between Boehme and the Kabbalah; he mentions it twice by name (*TQ* 3.34, 6.11). Kabbalistic writings had been introduced to the Christian world by Pico della Mirandola toward the end of the fifteenth century, and, as Stoudt notes, by the beginning of the seventeenth century "knowledge of Cabala was not unusual. Reuchlin's works were available for those unable to read the Hebrew, and it was not hard to find someone who had read him. Agrippa von Nettesheim and Paracelsus were also well known."[6]

Boehme was certainly so placed as to have access to a variety of esoteric approaches. While influences cannot, as such, be allocated to specific sources, suggestions may certainly be made. After 1612 and the circulation of his first work, *Aurora*, a group of learned friends and disciples gathered about him, through whom he might not only have come in touch with the thought and scholarly pursuits of his time, but also with mystical and Hermetic philosophy. Among his closest associates were the Paracelsan physician Tobias Kober, the Schwenkfeldian nobleman Carl von Ender, Johann Rothe, a student of alchemy, "Tauler, medieval mysticism, and Johann Arndt,"[7] and, in particular, Balthasar Walther, director of the chemical laboratory at Dresden, who was familiar with esoteric wisdom and the occult arts, and from whom, it has been suggested, Boehme received knowledge of the Kabbalah.[8] Boehme's home town itself counted among its populace scholars, physicians, men of learning, and alchemists. Görlitz was situated near the borders of Bohemia where, in the early part of the seventeenth century, there was a notable growth in esoteric interest, centered about Rudolph II's court in Prague. As documented by Frances Yates, this "Rosicrucian enlightenment" produced "a phase in which the Renaissance Hermetic-Cabalist tradition . . . received the influx of another Hermetic tradition—alchemy."[9] Similarly, in Görlitz there were groups of followers of the "inner light" thinkers Kaspar von Schwenkfeld, Sebastian Franck, and Valentin Weigel, in whose works there are notable affinities with Boehme.[10] As certain parallels and echoes testify, it would seem that through these three figures, through Martin Moller, the Lutheran Pastor of Görlitz at the beginning of the century[11] and through others, Boehme inherited the spiritual wisdom of medieval and Renaissance mysticism, of, in particular, Eckhart, Tauler, Suso, Ruusbroec, and the *Theologia Germanica*, even though he mentions none of these by name. It is possible that Boehme passed on aspects of this tradition to Blake. Moreover, among those interested in Schwenkfeld, Franck, and Weigel, Boehme would have found an influence more immediately pertinent to Blake, namely that of Paracelsus.

It has been argued with some justification that Paracelsus's influence on Blake was one that was mediated through Boehme. Bentley proposes that "the significance of Paracelsus for Blake is primarily his advocacy of ideas which Boehme later accepted. In Blake's time Paracelsus's personal significance was of far less importance than that of Boehme. In general it is likely that Blake acquired knowledge of and respect for Paracelsus through his interest in the works of Boehme."[12] It is certainly true that in his relationship with Paracelsus Boehme again manifests his creative independence, as Hans Popper underlines: "Boehme's treatment of Paracelsan ideas must be understood as, not merely a further development, but a complete re-interpretation."[13] Bryan Aubrey adds weight to the view that Blake drew upon a Behmenist Paracelsus, suggesting that much of the alchemical physician's work, particularly that which deals directly with Hermetic philosophy, might not have been readily available to the poet.[14] While there are significant differences between Boehme and Paracelsus, not least in that Lutheran theology was an important influence for the former, whereas it appears to have made little impact on the latter, they nonetheless participated in and passed on shared strands of esoteric thought, as Blake did after them, each adapting these traditions to their individual means and ends. Among these strands, Neoplatonism typifies perfectly the complexity and fecundity of the whole network of interrelationships, appearing as it does in various guises and degrees in Paracelsus, Boehme, and Blake, in Hermetic philosophy, alchemy, Kabbalism, and indeed in Christian mysticism in general, from St. Augustine, Dionysius the Areopagite and John Scotus Erigena onwards. Thus, although "Plato, Plotinus and other Neoplatonists were translated into English for the first time by Blake's contemporary and acquaintance Thomas Taylor the Platonist," as Kathleen Raine notes,[15] the poet could have received this strain of thought from a whole variety of sources, among whom Boehme can be included.

It is also very likely that Blake received aspects of and perhaps approaches to Behmenism through individuals and movements which Boehme himself influenced. William Law's interpretations of Boehme appeared in such works as *An Appeal to all that Doubt* and, in particular, *The Way to Divine*

Knowledge, which Law had intended as an introduction to his translation of Boehme. There are notable correspondences between the two English authors. Two of Law's associates, John Byrom and Henry Brooke, were also Behmenists: Byrom's poetry contains many clear references to and expositions of his thought,[16] and, as Howard Brinton notes, Brooke's "once famous novel the *Fool of Quality* . . . as well as his two long poems *Universal Beauty* (1735) and *Redemption* (1750) are full of Behmenist phrases."[17] Christopher Walton has noted that there were "many . . . savans of Germany and England" who were "students of Behmen," including Lavater, Spurzheim, and Berkeley,[18] whose works Blake annotated. Among the figures who feature prominently in Blake's own work, John Milton has been proposed as an heir to Boehme's thought, most notably by Margaret Lewis Bailey in *Milton and Jakob Boehme.* Bailey provides valuable historical background material, particularly in her portrayal of the dissemination of Behmenism in England, suggesting that Milton's "personality and writings alike hold up a mirror to the spiritual and intellectual progress of his time,"[19] and that he would accordingly have been receptive to the growth in Behmenist interest among his acquaintances and contemporaries. Rufus Jones has also argued in favor of Boehme's influence:

> Milton, without any doubt, had read the German mystic's account of the eternal war between the Light Principle and the Dark Principle, of the fall of Lucifer, of the loss of Paradise, and of the return of man in Christ to Paradise, and there are many passages in the great poet which look decidedly like germinations from the seed which Boehme sowed.[20]

Emanuel Swedenborg's name has also been associated with Boehme's. Even during his lifetime marked similarities were recognized. Among those attracted to his teachings when he was alive were people who were also advocates of Boehme's thought. Lavater, for instance, sent letters of admiration to the Swedish visionary. Dr. F. C. Oetinger, Bishop of Murrhard and a noted admirer of Boehme, corresponded with Swedenborg and translated certain of his works, including *Heaven and Hell* and *Arcana Coelestia*, into German. The Reverend Francis Okeley, a Moravian minister, friend of William Law and John Byrom, and author of *Memoirs of the Life of Jacob Behmen* (1780), became acquainted with Swedenborg and read the visionary's works "with mingled approval and dissent."[21] Accordingly, Swedenborg was prompted to stress:

> My opinion concerning the writings of Behmen . . . I have never read them, as I was prohibited reading dogmatic and systematic theology, before heaven was opened to me, by reason, that, unfounded opinions and inventions

might thereby easily have insinuated themselves, which with difficulty could afterwards have been extirpated.[22]

This statement was printed in *The New Jerusalem Magazine* in 1790, eighteen years after Swedenborg's death. In the same year, dissociating himself from Swedenborgianism, Blake began work on *The Marriage of Heaven and Hell*, which as seen declares Swedenborg's works to be "only the Contents or Index of already publish'd books," suggesting that as a "man of mechanical talents" Swedenborg drew "from the writings of Paracelsus and Jacob Behmen." Whether or not Blake was aware of Swedenborg's repudiation of any debt to Boehme, he was conscious of Behmenist strands of thought in Swedenborg's work. Despite Swedenborg's denial, it is probable, as Blake would have appreciated, that he nonetheless inherited elements of Boehme's theosophy indirectly, perhaps unwittingly, from the intricately woven network that unites the mystical tradition. As his writings illustrate, he was, for instance, familiar with Kabbalism.[23] It is also worth mentioning, as Overton notes, the existence of "the tradition that Swedenborg was first turned to spiritual subjects by reading Law's 'Appeal' and other [of his] early mystical writings."[24]

It is thus understandable that doubt has been voiced over the years as to the verity of Swedenborg's refutation of Boehme's influence upon him. It is certainly not surprising that Blake should have associated and compared the two visionaries. Among those attracted to Swedenborg in Blake's time were individuals who also shared an interest in Boehme. Jacob Duché, for example, an Anglican clergyman from Philadelphia who had moved to England in 1777, was a student of Boehme, Law and, by the early 1780's, Swedenborg. From about 1782 onwards, Duché gathered about him in his home in Lambeth a circle of associates interested in Swedenborg. As Erdman points out,[25] Duché might well have been known to Blake, for in 1779 the poet's name appeared among a list of subscribers to his *Discourses on Various Subjects*, a work in which the young Blake would have found Behmenist material. It is quite possible that Blake was more immediately familiar with Duché and, therefore, that he might have been party to "discourses" about Swedenborg and Boehme within his Lambeth circle. Indeed, Blake was friendly with at least one member of Duché's group, namely William Sharp the engraver.[26] Likewise, as has been ably documented,[27] the poet was well acquainted with Swedenborgians, his name appearing with his wife's in the minute book of the First General Conference of the New Jerusalem Church in 1789. It may well be that the publication of Swedenborg's denial of Boehme's influence, coinciding as it does with the beginnings of the New Church in London, underlines that Boehme's name was common currency among the Swedenborgians, that the declaration appeared so that Swedenborg's importance, his own divine inspiration, might not in any way be obscured.

Other individuals and sects also kept alive and nourished "the seed which Boehme sowed." Dr. John Pordage (1607–81) was one of the best known proponents of Boehme's vision during the seventeenth century, so much so that Richard Baxter, the Puritan, named him specifically when discussing the Behmenists and other sects.[28] Pordage's writings present devoted, simplified, sometimes confusing expositions of Boehme's thought, the most often cited being the posthumously published *Theologia Mystica or the Mystic Divinitie of the Aeternal Nature* (1683). During Blake's lifetime, two works in which Pordage's writings appear were published, *Theological and Practical Divinity: with Extracts of Several Treatises written by Jacob Behmen* (1769) and *A Compendious View of the Grounds of the Teutonic Philosophy* (1770).[29] In the early 1670s, Pordage became associated with Jane Lead (1623–1704), who, like him, was subject to "visions and revelations," and who probably first encountered Boehme through him. Lead wrote many books and pamphlets centering around Boehme's thought, such as *The Heavenly Cloud* (1681), *The Revelation of Revelations* (1683), and the four volumes of her spiritual diary, *A Fountain of Gardens* (1697–1701).[30] Continuing the Behmenist tradition established earlier in the century, she formed the Philadelphian Society (1697–1704) in London, with the aim of studying and explaining Boehme's writings. Most prominent in this society was Lead's "spiritual son" Francis Lee (1661–1719), an intellectual of some standing who edited and provided commentaries for her writings.[31] When William Law was seeking to further his knowledge and understanding of Boehme later in the eighteenth century, he became "deeply interested" in Lee's writings, borrowing many of his manuscripts from Lee's daughter and copying several of them out by hand.[32]

While the Philadelphians were a relatively small, perhaps self-contained group, the Behmenists as a whole in the seventeenth century were by no means isolated. Richard Baxter noted affinities with other sects of the period, particularly with the Quakers, writing of "the Behmenists, whose opinions go much towards the way of the former [the Quakers], for the sufficiency of the light of nature, the salvation of heathens as well as Christians, and a dependence on revelations."[33] This association was common among writers of the time on Quakerism.[34] While certain objections to the Behmenists were raised by the Quakers,[35] there were notable grounds of agreement between the two sects. The Quakers counted among their numbers people who were, or at least who had been followers of Boehme, such as Thomas Taylor the Seeker,[36] and Francis Ellington who regarded Boehme as "a prophet of the Lord;"[37] people who probably, as Robert Barclay argues, "exercised a subtle influence in giving a greater prominence to the mystical element which existed in early Quakerism."[38] Particularly significant are the parallels that have been noted between Boehme and George Fox (1624–91), the founder of the Society of Friends. As the Quaker Rufus Jones argues, although Fox mentions neither Boehme nor the Behmenists by name, the similarities between Fox's *Journal* and Boehme's works are such that "no careful student of both can doubt that there was some sort of influence, direct or indirect."[39] Jones points out an important way in which the spiritual tradition is propagated: "there are ideas expressed and experiences described in the *Journals* which look strangely like memories, conscious or subconscious, of ideas and expressions to be found in Boehme's writings."[40] It is possible that, like others before and after him, Fox received aspects of the spiritual tradition from sources and in ways that he might not always have recognized; that, in this case, he might have "imbibed ideas from an environment permeated with Boehme's influence."[41] In support of this view, Jones gives examples of verbal echoes of Boehme in Fox's *Journal* which make it "difficult to believe that Fox could have got his phraseology anywhere else than from Boehme."[42]

As suggested, echoes—verbal or otherwise—can often be traced with a little effort to a variety of sources. Nonetheless, apart from the fact that Jones's comparisons are valuable all the same, they are important in highlighting the fertile interaction that existed—at times in the form of contention—between the various dissenting sects that arose in the middle of the seventeenth century, and in which the Quakers played an integral part, both giving to and receiving from the upsurge in interest in spiritual regeneration. As Harry Emerson Wildes conveys in his portrayal of the milieu in which Fox moved, this interrelationship was one that was kept alive in the very language of the various sects: "Boehme's vividness of preaching and the vigor of his style so impressed his hearers that many of his turns of speech were already current, taking hold so tenaciously that Englishmen innocently adopted them as their own."[43] Although the Quakers as a body attempted to diminish Boehme's influence among them as they became more established—suggesting perhaps as Bailey argues "how generally prevalent this interest in Boehme had become"[44]—this sense of the creation of and participation in a living, sometimes "subconscious" tradition makes it possible to appreciate that the Quakers' affinities with and dissemination of Boehme's vision were in no way restricted to the early years of their movement. In fact, eighteenth-century Quakerism maintained characteristics thoroughly in keeping with the spirit of Boehme, such as the emphasis on the "inner light," the "intense conviction of the immediate contact of God with the soul," the overcoming of the "own-self," and the casting off of "the lead of human reason."[45] Such correspondences with Blake's own concerns underline the possibility that Quakerism played some part in his absorption of Boehme, both directly—for instance, through contemporary Quakerism and Quaker writings, most notably George Fox's *Journal*—and indirectly through the dissenting tradition to which Quakerism had contributed, and which was alive, if in a somewhat covert form, in the poet's time.

Boehme has often been regarded as an important influence upon the variety of groups that sprang to life in England in the 1640s: the Seekers, the Levellers, the Diggers, the Ranters, and the Muggletonians, alongside the Quakers. The Digger Gerrard Winstanley certainly seems to echo Boehme, and, significantly, points to Blake after him. His writings display such shared convictions as the injustice of the social order and the corrupting role played by the clergy, the primacy of personal experience and the direct apprehension of the spiritual life within, and the belief that "the whole Scriptures are but a report of spirituall mysteries, held forth to the eye of the flesh in words; but to be seene in the substantiall matter of them by the eye of the spirit."[46] Winstanley accordingly manifests a characteristic which is common among figures of certain strong, spiritual persuasions, the claim to speak from immediate divine direction rather than through the influence of others. Nonetheless, as George Sabine suggests, it is quite possible that this inspiration was mediated to a degree by Behmenism, not least on account of the manner and extent of the diffusion of thought such as Boehme's. Sabine presents a view of the movements in Winstanley's time which, in turn, may equally be applied to the dissemination of the Digger's own writings:

> the seventeenth century was very definitely an age of popularisation, at least in comparison with any preceding age, rapidly spreading both religious and political thought to a multitude of obscure and uneducated men. And as the ideas travelled, their individuality was worn off.[47]

Concurring with the relaxation of the censorship laws, from the beginning of the 1640s onward many works of a spiritually and politically radical nature were published and circulated, including the complete English translations of Boehme's works, which appeared between 1645 and 1662. Many of these writings were printed by Giles Calvert, "whose name on a title-page was in itself almost a political and religious manifesto,"[48] and whose industry was described by one contemporary critic as "that forge of the devil from whence so many blasphemous, lying, scandalous pamphlets for many years past have spread over the land."[49] It would appear that Calvert's endeavors provided a "unifying force" of sorts, a sense of identity between the various antinomian groups. Alongside Boehme's works, he printed "translations of Henry Niclaes . . . , the works of Saltmarsh, Dell, some Levellers, most of Winstanley, the Wellingborough broadsheet, many Ranters and very many Quakers."[50] Similarly, although opposed by the ecclesiastical authorities, Boehme might well have undergone popularization from the pulpit and pen of preachers like John Everard (1575-ca. 1650), a Cambridge doctor of theology who was well versed in the German mystic's thought and related sources. Everard was an immensely popular preacher, attracting large audiences to his sermons in London, so much so that after his death some of these sermons were gathered together, along with his translations of certain mystical texts, and published in three successive editions (1653, 1657, and 1659).

The English radical dissenting tradition was not detached from the esoteric "mainstream" of European mysticism and hermeticism. While much of its concern was political, focusing as it did on the "mean, poor and despised" of the world,[51] the views of men like Gerrard Winstanley, Abeizzer Coppe, and Joseph Salmon existed within a spiritual framework. Not only were aspects of European mysticism maintained by the inheritance which such writings as Boehme's brought with them, but they were also actively assimilated and propagated by figures like Everard, who studied and translated such mainsprings of the tradition as Tauler, Dionysius the Areopagite, the *Theologia Germanica,* Hans Denck, and Sebastian Franck, along with esoteric and alchemical works including *The Poimandres of Hermes Trismegistus.*

It is possible to trace certain tendencies among the "mean, poor and despised" of Blake's own time which, as Harrison remarks, "suggest that Boehme's influence, either directly or indirectly, was quite widespread among a certain type of seeker."[52] Stephen Penny, an acquaintance of William Law, wrote of those he had encountered who were interested in Boehme's writings: "what is remarkable . . . they are of the simple and illiterate sort. Others of school-learning despise us, and ridicule them. It was of the first sort the followers of the Saviour of the world consisted, when clothed with humanity."[53] Ralph Mather, an early Swedenborgian and ex-Quaker, supported this view in the survey he compiled in 1775 of those in Britain "in whose minds the light of God has arisen or is graciously arising," finding evidence of people who had, despite the inherent difficulties of the German visionary's theosophy, been influenced by Boehme and Law, notably among the "simple and low in the world."[54] Adding further detail to this, A. L. Morton notes that the beliefs and aspirations that had blossomed in the seventeenth century continued to exist, among the Quakers, Muggletonians, and Traskites for instance, and that "they persisted most strongly as they had sprung up originally, among the artisans and petty tradesmen of the thickly-peopled working-class quarters. These were exactly the social circles and the geographical areas in which Blake was born and in which his whole life was passed."[55] Existing as a faint undercurrent to their contemporary society, these groups continued to cherish and circulate among themselves the writings of their predecessors, "preserving their faith in little obscure conventicles," regarding themselves, as many of their ancestors over the centuries had done, as "the possessors and guardians of a secret doctrine, not to be lightly revealed to the uninitiated."[56] E. P. Thompson has lent strength to this argument in *Witness Against the Beast.* As exemplified by the Muggletonians, it would appear that the preservation of the tradition had become a guiding principle, an institution in the families of believers.

The millenarian doctrine of the Everlasting Gospel acted in its various forms as a touchstone, a rallying point for the ideas and hopes that had fired the radical dissenting groups. Blake's use of it, both as a phrase and as a concept, in the latter part of his life suggests his identification of himself with the tradition that had kept the Everlasting Gospel alive. Foremost among the writings treasured by the Muggletonians were those handed down to them by the leading spirits of their movement, Lodowick Muggleton (1609–98) and his cousin John Reeve (1608–58), two tailors who had proclaimed themselves the heralds of the Second Coming, following the divine "commission" given to Reeve in 1652. Central to their teachings were the doctrines of the "Three Commissions" and the "Two Seeds." The former divided the world into three ages or "commissions" of the Father, the Son, and the Spirit, with the third age completing the cycle that began with the Fall, manifesting itself through Muggleton and Reeve. The latter doctrine developed the common idea of the two "seeds" in man, a divine and a diabolical, the seed of Adam and faith, and the seed of Cain and reason, the lot of each individual being determined by whichever seed had ascendancy in him.[57] Later chapters illustrate that both of these teachings have clear antecedents in Boehme's writings, and also that they anticipate insights that lie at the foundations of much of Blake's work.

Although both Muggleton and Reeve came to dissociate themselves from Boehme's vision, probably on account of their belief in their being chosen above all men, both had studied his teachings with some enthusiasm. Their "commission" is also thoroughly in keeping with the whole Everlasting Gospel tradition, which may be traced at least as far back as the twelfth century to Joachim of Fiore, and in which Boehme played an important part, alongside such millenarians as Henry Niclaes and the Familists. In brief, this tradition also views the life of the world in terms of three "ages." The first is that of the Father, which extends form the Fall of Man to the birth or death of Christ, and finds expression in divine Wrath, the Law, and the Old Testament. The second belongs to the Son, an age of faith and loving humility which realizes itself through the New Testament. The third age is of the Spirit, an ever-present age in which the truth of the Everlasting Gospel, of the interrelationship of God and man is realized, revealing the seat of the divine as being within man. It is a revelation that sounds the advent of the New Jerusalem, the forgiveness of sins, and liberty through a spiritual as opposed to literal understanding of the Bible.

In England the Everlasting Gospel had appeared variously in the writings, for instance, of John Saltmarsh, William Erbery, Abeizzer Coppe, Gerrard Winstanley, Lawrence Clarkson, William Dell, Isaac Penington, and George Fox.[58] John Pordage had associated with and supported many prominent radicals of his time—he himself had been accused of being both a Ranter and a Familist—counting among those whom he had known Erbery, another admirer of Boehme, Coppe, Thomas Tany, and Richard Coppin.[59] The millenarianism he had inherited from Boehme, and which had possibly been nurtured by such interactions, was in turn kept alive by Jane Lead and the Philadelphians. Among the revelations which Lead had received was that of the Everlasting Gospel, "which was to be preached to the devil and his angels, after the restoration of the whole human race."[60] She had published the doctrine in works such as *The Enochian Walks with God* (1694), *The Wonders of God's Creation Manifested* (1695), and *A Revelation of the Everlasting Gospel-message* (1697). After her death the spirit of her Philadelphianism had been maintained by Richard Roach, another prominent member of the society and close friend of Francis Lee, who had reformed the Philadelphians in 1707, temporarily uniting them with the Camisards to announce the advent of the Last Days. Until his death in 1730, Roach proclaimed the millenarian message, as found in his work *The Great Crisis* (1725–27), which depicted the state of the world in the third age and envisaged London—as did Blake after him—as the New Jerusalem.

Naturally, the tradition of the Everlasting Gospel had often been interpreted literally as an imminent transformation to be made to, rather than within, the world. Among the English radical sects, among the Philadelphians, this inclination had certainly manifested itself. In Blake's time, the expectation of an "actual" Last Judgment and the overthrow of the ruling powers was typified by the popular millenarianism of Richard Brothers and Joanna Southcott, who, it may be noted in passing, included among their followers friends of the poet, William Sharp, John Gabriel Steadman, and William Owen Pugh. Believing himself to be under divine direction, Brothers proclaimed the date of the beginning of the millennium to be November 1795. As highlighted in the two volumes of his very popular *A Revealed*

Knowledge of the Prophecies and Times, he regarded his mission to be the leading of the "invisible Hebrews," the "descendants of the ten lost tribes of Israel, many of whom were living in England"—again suggesting Blake, outwardly at least—to the Holy Land to rebuild in bricks and mortar the city of the New Jerusalem.[61] Similarly, the followers of Joanna Southcott believed the Everlasting Gospel to be their prophetess's dispensation, that it was to be "the final revelation of [God's] will, previous to the destruction of Satan and the establishment of Christ's Kingdom," in which England would be "the place from whence the everlasting gospel will be sent to every habitable part of the globe."[62]

While both Blake and Boehme were engaged with social and ecclesiastical injustices, the spirit of the millennium undergoes a transformation in their works that is profound and as such less tangible. For both the revelation contained within the myth of the Everlasting Gospel has its center and finds its realization within the individual, and thus may occur within time in any moment: "whenever any Individual Rejects Error and Embraces Truth a Last Judgment passes upon that individual" (*VLJ* 562). The imminence of the third age, of the "Age of the Lily" as Boehme referred to it, is therefore one that has its basis in a living process and calls to the individual in every moment. Boehme wrote of this third age:

> that which is old and past above a thousand years agoe, is as nigh and as easily to be knowne in the light, as that which is done to day; for a thousand years before God are scarce so much as a minute, or the twinkling of an eye. (*Ep* 4:15)

This gives a fuller sense of the immediacy of Blake's "converse in the spirit . . . with spirits." "Within a Moment: a Pulsation of the Artery" (*Milton* 127, pl. 29, l. 3), the divine humanity within each individual coexists with that of others. In *On the New Birth* Boehme underlines the nature of this, stressing the primacy of the individual in relation to tradition:

> A Christian . . . has no sect. He can dwell among the sects, even appear in their services, and yet hang on to none. He has only a single knowledge and that is Christ in him. (*WC* "On the New Birth," 7.5)

From his early works to the productions of his later years, Blake preached the conviction that "All Religions are One," that

> All had originally one language, and one religion, this was the religion of Jesus, the everlasting Gospel. Antiquity preaches the Gospel of Jesus. (*DC* 543)

3
Communion, the Prophetic, and the Living Bible

PROGRESSIVE INDEPENDENCE

While Boehme's thought and understanding underwent changes and developments, each of his works does not so much mark a gradual shift in belief as represent a diligent, searching return to and reappraisal of the vision and experiences that inspired his spiritual endeavors, a forging of new forms, of a deeper, more subtle apprehension of the spiritual. He came to regard his first book, the *Aurora*, as the work of his spiritual childhood (*Ep* 12.56), an initial attempt to give expression to the intimations that had awoken within him. For all its crudities, it gave form to a process of personal sublimation, the turning inward and assimilation of the apparently disparate parts of his experience. Boehme himself recognized the ongoing nature of spiritual inquiry in the *Aurora*:

> the being of God is like a wheel, wherein many wheels are made *one in another*, upwards, downwards, crossways, and yet they continually turn, all of them together.
>
> . . .when a man beholdeth the *wheel*, he highly marvelleth at it, and, in its turning, cannot *at once* learn to conceive and *apprehend* it: But the more he beholdeth the wheel, the more he learneth its form of frame; and the more he learneth, the greater the longing he hath to the wheel; for he continually seeth somewhat that is more and more wonderful, so that a man can neither behold it, nor learn it *enough*. (*Aur* 21.64–65)

Such a vision makes it necessary to animate and integrate the written into a dynamic, living process, to direct it toward the inner drama of man's existence.

Blake's inheritance similarly represents a new development and creation of spiritual understanding, one that was also formed with diligence throughout his life. For instance, as is evident in the relationship between the three major epics, *The Four Zoas, Milton,* and *Jerusalem*, phrases, lines, and whole passages appear and reappear from previous pieces, reworked into different contexts, associations, significances, and so on, while maintaining a common core of vision. In turn, the achievements of each mystic, individually and in the light of one another, propose new possibilities, stressing the necessity for each individual to interpret and encounter anew the truths that "reside in the human breast" (*MHH* 38, pl. 11). Boehme speaks of this:

> one always understands otherwise than another, according as each is endued with the Wisdom; and so also he apprehends and explains it.
>
> Every one will not understand my writing according to my meaning and sense; indeed there may not be one who does so; but everyone will understand according to his gifts, for his benefit; one more than another, according as the Spirit has its property in him. (*Conf.* 110)

Again, the "worship of God is. Honouring his gifts in other men." Blake also perceived that "Vision or Imagination is a Representation of what Eternally Exists. Really and Unchangeably," and that as such vision is dependent upon the individual:

> The Last Judgment is one of the Stupendous Visions[.] I have represented it as I saw it[.] to different People it appears differently as every thing else does for tho on Earth things seem Permanent they are less permanent than a Shadow. (*VLJ* 554, 555)

This necessary independence in part explains why Blake and Boehme disapproved of the passive acceptance of another's thought and understanding, not least as it reduces the spiritual potential that might lie in another's works to "things . . . less permanent than a Shadow." With this in mind Blake declared "To Imitate I abhore" (*PA* 580): "<How ridiculous it would be to see the Sheep Endeavouring to walk like the Dog. or the Ox striving to trot like the Horse just as Ridiculous it is to see One Man Striving to Imitate Another Man varies from Man more than Animal from Animal of Different Species>" (*Ann. Ren.* 656). The wealth of different forms unites men: "As all are alike in outward form, So (and with the same infinite variety) all are alike in the Poetic Genius" (*ARAO* 1). A potent, mutually beneficial relationship exists between variety and unity. While "outward form" is not final reality, the external is not completely cut off from the inner, participating as it does in a subtle correspondence with the spiritual depths from which in fact it springs: "the Poetic Genius is the true Man. and . . . the body or outward form of Man is derived from the Poetic Genius. Likewise . . . the forms of all things are derived from their Genius. which by the Ancients was call'd an Angel and Spirit and Demon" (*ARAO* 1).

Given that "The human mind cannot go beyond the gift of God, the Holy Ghost," and that "Art cannot go beyond the finest specimens of Art" (*DC* 544), even the most inspired elucidations of the inner life cannot establish for it any final and incontrovertible form. It is always seeking new avenues of expression, and may appear in terms not usually associated with it. The interaction between outward and inward is one that is eternally fruitful. While the interactions of the spiritual tradition nourish diversity of expression, they draw its aspirants together in an imaginative communion, a Lord's Supper in which each gives individual form to that which "Eternally Exists. Really and Unchangeably." Blake's and Boehme's work is directed toward the revelation of the unitive and indwelling Christ, who, as Boehme believed, "brought the Divine Image into . . . the Soul": "And this is done by the Imagination, or Faith, for Faith is an eating of the Divine Body, and every body grows by eating" (*FQ* 7.24–25). As a man feeds, so he grows: "As the mouth is, so also is the food belonging to the mouth" (*WC* "On the New Birth," 6.9). Through tradition Blake was able to live through the imaginative lives of others, to create as those like Boehme had created before him, to strive to fulfill the spiritual imperatives that fired such minds; to live through an independent and responsive activity which, as such, may be seen as both paying tribute to and participating in the active, eternal reality of Boehme's individual existence.

PROPHETIC VISION AND ACTIVITY

In the autobiographical piece addressed to Flaxman, Boehme is placed in the company of two biblical figures, "Ezra" and "Isaiah the Prophet." This company highlights that Blake regarded himself as working within a biblical tradition, a tradition that was not exiled to some distant, irrecoverable past, but alive and working within all ages. It is likely that he saw Boehme as working and living within the same tradition, in particular within that which finds expression in the visions and aspirations of the prophets. Both visionaries identified themselves in various forms with the tradition of prophecy. As the poet underlined in his copy of Lavater's *Aphorisms*, "every great genius, every hero, is a prophet" (*Ann. Lav.* 592). In *The Marriage of Heaven and Hell* Blake suggests a sense of active companionship with the biblical prophets, writing that "Isaiah and Ezekiel dined with me," presenting an imaginative conversation that might nourish the spiritual understanding (38–39, pls. 12–13). The "dinner" suggests the spiritual and intellectual communion through which the liberty of divinity is realized. Just as vision is dependent on the individual, prophetic vision of the one "Divine Image" is united in the eternally fruitful variety of its manifestations, as Boehme understood:

> All the Prophets from the beginning of the World, have prophesied Christ in different forms, one thus, another so; they have not all concurred in one style, phrase, and forme; but each according as the Spirit of God hath revealed to him in the eternal Constellation of the soule, yet they have all spoken out of one Centre, and Ground. (*Ep* 2.33)

To return to Blake's tracts of 1788, suggesting, in part, the significant extent to which Boehme might have influenced these early pieces: "The Religions of all Nations are derived from each Nations different reception of the Poetic Genius which is everywhere call'd the spirit of Prophecy" (*ARAO* 1). Through the individual prophet a voice is given to the spiritual source of existence, a voice which speaks through the diverse manifestations of man's religious needs, calling him back to his eternal "Ground." Rather than being restricted to a literal, biblical past, prophetic activity, its creation, in Blake's words, of "various sublime and Divine Images" (*VLJ* 555), seeks out and encourages new prophetic endeavors in all ages. Boehme wrote "of the Prophets, and their successors": as "were the prophets" in the past, "such they still are in the present day" (*MM* 63.42; *EOG[E]* 12.65). In *The Marriage* Blake recalls: "After dinner I asked Isaiah to favour the world with his lost works, he said none of equal value was lost. Ezekiel said the same of his" (39, pl. 13). The prophet, like the artist, "cannot go beyond the gift of God." Spiritual genius persists throughout the centuries. As seen, the phrase "of equal value" is repeated in a later plate of *The Marriage*: "Any man of mechanical talents may from the writings of Paracelsus or Jacob Behmen, produce ten thousand volumes of equal value with Swedenborg's." The repetition of the phrase in this context suggests a specific association in the poet's mind of Boehme and Paracelsus with the prophetic tradition. If one of merely "mechanical" "gifts" is able through works such as Boehme's to produce writings of a parity with those of Swedenborg, someone of such "talents" as Blake was certainly in a position to respond creatively to the profoundly prophetic quality of Boehme's works, to recognize and participate in their subtle yet energetic promotion of the underlying unity and equality of vision that draws together the true prophets of the world. As Blake extended his conception of the prophetic artist to embrace a diversity of pursuits and approaches, Boehme believed, for instance, that the Philosopher's Stone, the cornerstone of the alchemical tradition that played an important role in each mystic's works, was known by and, consequently, united all prophets (*TLM* 7.39–40).

The spiritual life that sustains and unites the prophetic tradition can be a source of inner strength, of determination for the individual's endeavors. Both Blake and Boehme manifest this strength. Blake "asked" "The Prophets Isaiah and Ezekiel . . . how they dared so roundly assert that God spake to them." "Isaiah answer'd" in the spirit of creative, personal knowledge: "I saw no God. nor heard any, in a finite organical perception; but my senses discovered the infinite in every thing. . . . I was then perswaded. and remain confirm'd" (*MHH* 38, pl. 12). In the same spirit Boehme asserted his right to speak, for instance, of the fall of Lucifer:

> Although *self-reason* might here cavil at us, and say we were not by when this was done , yet we say that we in a *magical Manner*, according to the Right of Eternity, were really there, and saw this; but not I, who am I, have seen it; for I was not *as yet* a Creature; but we have seen it in the *Essence* of the Soul which God breathed into *Adam*. (*MM[L]* 9.1)

Blake spoke of "The strong man" who "acts from conscious superiority, and marches on in fearless dependence on the divine decrees, raging with the inspirations of a prophetic mind" (*DC* 545). In his faith, the prophet knows imaginatively that "the vioice [*sic*] of honest indignation is the voice of God" (*MHH* 38, pl.12). Although Boehme regarded himself as humble he often speaks with a voice that is anything but. Neither Boehme nor Blake thought that humility was the same as acceptance of social and ecclesiastical authority. Blake's loathing and denunciation of the "Creeping Jesus" of the "crawlers" who are "but mimickers of humility and love," of the "sneaking serpent" that would enslave man (*EG* [k] 519, pl. 55; *Ann. Lav* 586; *MHH* 33, pl. 2, l.17), finds support and resonance in Boehme's outspoken faith in the truth of his own vision and in his fiery criticism of the earthly state: "Behold, thou immodest vile whorish World, here thou shalt find a Glass; behold thyself [and see] what thou art" (*TP* 20.45). Man "is to consider how, with body and soul, he lies captive ... in God's wrath, in the jaws of hell's abyss; how God's wrath burns in him, in soul and body" (*WC* "On True Repentance," par. 3).

As the true prophets are those "in whom Christ has become man," the false are those "who interpret by the letter without knowledge" (*EOG[E]* 12.60–61). Boehme states "Ye shall with your conclusions of reason, without the blood of Christ in you, obtain nothing . . . ye shall be taken prisoner in God's severe righteousness in your rationalistic inferences, and chosen to be false prophets" (*EOG[E]* 12.64). By contrast with the prophetic, which embraces the diversity of gifts in others, Blake's reasoning Angel in *The Marriage* can neither inspire nor take part in any truly potent, mutually beneficial "converse" of independent spirits: "I have always found that Angels have the vanity to speak of themselves as the only wise; this they do with a confident insolence sprouting from systematic reasoning" (*MHH* 42, pl. 21). It is quite possible that by the time of *The Marriage* Blake had come to see the distinction between the true and false prophet drawn in his respective readings of Boehme and Swedenborg, that is, between one possessed of an "honest indignation" that might inspire creative newness in others, and one of "confident insolence" who "boasts that what he writes is new; tho' it is only the Contents or Index of already publish'd books" (*MHH* 42, pl. 21). As with the Angel—or rather, perhaps, "as" the Angel—Blake's Swedenborg succumbed to a premature and illusory sense of his own independence, mistaking the apparent source of the spiritual life for the real. For Blake Swedenborg revered a mode of apprehension that merely limited the individual to his weaknesses, severing the fallen man from the possibility of a world of energetic correspondence and creation beyond the constraints of the outward, reasoning self:

> he imagines that all are religious. and himself the single one on earth that ever broke a net.
>
> Now hear a plain fact: Swedenborg has not written one new truth: Now hear another: he has written all the old falshoods.
>
> And now hear the reason. He conversed with Angels who are all religious, and conversed not with Devils who all hate religion, for he was incapable thro' his conceited notions. (*MHH* 43, pls. 21–22)

Where Blake saw the worldly "Angels" as governing through a false, abstract religion, Boehme, true to the prophetic voice, repeatedly denounced the Church for deceiving and leading man away from the unifying ground of divine inspiration, targeting its pomp and self-importance: "Your own authority, and the climbing up of your *Tyrannical* Power (which you yourself have erected) is your *Beast*; in that you have set up a wicked compulsion, forcing and oppressing . . . poor people" (*TLM* 3.62). As the prophet would deliver man from this "compulsion," Boehme urged,

> behold, dear brethren, how very Thievishly they have delt with you, they have set themselves up over the Earth, and have drawn to themselves all Power, might, and honour, and ascribe all authority to themselves, and have blinded you with flattering *Hypocrisy*. . . . they have stirred you up to Contention and Wars, so that you have murdered one another. (*TLM* 12.19)

Following Boehme's unsparing indignation at those of "earthly Babel" who "consumest the Sweat and Blood of the Needy" (*TP* 19.47), Blake forces the Angel to behold the "wicked compulsion," the "Contention" that springs from "systematic reasoning." For the Angel's "vanity" would reduce the "infinite variety" of man to a "species," a generalization, "a number of monkeys . . . chained by the middle, grinning and snatching at one another" (*MHH* 42, pl. 20).

As this suggests, the prophet does not present what is merely palatable. This is because "another man liveth in him, which is not like and comfortable to the outward mortall man; and so God's Justice executeth its judgment . . . upon the house of sinne" (*Ep.* 1.26). Blake echoes this "judgment": "Jesus did not wish to unite but to seperate [*sic*] . . . as in the Parable of the sheep and goats! and he says I came not to send Peace but a Sword" (*MHH* 40, pl. 17). Boehme understood that the prophet should work through this separative "Sword": "all Prophets speak from the *Turba*; they discover that which is false; and declare what is better, which enters into the will of God" (FQ 38.3). The *Turba* is

> the aroused and awakened ferocity of the inner ground, where the hellish foundation is manifest in the spirit of this world, from which great plagues and sicknesses arise. It is also the awakened ferocity of outward nature, as may be seen in the downpour of violent storms, where fire is manifest in water. It is a pouring out of the anger of God, by which nature is troubled. (*The Key* 133)

Such an insight into man's "inner ground" cannot be seen in the literal terms of the "Corporeal or Vegetative Eye," as Blake appreciated: "The roaring of lions, the howling of wolves, the raging of the stormy sea, and the destructive sword. are portions of eternity too great for the eye of man" (*MHH* 36, pl. 8, l. 27). This fiery energetic "ground" from and of which the prophet speaks is the source of much that is potent and distinctive in Boehme's works. It is the prophet's task to find forms through which the destructive "portion" of man's being may be "married" to the creative; forms that liberate rather than confine the essential energies of life.

To return to the letter to Flaxman, it would seem that Blake was highly responsive to the fiery quality that animated his seventeenth-century counterpart: "Behmen appeard to me. terrors appeard in the Heavens above / And in Hell beneath and a mighty and awful change threatend the Earth" (*Letters* 707–8). "The Tyger" similarly speaks of the "ferocity of the inner ground" and the necessity attendant upon it, asking "What immortal hand or eye, / Dare frame thy fearful symmetry?" (*SoE* 25, ll. 23–24). As Boehme speaks "from the *Turba*," he may be seen to have "dared" to "frame" the "Tyger." In the creation of the poem, the prophetic giving of form, Blake may also be said to have done so. From this it may be argued that Boehme himself is, in a manner of speaking, present in the piece, that the poem "frames" the potent energies that "appeard" to Blake through the spiritual form of "Behmen." Just as Boehme's advent is associated with profound upheavals "in the Heavens above / And in Hell beneath," in "The Tyger" the poet's voice asks, "In what distant deeps or skies. / Burnt the fire of thine eyes?" (*SoE* 24, ll. 5–6). In each case, the fiery, energetic figure's activities are not restricted to either "Heaven" or "Hell." In the realm of possibility, each may "appear" in the "deeps or skies," or, rather, in both, drawing the apparently fixed opposites together into a relationship of such consequence, a "marriage" of such revolutionary significance for "the Earth" as to be fearful. It is notable that both Boehme and the "Tyger" are associated with the same word: "terrors." There is an air of such imminent potency and "change," of revelation in the evocation of each as to suggest that Blake perceived in both the workings of God's "judgment," and that as such he might well have apprehended an immediate, active correspondence between the two. Thus, as the "Tyger," like Boehme, expresses the wrathful aspect of prophetic activity, the question "In what distant deeps or skies. / Burnt the fire of thine eyes?" may be seen to encompass and address the Tyger's formative energies—the energies that give it form and life—as they "Burnt" and found manifestation in Boehme and those like him. In addition, it may be seen that Blake was also addressing himself here, that he was attempting to confront and understand that within himself which was "distant," "not like and comfortable to the outward mortall man," as if the "Tyger" were as Boehme's prophetic "Glass," a mirror through which the poet and those like him might find manifestation. The "judgment" effected through such "mighty and awful" revelation expresses the necessity of the "awakened" fiery "portion" of man's being. The "ferocity of the inner ground" may therefore be imaginatively embraced, as Blake discovered: "I was walking among the fires of hell, delighted with the enjoyments of Genius; which to Angels look like torment or insanity" (*MHH* 35, pl. 6). As the Duke of Orleans states in *The French Revolution*, the individual need not be "consumed" by "the fires / Of another's high flaming rich bosom," "for fire delights in its form" (294, ll. 191–92, 189). It seems quite probable that Blake "delighted" in the "mighty and awful" "fires" that "appeard" in the energetic "form" of Boehme.

Boehme and Blake conceived prophetic activity as working through an energetic, guiding structure, through a "framing" voice. This "frame" appears in Boehme:

> Every prophet is a limit {or boundary}, wherein a time is included or an age comprehended; and he is the mouth of that kingdom or dominion; that is, when that kingdom hath awakened and generated the turba in it, then is he the mouth of the inward ground, which declareth . . . the vanity {of confusion}. (*MM* 67.9)[1]

The fiery "ground" thus demands a reevaluation of the prophetic role; one that again stresses the importance of individual "gifts," as Blake understood:

> Prophets in the modern sense of the word have never existed Jonah was no prophet in the modern sense for his prophecy of Nineveh failed Every

> honest man is a Prophet he utters his opinion both of private and public matters/Thus/If you go on So/the Result is So/ He never says such a thing shall happen let you do what you will. a Prophet is a Seer not an Arbitrary Dictator. It is man's fault if God is not able to do him good. for he gives to the just and to the unjust but the unjust reject his gift. (*Ann. Wat.* 617)

Understanding with Boehme that the prophetic is not bound to the "time" of its activity, that it works from an eternal ground, Blake emphasized the necessity of paying heed to prophetic utterance, underlining the importance of fruitful spiritual interaction:

> O What Wonders are the Children of Men! Would to God that they would Consider it That they would Consider their Spiritual Life Regardless of that faint Shadow Calld Natural Life. and that they would Promote Each others Spiritual Labours. Each according to its Rank and that they would know that. Receiving a Prophet As a Prophet is a Duty which If omitted is more Severely Avenged than Every Sin and Wickedness beside. It is the Greatest of Crimes to Depress True Art and Science. (*Letters* 767)

Blake would have "received" Boehme "As a Prophet."

HUSKS, HISTORIES, AND THE INNER BIBLE

In the spirit of individual prophetic activity, Boehme believed that

> in the greatest Part of the Books of the Divines, there is nothing but the History that such a Thing has been done, and that we should be regenerated in Christ. But what do I understand from hence? Nothing, but only the History, that such a Thing has been done, and done again, and ought to be done.
>
> Our Divines set themselves Hand and Foot with Might and Main, with their utmost Endeavour, by Persecution and Reproach, against this, [and say,] that man must not [dare to] search into the deep Grounds what God is; Men must not search nor curiously pry into the Deity. (*TP* 3.5–6)

The contention of "Babel" stands in opposition to the "Honouring" of God's "gifts in other men": "in the churches nothing but contention, disputation, scorn and blasphemy is exercised and taught, that one brother despiseth the other, calleth him heretic, and damneth him to hell fire for an opinion's sake, whereby all love, truth, unity and concord is vanished" (*MM* 63.41). Boehme declared his own desire for active, illuminating converse:

> Dear brothers; We wish to speak with you . . . out of our pearl, out of Christian essence and knowledge, not from husks and histories, but out of a childlike spirit, out of Christ's knowledge. . . .

> Now man binds us . . . to the stone churches, which in their value would indeed be good if man also brought Christ's temple into them. (*WC* "On the New Birth," 6.1–2)

There are therefore "two . . . Churches upon the earth; one which seeketh only worldly pleasure, might, honour, and the outward god . . . therein . . . lodgeth the Serpent's child. The other, which seeketh the virgin-child and God's kingdom, and must suffer itself to be persecuted, reviled, reproached, and killed by the Cainical Church." If "the virgin's child . . . be not manifest . . . then the devil is" (*MM* 26.25–26). Blake argued in agreement with this in *Jerusalem*:

> Man must and will have Some Religion; if he has not the Religion of Jesus, he will have the Religion of Satan, and will erect the Synagogue of Satan, calling the Prince of this World, God; and destroying all who do not worship Satan under the Name God. (201, pl. 52, "To the Deists")

Boehme's view that the worldly "stone church" "is a spiritual whore-house, which a man must distinguish from the temple of JESUS CHRIST" (*MM* 63.45) is echoed in Blake's that "Brothels" are built "with bricks of religion" (*MHH* 36, pl. 8, l. 21).

The Church would have its place "if man did not hang onto the husks" of understanding: "Many a man goes to church for twenty or thirty years, hears sermons, uses the sacraments, allows himself to be absolved and is still [just as bad a] beast of the devil (and of vanity) as the rest. A beast goes into the church and to the Lord's Supper, and a beast goes from there again" (*WC* "On the New Birth," 6.4). Responsibility lies with the individual:

> Man can undertake nothing from the Beginning of his Youth, nor in the whole Course of his Time in this World, that is more profitable and necessary for him, than to learn to know himself; what he is, out of what, from whence, and for what he is created, and what his Office is. (*TP* "The Author's Preface," par. 1)

Boehme repeatedly points to the "Mouth-Hypocrisy" of those who were unresponsive to the indwelling spiritual life, the "Lip-Christians," the "History-Priests" who had perverted the truths that lie in the Bible:

> the Temple of Christ was turned into Temples made of Stones, and out of the Testimony of the Holy Ghost a worldly Law was made. Then the Holy Ghost spoke no more freely, but he must speak according to their Laws . . . and so the Temple of Christ in Man's Knowledge became very obscure. (*TP* 26.27)

This is echoed in Blake's depiction of Urizen, who arises "A wide world of solid obstruction":

> Here alone I in books formd of metals
> Have written the secrets of wisdom
> The secrets of dark contemplation
> . . . .
>
> Lo! I unfold my darkness: and on
> This rock, place with strong hand the Book
> Of eternal brass, written in my solitude.
>
> Laws of peace, of love, of unity:
> Of pity, compassion, forgiveness.
> Let each chuse one habitation:
> His ancient infinite mansion:
> One command, one joy, one desire,
> One curse, one weight, one measure
> One King, one God, One Law.
>
> (*BU* 72, pl. 4, ll. 24–40)

Blake and Boehme believed that "One Law for the Lion and Ox is Oppression" (*MHH* 44, pl. 24).

Nonetheless, both regarded the Bible as their primary written source of inspiration. Working through imagination, Boehme opposed the literal interpretation of the Bible, believing that the view that regards it as a distant "History" in which "such a Thing has been done, and done again, and ought to be done" is backward looking, denying the ongoing ever renewing movement of the spiritual. His standpoint takes account of the fact that the Bible itself has been and will be determined and changed by the passage of time and the subtle impositions of "History":

> men understand nothing at all more of the Holy Ghost's language, what the spirit of God hath spoken in Moses and the Prophets. . . . Men cleave merely to an historical action, and see not what is signified by this or that action.
>
> . . . God's spirit hath not done such wonders for the history's sake of a plain and simple shepherd, as it stands in the outward form of it. . . . No, sure: but for this cause; that under such plain, simple, historical relations is signified . . . that which is future, eternal. (*MM* 60.49–50)

Blake reaffirmed this:

> If Moses did not write the history of his acts. it takes away the authority altogether it ceases to be history and becomes a Poem of probable impossibilities fabricated for pleasure as moderns say but I say by Inspiration . . .

> Nothing can be more contemptible than to suppose Public RECORDS to be True Read them and Judge. if you are not a Fool.
>
> Of what consequence is it whether Moses wrote the Pentateuch or no. (*Ann. Wat.* 616–17)

This opens up the possibilities of the creative. In works such as *The Book of Urizen*, Blake consciously mirrored the form and style of biblical verse. In this he was creating from the truths embodied in the Bible anew, as the biblical prophets "and their successors" had done before him, casting off the "one Law." In this he is at one with Boehme:

> the Spirit of Christ in his children is not bound to any certain form . . . as the spirit in the Apostles was free, and they spake not all one and the same words, but from one spirit and ground they did all speak, every one as the spirit gave him utterance. Even thus likewise the spirit speaketh yet out of its children, it needeth no form aforehand composed and gathered together out of the literal word. (*MM* 28.52)

In other words, "the prophetic spirit seeth through God's seeing . . . And then the Word expresseth, declareth and expoundeth . . . through the prophetic spirit" (*MM* 67.11). Morton D. Paley has noted in respect of Blake that "The appropriation of the Bible in parts of *Jerusalem* goes far beyond mere imitation; it is the product of a remarkable assimilation of biblical texts that can then be recast into new forms of utterance."[2] Like Boehme, Blake perceived and worked through the immense possibilities he found in the Bible: "The Old and New Testaments are the Great Code of Art" (*Laocoön* 274). He asked,

> Why is the Bible more Entertaining and Instructive than any other book. Is it not because . . . {it is} addressed to the Imagination which is Spiritual Sensation and but mediately to the Understanding or Reason. (*Letters* 702-3)

Envisioning prophetic activity as a merciful "limit" or boundary, Boehme understood that the

> literal word is only a manuduction and manifestation of Christ; that we should have the same before us, as a testimony and witness of Christ, [shewing] what he is, and what he hath done for us, that we should conceive, let and fasten our faith therein; and yet with the desire enter into the living Word, Christ. (*MM* 28.53)

Blake also believed that "the Hebrew Bible and the Greek Gospel are . . . Preservd by the Saviours Mercy." He adds, "The Nature of my Work is Visionary or Imaginative it is an Endeavour to Restore <what the Ancients calld >

the Golden Age" (*VLJ* 555). Working within biblical and prophetic traditions, he strove to reveal the eternal Bible that resides as inexhaustible potential within the outward form of the Old and New Testaments, to bring to light in the individual the ever present third age of the Everlasting Gospel, Boehme's "Age of the Lily."

Just as Blake's Isaiah and Ezekiel stated of their "lost works" in *The Marriage* that "none of equal value was lost," he declares in *Milton* that

> The Stolen and Perverted Writings of Homer and Ovid: of Plato and Cicero. which all Men ought to contemn: are set up by artifice against the Sublime of the Bible. but when the New Age is at leisure to Pronounce; all will be set right; and those Grand Works of the more ancient and consciously and professedly Inspired Men, will hold their proper rank. (*Milton* 95, "Preface")

The "divinely inspired" Boehme's writings were probably among the "Grand Works" of those who had been illuminated by the Bible and, consequently, who had cast new light on it. In *A Vision of the Last Judgment* Blake wrote that "The Hebrew Bible and the Gospel of Jesus are not Allegory but Eternal Vision or Imagination of All that Exists" (554). Boehme's works stand as a model of a reading of the Bible in this creative spiritual sense. Like Blake, he understood that its inner truths are elusive and as such demand an active, imaginative approach: "the Words of Scripture are true; but there is required an *Understanding* to discern them, not an outward Supposition or Conceit, whereby Men tattle of a foreign strange God who dwells somewhere above, in a Heaven afar off" (*EOG* 7.68).

Sharing Blake's view that the outward is engaged with the inner life in a persistent creative interaction, Boehme located the true Bible within the individual:

> I have written out of my own Book which was opened in me, being the Noble similitude of God, the Booke of the Noble and precious Image (understand God's owne similitude or likenesse) was bestowed upon me, to Read . . .
>
> . . . I can find therein the foundation of the World, and all Mysteries; yet not I, but the Spirit of God doth it according to the measure, as he pleaseth. (*Ep* 2.14–15)

Accordingly, the active, imaginative reading of spiritual writings can be a reading and creation of one's own spiritual possibilities, a living experience that overcomes all simple delineations of subject and object, of self and other. Desiring that the individual might realize the indwelling body of Christ and so join in spiritual communion with the poet and those like him, Blake wrote at the beginning of *Jerusalem*: "I . . . hope the Reader will be with me, wholly One in Jesus our Lord, who is the God [*of Fire*] and Lord [*of Love*] to whom the Ancients look'd and saw his day afar off, with trembling and amazement" (145, pl. 3 "To the Public"). The opening of the "book" of oneself may be an opening up of oneself to the "terrors" and awe of prophetic vision, of the perception of God's "Fire" and "Love," of destruction and creation, of the temporal and the eternal; a "judgment": "What immortal hand or eye, / Dare frame *thy* fearful symmetry?" (emphasis added). The outward, written Bible does not simply "frame" its internal sense *as* the body "frames" the spirit; the literal word and the body are external and distinct from one another, while the spirit of the internal sense of the Bible and the indwelling spirit in man are one. The spiritual life was not for Blake and Boehme isolated within man, separate from an external world that remained impassive and untouched by it, or mere solipsism. It lived through man's apparently separate internal and external worlds in such a way as to realize the unifying love of man in Christ, "For every thing that lives is Holy" (*MHH* 45, pl. 27). Boehme writes :

> If I had no other book than only the book which I am myself so I have books enough. The whole Bible lies in me if I have Christ's spirit. If I read myself I read God's book and you my brothers are the alphabet which I read in myself, for my mind and will finds you within me. I wish from my heart that you would also find me. (*Rem.* "Apol. Tilcken," par. 298)

It would seem that Blake "found" Boehme.

4
Obscurity, Difficulty, and Awakening

NECESSARY OBSCURITY

Throughout his writings Boehme stresses that he "may happen not to be understood clearly enough by the desirous Reader," and that he "shall be as one that is altogether dumb to the unenlightened" (*TP* 5.1). Believing with Blake that all men are fallen; that, to quote the poet, while man would "live in Paradise and Liberty," he "may do so in Spirit but not in the <Mortal> Body" (*VLJ* 564), Boehme repeatedly states that even the most diligent reader may at times misconceive him, for "in this World there is no true Understanding, either in the Stars, or in the Elements; and also in all its Creatures" (*TP* 5.12). Boehme's writings can be ill expressed, chaotic, subject to misleading rationalizations, and confusing. However, many of the difficulties and obscurities stem from the difference between the literal word and the spiritual sense, from the apprehension that "in this World there is no true Understanding." Blake's reading of Boehme would not have been restricted to the outward form. Appreciative of the spiritual sense, he would have been aware that much of the supposed confusion and unintelligibility was more apparent than real. As Peter Malekin remarks of Boehme, "What will seem self-evident absurdity to one reader will be everyday experience to another."[1] Blake himself was also engaged with an approach that involved obscurity and difficulty, an approach which in his case led to increasing complexity and density in his work. Blake's "converse" with such figures as Boehme, the persistent forging and reforging of vision that breathes life into spiritual interaction, might well have nourished and even guided him into the greater abstruseness of his later works.

For all the difficulties of Boehme's writings, there is in their very chaotic quality, in the energy of their struggle for expression something which speaks directly and forcefully of the fiery "inner ground" of which the prophet speaks. Identifying Boehme's earliest works, the *Aurora* (1612), *The Three Principles of the Divine Essence* (1619), and *The Threefold Life of Man* (1620), as being the most problematic, Bryan Aubrey writes: "there is a strange irony here. The very works which are the most chaotic in style are also the ones which have the greatest immediacy; the words seem to pour out with the eruptive force of a volcano, as if a voice was speaking, breathlessly, from the very roots of being."[2] Boehme's is a voice that would make itself known. There is an air of freshness and newness born of his struggle for expression that reproduces the necessary fecundity and newness of spiritual discovery and understanding; an air which, as suggested by the immediacy of Blake's apprehension of "Behmen" "in the Heavens above / And in Hell beneath," might well have readily enhanced the creative possibilities of Blake's "communion" with him.

In this spirit of freshness and newness, both Boehme and Blake stressed the importance of simplicity, particularly in terms of the purity and clarity of apprehension of innocence and childhood. Desiring to speak "not from husks and histories, but out of a childlike spirit," Boehme turned to the child as a spiritual guide:

> the corrupted nature in this world *labours* in its utmost power and diligence, that it might bring forth heavenly forms, and many times little children might be their parents' schoolmasters and *teachers*, if parents could but understand, or would take *notice* of them. (*Aur* 12.89)

This sentiment echoes clearly throughout the poet's *Songs of Innocence and of Experience*. Responding to Dr. Trusler's charge that his works were in need of explanation, Blake argued that his "Visions" had "Particularly . . . been Elucidated by Children who have taken a greater delight in contemplating my Pictures than I even hoped. Neither Youth nor Childhood is Folly or Incapacity" (*Letters* 703). The simplicity of innocence was for them possessed of the same potent clarity of vision as that which is able to distinguish imaginatively between the spiritual and the merely natural, the inward and the outward, the eternal and the temporal. Blake drew the distinction in *Milton*: "How wide the Gulf and Unpassable between Simplicity and Insipidity" (129, pl. 30). He told Dr. Trusler,

> You say that I want somebody to Elucidate my Ideas. But you ought to know that What is Grand is necessarily obscure to Weak men. That which can be made Explicit to the Idiot is not worth my care. (*Letters* 702)

The "necessarily obscure" defines the visionary's stance. Blake wrote with distaste of the supposed artist who is, in truth, a "Hired Knave" who "cares not for the Few. His Eye is on the Many. or rather on the Money" (*Ann. Ren.* 655). "If you Endeavour to Please the Worst you will never Please the Best To please All is Impossible" (*Ann. Ren.* 661). For Blake and Boehme it was a duty not to simplify spiritual truth. Boehme wrote of the energetic inner necessity that gave form to his works, "I have not dared to write otherwise than was given and indicated to me. I have continually written as the Spirit dictated and have not given place to Reason" (*Ep* 3.15). It is very possible that Boehme's refusal to compromise his vision for the sake of general understanding reinforced for Blake, who believed that "General Knowledge is Remote Knowledge" (*VLJ* 560), the importance of his "converse" with like-minded spirits "in the Heavens." After the years at Felpham under Hayley's patronage had proved far less conducive than he had hoped, he wrote to Thomas Butts:

> Now I may say to you what perhaps I should not dare to say to any one else. That I can alone carry on my visionary studies in London unannoyd and that I may converse with my friends in Eternity. See Visions, Dream Dreams, and prophecy and speak Parables unobserv'd and at liberty from the Doubts of other Mortals. (*Letters* 728)

The nature of the life of the spirit defines the visionary stance. Boehme and Blake perceived that the spirit should not, as it could not truly be apprehended as either an object of knowledge or a merely subjective state. It could not be readily "framed," as Boehme understood: "the spirit cannot be written down, being no creature, but the moving, flowing, boiling power of God" (*Aur* 3.64). Spiritual truth was not something that could be simply proved or disproved. For either to have attempted to show openly the truths revealed in spiritual experience, and through this verify those truths, would have been as good as submitting to the Spectre of "demonstration" that Blake persistently attacks. The spirit imposed its own limitations. The "necessarily obscure" was determined by a sublime inner necessity. Boehme, like Blake after him, understood that human reason of itself could not, for all its assertions to the contrary, penetrate this sublimity. He wrote of his own work that "a Man's own Reason, without the light of God, cannot come into the Ground [of them,] it is impossible; let his Wit be ever so high and subtle, it apprehends but as it were the Shadow of it in a Glass" (*Clavis* 2). Boehme distinguished between a lower form of understanding that is bound to the "natural life, whose ground lies in a temporal beginning and end," and a higher, living, imaginative knowledge that is able to "enter into the supernatural ground wherein God is understood" (*SP* "Theoscopia," 1.2). This distinction also appears in Blake in "the Mighty difference" he discerned between a mental process that is limited to "the Vanities of Time and Space," seeing only itself in the shadowy "Vegetable Glass of Nature," and the "Eternal . . . Worlds of Vision" revealed in the creative knowledge of "Spiritual Mystery" (*VLJ* 555). He wrote, with a rare and perhaps misleading use of the word "Allegory," "Allegory addressd to the Intellectual powers while it is altogether hidden from the Corporeal Understanding is My Definition of the Most Sublime Poetry" (*Letters* 730).

As Boehme had "continually written as the Spirit dictated," Blake wrote that he himself was "compelld by my Genius or Angel to follow where he led if I were to act otherwise it would not fulfill the purpose for which alone I live" (*Letters* 701). In his distinction between the "Intellectual powers" of the spiritual life and "Corporeal Understanding," he wrote of *Milton*, "I may praise it since I dare not pretend to be any other than the Secretary the Authors are in Eternity" (*Letters* 730). Boehme, the spiritual as opposed to the "natural man," may well be apprehended as one of Blake's "Authors . . . in Eternity." As "it is impossible to know God or heavenly things without conjunction with those who know God and heavenly things" (*Ann. Lav* 600), as Blake believed, the dependency on the spirit for illumination is a dependency that extends to and embraces all those who were advanced in experience of the spiritual life. Boehme had shown that the Holy Spirit made possible this union of understanding:

> without the illumination thereof you will not *understand* this Mystery; for there is a strong lock and bar before it *in the spirit of man*, that must be first unlocked or opened; and that, *no man* can do, for the Holy Ghost is the *only* key to do it withal. (*Aur* 13.31)

Blake had also found himself "in the predicament of that prophet," namely Balaam, "who says," "I cannot go beyond the commandment of the LORD, to do *either* good or bad of mine own mind; *but* what the LORD saith, that will I speak" (*Letters* 701).[3] The visionary clearly apprehended both his extensive spiritual possibilities and, by no means in contradiction of this potential, the limitations and necessary obscurities to which he himself as a human was subject. Boehme saw this:

> I do *not borrow* of other men in my writings . . . all is written by God in my mind, so that I *absolutely* and infallibly believe, know and see it; yet not in the flesh, but in the spirit, in the impulse and motion of God . . .
>
> Nor is this my *natural will*, that I could do it by my own small ability; for if the spirit were withdrawn from me, then I could neither know nor understand *my own writings*.
>
> (*Aur* 3.110, 112)

As may be seen in this, the difficulties and obscurities of Blake's and Boehme's vision give expression to and actively participate in an important aspect of the spiritual life; an aspect that may best be described as a spirit of dynamic paradox. Boehme evokes this in two passages in *The Treatise of the Incarnation*:

> God dwells not in this World in the Outward Principle, but in the *Inward*: he dwells indeed in the Place of this world, but this world apprehends him not;

how then will the Earthly Man apprehend the secret Mysteries of God. (1.2.43)

> Paradise springs no more through the Earth, for it is become a Mystery, and yet is *continually there*. . . .
>
> It is *in* this World, and yet is *out* of this World. (1.6.84, 86)

In *Psychology and Alchemy* Jung asks,

> Has it not yet been observed that all religious statements contain logical contradictions and assertions that are impossible in principle, that this is in fact the very essence of religious assertion? . . . the paradox is one of our most valuable spiritual possessions, while uniformity of meaning is a sign of weakness. Hence a religion becomes inwardly impoverished when it loses or waters down its paradoxes; but their multiplication enriches because only the paradox comes anywhere near to comprehending the fulness of life.[4]

At the beginning of *The Four Zoas* Tharmas speaks of this fullness to Enion:

> Why wilt thou Examine every little fibre of my soul
> Spreading them out before the Sun like Stalks of flax to dry
> The infant joy is beautiful but its anatomy
> Horrible Ghast and Deadly nought shalt thou find in it
> But Death Despair and Everlasting brooding Melancholy.
>
> (302, Night 1, ll. 48–52)

"Spiritual Mystery" refuses any final restrictive form imposed on life. Blake and Boehme exhort a living process in which the reader is to be actively involved. As Evelyn Underhill perceived, "True Mysticism is active and practical, not passive and theoretical. It is an organic life-process, a something which the whole self does; not something as to which its intellect holds an opinion."[5] Blake expressed this in words that may be seen as conveying the whole spirit that underlies and gives form to the "necessarily obscure":

> He who binds to himself a joy
> Does the winged life destroy
> But he who kisses the joy as it flies
> Lives in eternity's sunrise.
>
> (*SB* 470, "Eternity")

William Law said of Boehme that

> His style is what it is, strange and uncommon; not because he wanted learning and skill in words, but because what he saw and conceived was quite new and strange, never seen or spoken of before; and therefore if he was to put it

> down in writing, words must be used to signify that which they had never done before.[6]

This demands an inward mental alertness. As Boehme urged, man must "not be a lazy sleeper" but "as a soldier that stands before his enemy": "fighting must be the watchword, not with tongue and sword, but with mind and spirit; and not give over" (*SP* "Six Theosophic Points," 10.23, 25). With the same alertness Blake exhorts the "Young Men of the New Age" in the hymn at the beginning of *Milton*:

> Bring me my Bow of burning gold:
> Bring me my Arrows of desire:
> Bring me my Spear: O clouds unfold!
> Bring me my Chariot of fire!
>
> I will not cease from Mental Fight,
> Nor shall my Sword sleep in my hand.
> (95, "Preface," ll. 9–14)

"Mental Fight" is necessary to defend that which the necessarily obscure keeps alive. Blake spoke of "having Spiritual Enemies of . . . formidable magnitude" (*Letters* 723), a magnitude Boehme repeatedly stresses: "the human flesh is very young and tender, and the *devil* is rough and hard" (*Aur* 13.29). After Boehme's first moment of illumination in 1600 almost twelve years passed before he was able to write his first work, the *Aurora*. He described those years:

> It was with me as with a young tree that is planted in the ground, and at first is young and *tender*, and flourishing to the eye, especially if it comes on lustily in its growing. But [it] doth not bear fruit at once; and though it blossoms, the blossoms fall off; also many a cold wind, frost and snow pass upon it, *before* it comes to any growth and bearing fruit.
>
> So also it went with this spirit: The first fire was but a *seed*, and not a constant lasting light: *Since that time* many a cold wind blew upon it. (*Aur* 19.15–16)

From this experience he was able to act as a source of guidance and support:

> I write . . . not for mine own glory, but for a *comfort* to the Reader, so that if perhaps he be minded to walk with me upon my *narrow* bridge, he should not suddenly be discouraged, dismayed and distrustful, when the gates of hell and God's wrath meet him, and *present* themselves before him. (*Aur* 19.22)

Paradoxically, the very difficulties of the spiritual life enhanced its vitality for Blake and Boehme. This lies at the core of *The Marriage of Heaven and Hell*:

"Without Contraries is no progression. Attraction and Repulsion, Reason and Energy, Love and Hate, are necessary to Human existence" (34, pl. 3).

ROUSING THE FACULTIES TO ACT

Blake and Boehme demand that the reader discover "new and strange" ways of perceiving, understanding, and reading. Boehme desired "that the formed and conceived word in God's children may be stirred up, whetted and exercised, and the truth come forth to light" (*MM* 22.55). Blake pointed out this desire in his letter to Dr. Trusler:

> You say that I want somebody to Elucidate my Ideas. But you ought to know that What is Grand is necessarily obscure to Weak men. That which can be made Explicit to the Idiot is not worth my care. The wisest of the Ancients considerd what is not too Explicit as the fittest for Instruction because it rouzes the faculties to act." (*Letters* 702).

In *The Marriage* this activity is associated with prophetic activity:

> I . . . asked Isaiah what made him go naked and barefoot three years? He answerd, the same that made our friend Diogenes the Grecian.
>
> I then asked Ezekiel. why he eat dung, and lay so long on his right and left side? He answerd. the desire of raising other men into a perception of the infinite. (39, pl. 13)

There is always more to life. Boehme repeatedly states of his work, "You must elevate your sense or mind in the *spirit*, if you intend to understand or *apprehend* it" (*Aur* 8.43), and thus "I will so write in a divine, and also in a creaturely Way, that I might stir up any one to desire and long after the Consideration of the high Things . . . for Christ biddeth us to pray, seek, and knock, and then it shall be opened unto us" (*TP* 2.5). Blake's much-quoted maxim, "If the doors of perception were cleansed every thing would appear to man as it is: infinite" (*MHH* 39, pl. 14), clearly echoes the propositions that appear repeatedly in Boehme's writings; so much so as to suggest that he was consciously reaffirming Boehme's exhortations:

> if . . . thy Eyes were opened, then in that very Place where thou standest, sittest or liest, thou shouldst see the glorious Countenance or Face of God, and the whole heavenly Gate. (*Aur* 10.98)

Paradise is not in the world,

> yet as it were swallowed up in the Mystery; but it is nor altered in itself, it is only withdrawn from our Sight and our Source; for if our Eyes were opened, we should see it. (*FQ* 39.1)

Both visionaries worked through the compelling possibilities revealed in their respective use of the word "If."

Following the dictates of the spirit Boehme asserted that "one cannot lend the Key to another to [unlock] this [withal;] and if one has a Key, he cannot open it to another . . . every one must unlock it with his own Key, or else he cannot enter therein. For the Holy Ghost is the Key, when he has that Key, then he may go both in and out" (*TP* 9.26). The rousing of the faculties to act is to the individual participation in "Spiritual Mystery." Both visionaries sought to awaken the mind from its habitual, natural processes toward a real and living awareness of the limited and accepted terms through which life is normally lived. This is manifest in the vehemence of Boehme's prophetic proclamations, and in the spirit of provocation inherent in Blake's assertions such as "Sooner murder an infant in its cradle than nurse unacted desires," and that "no virtue can exist without breaking these ten commandments: Jesus was all virtue, and acted from impulse: not from rules" (*MHH* 38, pl. 10, l. 67; 43, pls. 23–24). This brings with it the necessity of reevaluation, of the pair Good and Evil for instance, as is apparent in such works as *The Marriage* and *The Everlasting Gospel*. In part, this subversive desire springs from the recognition that the prevalent religion in "this World," whether spiritual or secular, was for Blake and Boehme the opposite of what it presented itself to be. This is encapsulated in Blake's assertion that "The Modern Church Crucifies Christ with the Head Downwards" (*VLJ* 564). This is the Satanic cross and has clear precedents in Boehme, who believed that man had "hitherto accounted" the Antichrist "a God":

> Observe it, ye children of God, for I myself formerly, before the time of my high knowledge, did thus *reverence* and honour him, and supposed it was according to God's will; for I was taught no otherwise, and the whole world is in the same conceit. (*TLM* 11.51–52)

Blake wrote of "what the religious call Good and Evil. Good is the passive that obeys Reason[.] Evil is the active springing from Energy" (*MHH* 34, pl. 3). In reaction to Thornton's "Tory" translation of The Lord's Prayer, he was able to say that "God is the Ghost of the Priest and King who Exist whereas God exists not except from their Effluvia" (*Ann. Thorn.* 669). He declared

> The Vision of Christ that thou dost see
> Is my Visions Greatest Enemy
> Thine has a great hook nose like thine
> Mine has a snub nose like to mine
> Thine is the Friend of All Mankind
> Mine speaks in parables to the Blind
> Thine loves the same world that mine hates

> Thy Heaven doors are my Hell Gates
> . . . .
> . . . thou readst black where I read white.
>
> (*EG* [e] 524, ll. 1–8, 14)

This is again in the Antinomian tradition of the Everlasting Gospel. The potent "fires" revealed to Blake in his "converse" with those such as Boehme, as in the "framing" of "The Tyger," inflamed and gave form to his own desires. His reading of Boehme would have been a matter of "Mental Fight," one in which Boehme, as one of the "Ancients," roused his faculties to act. Boehme was conscious that this interaction was one that could be mutually beneficial, anticipating those who would come after him: "Seeing then that my Knowledge has been received by seeking and knocking, I therefore write it down for a Memorial, that I might occasion a Desire in any to seek after them, and thereby my Talent might be improved, and not be hid in the Earth" (*TP* 2.6). Anticipation of the possibilities of others can be form-giving to oneself. As an indication of the high level of imaginative communication to which Blake and Boehme aspired, he wrote "Loving Reader, I had need have an angelical Tongue . . . and thou an angelical Mind, and then we should well understand one another" (*TP* 12.1). In *The Signature of All Things* he adds:

> though I see one to speak, teach, preach, and write of God, and though I hear and read the same, yet this is not sufficient for me to understand him; but if his sound and spirit out of his signature and similitude enter into my own similitude, and imprint his similitude into mine, then I may understand him really and fundamentally, be it either spoken or written, if he has the hammer that can strike my bell. (*SR* 1.1)

Paley has argued that Boehme's "hammer" is given new voice in the "hammer" of Blake's Los, an agent of "psychic transformation" which is also able to give form to, quoting Boehme, "the Longing of Love, *viz.* the Longing of the Soul's Spirit" (*TLM* 18.49): "Blake's furnace is a perpetual source of power for transforming a dead world. The hammer, the active force of the Logos, beats out the changes."[7] As Los is persistently at the "forge" with his "hammer," Boehme wields the life-giving hammer throughout his works, exhorting the reader to imaginative engagement:

> If you have not the *right hammer*, you cannot strike the Clock that awakens the poor captive soul; Heaven and Earth and *Every Thing lie in Man*, you need but to use the right Hammer, if you will strike his Clock and awaken him out of his sleep: your *Crying aloud* will not do it, you will not be able to beat the Divine sound into him, if you yourself have it *not*: But those that

> have the right Hammer, they awaken him indeed: therefore *all Teachers without God's Hammer*, are but Jugglers, Hammers for the Belly, Hammers for the Ear, and no Hammers for the Soul. (*TLM* 18.33)

The spiritual could only be known by the spiritual. Given the suggestion of the importance of communion here, it can be seen that the difficulty of reading each visionary is considerably lessened if each is read in the light of each other. To an extent, Blake and Boehme may, through "the Holy Ghost . . . the *only* Key," be seen as a key to each other.

The prophetic "tygers of wrath are wiser than" the uninspired "horses of instruction" (*MHH* 37, pl. 9, l.44). The prophetic task is not so much to teach what is not known, as to rouse the individual to the infinite spiritual potential that resides "in the human breast" (*MHH* 38, pl. 11):

> <Reynolds Thinks that Man Learns all that he Knows I say on the Contrary That Man Brings All that he has or Can have Into the World with him. Man is Born like a Garden ready Planted and Sown. This World is too poor to produce one Seed> (*Ann. Ren.* 656)

In response to Joshua Reynolds' assertion that "The mind is but a barren soil; a soil which is soon exhausted, and will produce no crop," Blake adds:

> <The Mind that could have produced this Sentence must have been a Pitiful a Pitiable Imbecility. I always thought that the Human Mind was the most Prolific of All Things and Inexhaustible> (*Ann. Ren.* 656)

In this Blake thoroughly agrees with Boehme: "In *Man* lyes *all* whatsoever the Sun shines upon, or Heaven contains, as also Hell and all the Deeps; he is an inexhaustible Fountain, that cannot be drawn dry" (*EOG* 13.79). Spiritual awakening, the realization of the similitude, has about it an element of recognition and identification, in which the individual perceives what he has always known in his innermost being. Blake writes in *A Vision of the Last Judgment*:

> If the Spectator could Enter into these Images in his Imagination approaching them on the Fiery Chariot of his Contemplative Thought if he could Enter into Noahs Rainbow or into his bosom or could make a Friend and Companion of one of these Images of wonder which always intreats him to leave mortal things as he must know then would he arise from his Grave then would he meet the Lord in the Air and then he would be happy. (560)

The rousing of the faculties to act would inspire a living conception of spiritual unity. It is a call to "Mental Fight":

> Go . . . overthrow their cup,
> Their bread, their altar-table, their incense and their oath:
> Their marriage and their baptism, their burial and consecration:
> I have tried to make friends by corporeal gifts but have only
> Made enemies: I never made friends but by spiritual gifts;
> By severe contentions of friendship and the burning fire of thought.
> He who would see the Divinity must see him in his Children.
>
> (*Jer* 251, pl. 91, ll. 12–18)

As Boehme wrote of this rigorous activity, of the "moment" when the "veil" of the "necessarily obscure" is lifted from man's understanding,

> *there is but one God*; but when the veil is put away from thy eyes, so that thou seest and knowest *him*, then thou wilt also see and know *all* thy brethren, whether they be *Christians, Jews, Turks,* or *Heathen.* (*Aur* 11.58)

5

Expression, Creation, and Manifestation

SYMBOLIC VISION AND THE STUBBORN STRUCTURE

Before discussing further the forces that shaped Blake's and Boehme's endeavors, and the necessities and possibilities each perceived in expression, it is necessary to look briefly at the fact that both viewed the outward world as symbolic. In *The Signature of All Things*, in one of his better known passages, Boehme wrote:

> The whole outward visible world with all its being is a signature or figure of the inward spiritual world . . .
>
> This formed world {i.e. "the inward spiritual world"} has manifested itself with the motion of all forms with this visible world, as with a visible likeness, so that the spiritual being might be manifest in a corporeal comprehensive essence . . . the internal holds the external before it as a glass, wherein it beholds itself . . . the external is its signature. (9.1–3)

In a similar vein, Blake perceived that "Mental Things are alone Real" (*VLJ* 565) and that

> This World <of Imagination> is Infinite and Eternal whereas the world of Generation or Vegetation is Finite and [*for a small moment*] Temporal There Exist in that Eternal World the Permanent Realities of Every Thing which we see reflected in this Vegetable Glass of Nature. (*VLJ* 555)

Aubrey has noted that Blake's understanding that "Eternity is in love with productions of time" (*MHH* 36, pl. 7, l. 10) corresponds with Boehme's that "In every external thing there are two properties; one from time, the other from eternity; the first property of time is manifest; and the other is hidden, yet it sets forth a likeness after itself in each thing" (*SR* 4.18).[1]

This again gives form to the sublime relationship both envisioned between the finite and the eternal, an interdependency in which the manifest plays a potentially merciful if paradoxical role: "Without the light of Nature there is no understanding of divine mysteries" (*Ep* 4.13). Boehme perceived that if a man "be born of God, he may know in every Spire of Grass, his Creator in whom he lives" (*TP* 8.9). Blake responded to Lavater's statement that "Whatever is visible is the vessel or veil of the invisible past, present, future —as man penetrates to this more or perceives it less, he raises or depresses his dignity of being," declaring it "A vision of the Eternal Now" (*Ann. Lav.* 592). This relationship is a source of that which is "quite new and strange" "and uncommon" in each visionary's works. As Caroline Spurgeon suggests, "If we consider all material things as symbols, their suggestiveness, and consequently their reality, is continually expanding."[2] The view that "Eternity is in love with the productions of time" realizes eternity as an exhortation to creativity.

This expansiveness compelled Blake and Boehme to find a system that, in contrast with the usual monolithic and restrictive character of systems, was not closed and fixed, but moving, expanding, self-generating as it were, and perpetually proposing and encouraging new possibilities. Émile Boutroux captures this in his observation of Boehme: "A living method, alone, enables us to penetrate into the mysteries of life. Being, alone, knows being; we must generate with God in order to understand generation."[3] Boehme stated, "let every one seek and find himself . . . for all things are generated out of imagination . . . and every imagination reaps its own work which it has wrought" (*SR* 15.41). The Antinomian in Boehme believed that the "Spirit of Christ in God, *will not be bound* to any Laws" (*TLM* 3.67); Man in Paradise "had no Law, but only the Law of the *Imagination*" (*ToI* 1.4.60). Again, "God's Spirit is not to be judged by reason" (*EOG[E]* 12.70). From the liberating possibilities of this understanding Los asserts the imperatives exhorted by eternity: "I must Create a System, or be enslav'd by another Mans / I will not Reason and Compare: my business is to Create" (*Jer* 153, pl. 10, ll. 20–21). Like Los, both visionaries may be seen to be "Striving with Systems to deliver Individuals from those Systems" (154, pl. 11, l. 5). As Boehme aspired to re-express the movements of the wheel of God, in which man "continually seeth somewhat that is more and more wonderful," it seems likely that Blake would have been highly responsive to the marked contrast between Boehme's "System" and the systems of figures such as Bacon, Newton, and Locke, as evoked in:

> their terrors hang
> Like iron scourges over Albion, Reasonings like vast Serpents
> Infold around my limbs, bruising my minute articulations
>
> I turn my eyes to the Schools and Universities of Europe
> And there behold the Loom of Locke whose Woof rages dire
> Washd by the Water-wheels of Newton. black the cloth
> In heavy wreathes folds over every Nation; cruel Works

> Of many Wheels I view, wheel without wheel, with cogs tyrannic
> Moving by compulsion each other: not as those in Eden: which
> Wheel within Wheel in freedom revolve in harmony and peace.
> (*Jer* 159, pl. 15, ll. 11–20)

The necessity of creating a visionary and symbolic system was driven by Boehme's understanding that "Every Spirit without a body, is empty, and knows not itself, and therefore every spirit desires a Body for its food and for its habitation" (*FQ* 4.1). Boehme and Blake worked in response to the dangers they perceived in formlessness and abstraction. In *The Book of Urizen*, Los is confronted with the "abdominable void," the "soul-shudd'ring vacuum"; he is "affrighted / At the formless immeasurable death" (70, pl. 3, ll. 4–5; 74, pl. 7, ll. 8–9). Commenting on this, Christine Gallant argues that the endeavor to "assimilate chaos" into an "imaginative order" is the "fundamental issue with which all myth may be said to be concerned."[4] Blake wrote of the imaginatively determinate:

> The great and golden rule of art, as well as of life, is this: That the more distinct, sharp, and wirey the bounding line, the more perfect the work of art. . . . The want of this determinate and bounding form evidences the want of idea in the artist's mind, and the pretence of the plagiary in all its branches. How do we distinguish the oak from the beech, the horse from the ox, but by the bounding outline? How do we distinguish one face or countenance from another, but by the bounding line and its infinite inflexions and movements? . . . Leave out this l[i]ne and you leave out life itself; all is chaos again, and the line of the almighty must be drawn out upon it before man or beast can exist. (*DC* 550)

The distinction drawn is between abstraction, fear, and doubt on the one hand, and affirmation and faith on the other. Expression is necessary, as Boehme acknowledged, describing his own writings as "an exercise of Faith" (*ToI* 1.16.18). As Blake wrote in *Jerusalem*, "Los built the stubborn structure of the Language, acting against / Albion's melancholy, who must else have been a Dumb despair" (183, pl. 36, ll. 59–60). Boehme had also given a voice to the "stubborn structure" that speaks in defiance of the "void":

> Every prophet is a limit {or boundary}, wherein a time is included or an age comprehended; and he is the mouth of that kingdom or dominion; that is, when that kingdom hath awakened and generated the turba {or confusion} in it, then is he the mouth of the inward ground, which declareth and expresseth the vanity {of confusion}. (*MM* 67.9)

In *the Signature of All Things* he speaks further of the "stubborn structure":

> A true Christian is in the spirit a Christian, and in continual exercise to bring forth its own form, not only with words in sound and shew, but in the power of the work, as a visible palpable form . . . as a servant of God in God's deeds of wonder; a helping to strike his instrument in God's will, and be a true sounding string in God's harmonious concert; a continual making word in God's voice. (*SR* 15.38)

To expand upon this, as the "Outward Creation" should be perceived symbolically, as the "Vegetable Glass of Nature," Blake's and Boehme's works may themselves be regarded as a mirror of sorts. This "Glass" reflects both the writer and the reader, as Boehme saw:

> I am known to myself, but not in my self-hood, but in his {God's} mirror which of grace he has put into me . . . and so likewise, dear brethren, it shall again be represented to you out of his glass, which he has set forth through my capacity in him, as his instrument. (*SR* 12.18)

Several points arise immediately from this. The "Glass" is in many respects necessary: understanding that "the spirit cannot be written down," Boehme asserted that "if we intend to speak of God, we must use *similitudes*" (*Aur* 3.29). As he wrote of fallen man and specifically of imagination and its possibilities: "In God's holiness it cannot take hold; for the will was rent off from that; therefore there must now be a similitude wherein the imagination of the human nature may take hold" (*OCT* 2.33). The similitude reiterates the "stubborn structure." The "Separation" that "rent" man from "God's holiness" actively proposes expression as a medium "wherein the imagination . . . may take hold." The written similitude may thus be seen as a manifestation of Grace, as underlined in the identification of Boehme's "Glass" with that of God. With this in mind it may be noted that throughout his own works Blake endeavors to manifest "The Divine Image" (*SoI* 12–13). The "Glass" in which similitude finds form may be spoken of as a "frame," as in that which gives form to Blake's "Tyger." Blake wrote of the measure of this "frame," reiterating Boehme's perception that man "cannot take hold" of "God's holiness" save through a similitude":

> Man can have no idea of anything greater than Man as a cup cannot contain more than its capaciousness. . . .
>
> Think of a white cloud. as being holy you cannot love it but think of a holy man within the cloud love springs up in your thought. for to think of holiness distinct from man is impossible to the affections. (*Ann. DLDW* 603)

A similitude of the divine, the soul, as Boehme saw it, "co-operates in the heavenly Imaging or Framing: And therefore it makes a Description,

Draught, Platform or Model . . . showing how a Thing should be imaged or framed" (*Aur* 15.55). In brief, the compulsion to find expression is a desire for manifestation: "the spiritual substance must needs bring itself into a material ground, wherein it may so figure and form itself" (*Clavis* 167). This desire for manifestation both gave shape to and found expression in Boehme's and Blake's works. Their work is their signature.

To build upon this, as the act of writing and creation was for both an integral part of the spiritual life, the process of life itself may be understood in terms of manifestation. As Martensen wrote of Boehme, in words that may equally be applied to Blake:

> Life is an unfolding from darkness to light, from the hidden, indefinite and unknowable to the manifested, definite and knowable. But Life and Manifestation . . . can only be conceived of as a movement between contrasts, and as the mediation of these. Without contrasts, there is neither life nor manifestation.[5]

"Without Contraries is no progression." Boehme set out this view clearly:

> Nothing without contrariety can become manifest to itself; for it has nothing to resist it, it goes continually of itself outwards, and returns not again into itself. But if it returns not again into itself, as into that out of which it originally went, it knows nothing of its primal being.
>
> If the natural life had no contrariety, and were without a limit, it would never inquire after its ground from which it arose; and hence the hidden God would remain unknown to the natural life. Moreover, were there no contrariety in life, there would be no sensibility, nor will, nor efficacy therein, also neither understanding nor science. For a thing that has only one will has no divisibility. If it find not a contrary will, which gives occasion to it exercising motion, it stands still. A single thing can know nothing more than a one. (*SP* "Theoscopia," 1.8–9)

This highlights the significance of the written as a mirror; that the act of writing can be an active and creative engagement with the processes and possibilities of manifestation. In this, the "stubborn structure" may be understood as the necessary contrary of that which seeks expression; as that without which the desire for expression would not realize itself, would not return "again into itself." Such contrariety is thus a matter, as Blake put it, of "organisation," resisting as it does the dissipation, the mere out-going of the desire for expression. As Boehme wrote of the state of spiritual inquiry in the world, "Babel . . . has broken the Looking-Glass, and sees with Spectacles" (*FQ* 21.23); that is, such inquiry "goes continually of itself outwards" and thus does not truly participate in the moving life of the spirit. In response, Boehme and Blake endeavored through the "stubborn structure" of contrariety to reinstate the "Looking-Glass." Their approach to writing is one that is engaged with a heightened form of the movements that give life to all perception, "sensibility," and "understanding." The act of writing provided each with the possibility of more certain and fruitful ways of manifestation, of knowing his "primal being," with possibilities that in turn offer themselves to the reader. The contrariety set in motion by the "stubborn structure" once more underlines the importance of "Mental Fight," not least because it "rouzes" that which is dormant in man "to act": "without a limit, it would never inquire after its ground." Through creative engagement with the written similitude, the individual can move beyond a passive relationship to that which is external to him or her, beyond that which "goes continually . . . outwards" and takes man away from his innermost being. This adds immense weight to the point that Blake's Los *must* "Create a System, or be enslav'd by another Man's."

The "Looking-Glass" of the written highlights the importance of individual endeavor, of creating anew. Up to a point, while the "frame" is Boehme's or Blake's, the reader sees something of himself in their "Glass." As Boehme stated:

> Every one says, "Shew me the way to the manifestation of the good." Hear and observe well, dear reason; thou must thyself be the way, the understanding must be born in thee, otherwise I cannot show it thee; thou must enter into it, so that the understanding of the work in its practic art. . . . may be opened to thee. (*SR* 14.1)

Blake's belief that "God only Acts and Is, in existing beings or Men" is also in Boehme, who argued that God "hath manifested himself by the externall World in a similitude, that the spirit might see it selfe in the Being essentially, and not so onely, but that the Creature likewise might contemplate and behold the being of God in the Figure, and know it" (*Ep* 5.14). In the light of this understanding that points to Christ as the similitude, the "Divine Image," a more specific manifestation of similitude may now be identified in Blake's work. Towards the end of *Jerusalem* Jesus appears

> standing by Albion as the Good Shepherd
> By the lost Sheep that he hath found and Albion knew that it
> Was the Lord the Universal Humanity, and Albion saw his Form
> A Man. and they conversed as Man with Man, in Ages of Eternity
> And the Divine Appearance was the likeness and similitude of Los.
> (255, pl. 96, ll. 3–7)

Again, "Man can have no idea of anything greater than Man." Through the "Figure" of Los, Blake actively explored the possibilities of similitude and identification in his work, as is underlined by the fact that Los is realized as a similitude of Blake:

> I bound my sandals
> On; to walk forward thro' Eternity, Los descended to me:
> And Los behind me stood; a terrible flaming Sun: just close
> Behind my back; I turned round in terror, and behold.
> Los stood in that fierce glowing fire; and he also stoop'd down
> And bound my sandals on in Udan-Adan; trembling I stood
> Exceedingly with fear and terror, standing in the Vale
> Of Lambeth: but he kissed me and wishd me health.
> And I became One Man with him arising in my strength:
> Twas too late now to recede. Los had entered into my soul:
> His terrors now possess'd me whole! I arose in fury and strength.
> (*Milton* 116–17, pl. 22, ll. 4–14)

Los is that "wherein the imagination . . . may take hold," is that through which Blake was able to "return" again "into" himself, and is thus "as the Good Shepherd / By the lost Sheep that he hath found." The fierce glowing fire in which Los stands may in part be understood as the fiery impulse to write, the compulsion that finds its life and movement in the essential contrariety, the "terrors" of expression: "Twas too late now to recede." In turn, the similitude, the unitive "Divine Image," made possible Blake's "converse" with Boehme. His appearance "in the Heavens above" and in "the fierce glowing fire" of "Hell beneath" is one in which "the imagination . . . may take hold."

CREATION AND THE INDIVIDUAL

The relationship between the individual and creation is given particular significance in both Blake's and Boehme's work, as is encapsulated in Boehme's perception that "the soul . . . co-operates in the heavenly Imaging or Framing." It seems probable that Blake would have seen in Boehme that which nurtures creative and artistic possibilities. As seen, Friedrich Schlegel identified that in Boehme which was in accord with Blake's needs, the "poetic imagination," the "strange spirit," the concern with "supersensual things," the "richness of his fancy and the depth of his feeling." As proposed by the imaginative and thoroughly mythological character that gives life to all of Boehme's works, and by the profound relationship he perceived between the individual and God, that "A true Christian is a continual making word in God's voice," Blake would have regarded Boehme as creative and "poetic," as a true "Artist," not least, as suggested, because of the expansiveness of Blake's conception of that role: "A Poet a Painter a Musician an Architect: the Man / Or Woman who is not one of these is not a Christian" (*Laocoön* 274). As is evident in the symbolic view of the world, both believed that life was not given and fixed, that man is not merely a *tabula rasa* on which reality writes itself, that life is in many respects a process in which the individual creates the world, for better or worse. Blake's view that "As a man is So he Sees" (*Letters* 702) is also Boehme's. The individual need not be limited by the ways of thinking, feeling, and perceiving predominant in the time in which he or she lives. This stresses the necessity of an actively creative approach to existence. A reading of their work is one that participates in the creative process. As Blake declared: "Let every Christian as much as in him lies engage himself openly and publicly before all the World in some Mental pursuit for the Building up of Jerusalem (*Jer* 232, pl. 77, "To the Christians"). As will become clearer, Blake and Boehme may be seen as co-builders of Jerusalem.

It may now be suggested that as Blake extended art beyond its normal boundaries, both visionaries extended expression in such a way as to make the act of writing participate in the creation of the world. Their approach to expression is one that is magical in the fullest sense of the word; that is, it is an activity that is understood in terms of symbolic vision, as opposed to one that is realized in the phenomenal. There is in both a potent and close interrelationship between creative activity and the eternal which may seem to be contradictory, in that the eternal may be seen as something that cannot be added to, and the creative as something that adds. However, this view regards eternity as fixed and finished, and in so doing reduces it to the level of the temporal, as if it were something that happened and was established in the past. For both the eternal embraced possibility, not least that given new expression and form by creative activity.

Boehme's works persistently propose the sublime correspondence noted by Yeats in "The Symbolism of Poetry": "the laws of art. . . . are the hidden laws of the world."[6] As Bailey wrote of Boehme's perception of the individual as a creator, "That there was in Boehme a Titanic, a Promethean element, an element that later culminated in Goethe's *Prometheus*, was felt instinctively by some of the philosopher's orthodox opponents."[7] It may equally be said that the same element was felt instinctively and favorably by his more heterodox readers. For instance, the "Titanic . . . Promethean element" in Boehme draws notable parallels with Blake's "Prolific," as given Titanic form in *The Marriage*: "The Giants who formed this world into its sensual existence . . . are in truth. the causes of its life and the sources of all activity" (*MHH* 40, pl. 16). More importantly, the creative role of the individual in Boehme's work explores the relationship between God and man:

> You have poured Your holy Name into my soul and mind. Yes, out of Your Name has it sprung, and You have given me authority to rule over all things with Your Name so that out of my mouth by Your power it is to flow forth and rule all things: Yes, I was to form and fashion holy figures and images with my mouth and expression; even as You, O eternal God, have formed and fashioned everything through Your holy Name. (*WC* "On Holy Prayer" 53)

The relationship between God and man may thus be said, with qualifications, to be one of interdependence.

To begin to elaborate on this, Boehme regarded that outward world as "only a formed Model or Platform, wherein the Great Mind of Divine Manifestation beholds itself in a Time, and plays with itself" (*MM[L]* 7.19). This underlines the extent to which the desire for manifestation underlies all existence. Boehme identified that in which the "Great Mind . . . beholds itself" as Sophia, the mirror of Wisdom:

> she is the *Substantiality* of the spirit, which the Spirit of God putteth on as a Garment, whereby he manifesteth himself, or else his form would not be known: for she is the Spirit's Corporeity, and though she is not a corporeal palpable substance, like us Men, yet she is substantial and visible, but the Spirit is *not* substantial.
>
> For we Men can, in Eternity, see no more of the Spirit of God, but only the *Glance* of the Majesty: and his glorious *power* we feel in us, for it is our life, and conducteth us.
>
> But we know the Virgin in all her heavenly Similitudes or Images: whereas she giveth a *body* to all fruits, she is not the Corporeity of the fruit, but the Ornament and Luster. (*TLM* 5.50–52)

Blake's Jerusalem, his own Sophia, appears in a similar light:

> In Great Eternity, every particular Form gives forth or Emanates
> Its own peculiar Light, and the Form is the Divine Vision
> And the Light is his Garment This is Jerusalem in every Man.
> (*Jer* 203, pl. 54, ll. 1–3)

As the essential contrariety of the "stubborn structure of the Language" provides the individual with the potential of manifestation, God's relationship to Sophia underlines the affinity between the movements of the "Great Mind" and those of the creative individual. Howard Brinton draws the correspondence:

> She is the . . . vision the artist has of his picture before he paints it, or the author's idea of his book before he writes it. She is the objective, the ideational, the constitutive; the will is the subjective, the affective, the evaluative. As the will brings her to reality, she determines the will and is determined by it, and

> creation proceeds as the dual product of the subjective impulse and the objective vision.[8]

Sophia, as that through which the "Artist" works, may be seen to highlight the necessity of creative activity, of expression, for without her the individual cannot realize the fullness of manifestation. From this Blake speaks of

> The Mystic Union of the Emanation in the Lord; Because
> Man divided from his Emanation is a dark Spectre
> His Emanation is an ever-weeping melancholy Shadow.
>
> (*Jer* 203, pl. 53, ll. 24–26)

It is through Boehme's and Blake's apprehension of the mirror of Wisdom that the two may be seen as co-builders of the holy city of Jerusalem, for "Man is adjoind to Man by his Emanative portion: / Who is Jerusalem in every individual Man" (*Jer* 187, pl. 39, ll. 38–39).

Given the affinity between God's and man's creations, Boehme perceived in creative activity that in which God finds manifestation:

> As a limner that pourtrays his own image, and does thereby behold what he is, and how his form and features are; or as a musician composes a curious lesson or song, and so plays and melodises with his life . . .
>
> Thus likewise God created us to his love-consort to his joy and glory, whereby he exalts his speaking eternal word, or plays in the same with us as with his instrument. (*SR* 10.44–45)

In other words, man's creative activities are necessary for the manifestation of God to man. God's relationship to man illuminates the depth of the fiery compulsion to find expression: "*in God's will* we are able to do ALL; our own Nature must not do it; but God himself is Zealous in Us, and he is our doing if we work any Wonder" (*TLM* 10.32). God urges man to write in order that He may write through him. Los is told in *Jerusalem*: "Shudder not, but Write, and the hand of God will assist you" (196, pl. 47, l. 17). Blake writes at the opening of *Jerusalem*:

> Reader! [*lover*] of books! [*lover*] of heaven,
> And of that God from whom [*all books are given*]
> Who in mysterious Sinais awful cave
> To Man the wond'rous art of writing gave
> Again he speaks in thunder and in fire!
> Thunder of Thought, and flames of fierce desire:
> Even from the depths of Hell his voice I hear,
> Within the unfathomd caverns of my Ear.
> Therefore I print.
>
> (145, pl. 3, ll. 1–9)

It is only through such terms, through Boehme's understanding that "the human soul is a spark out of the eternal-speaking Word of the divine" (*MM* "The Author's Preface," par. 9), that it is possible to appreciate fully the significance of his insight that "God must become man, man must become God; heaven must become one thing with the earth, the earth must be turned to heaven: If you will make heaven out of the earth, then give the earth the heaven's food" (*SR* 10.53). The truly creative is the fruit of eternity. Boehme writes of this relationship in *Mysterium Magnum*: "nothing comprehends him but the true Understanding, which is God himself" (*[L]* 1.8). The interdependency of God and man may thus be seen as one in which God urges man to renovate his means of expression, his creativity, to explore new ways of seeing that which has formerly been known as God. Such an understanding informs the immense spiritual significance Blake perceived in creative, imaginative activity:

> I know of no other Christianity and of no other Gospel than the liberty both of body and mind to exercise the Divine Arts of Imagination. . . .
>
> . . .What is the Life of Man but Art and Science? (*Jer* 231–32, pl. 77, "To the Christians")

Boehme agreed:

> when man, understand the inward . . . spiritual man, is married to Christ, then God eateth of man's will and words; and again man eateth of God's will and words. They sit at one feast, and then 'tis truly said and applied, *Whosoever heareth you, he heareth me.* Whosoever heareth these men to teach and speak of God, he heareth God speak, for they speak in the power of the Holy Spirit's spices, and eat together of the great supper of Christ. (*MM* 50.49)

PART II

6

Theogony: From Nothing to Something

INTRODUCTION

Part II works through an overall view of Boehme's symbolic system, introducing his vision of God's manifestation out of the *Ungrund*, of Eternal Nature, of the seven properties of nature and three principles, and of the movements from the Creation and Fall to the Last Judgment. Chapter 6 focuses on Boehme's theogony, laying the foundation for the unfolding in subsequent chapters of his complex visionary scheme and comparisons with Blake. As Part II progresses and the character of Boehme's system becomes clearer, discussion of Blake's work in the light of Boehme is increasingly introduced, to the point where the focus moves from Boehme to Blake. The significance of what is drawn in this chapter will be picked up and developed in the subsequent chapters.

Certain aspects of Boehme's system do not have immediate counterparts in Blake's work. The lack of correspondence is in many respects, however, more apparent than real. As will be seen in particular in the discussion of the seven natural properties and the three principles, Boehme's visionary system is one that embraces seemingly inexhaustible possibilities, nurturing a progressive, ever deepening and creative understanding, and in so doing proposing insights and consequences not immediately apparent in its outward form. As seen, Boehme and Blake distinguished between outward and inward form, regarding the latter as the unifying ground which is the source of the creative. Boehme's visionary system is like Los's furnaces, in that it too is "living: self-moving" (*Jer* 228, pl. 73, l. 2). Hans Popper has noted that Boehme's seven properties "assimilate chaos" and give form to the similitude, and as a result should not be apprehended

> as if they were entities on a par with either objects of sense-experience, or simply abstract notions, constructed by the mind. For they are principles, or modes of being, as well as forces, shaping the particular forms of existence.... they are not the "blue-print" or the "grammar" of all being; rather do they set out to be its mirror, or even its interlocutor. They are creatively active, form-

> ing articulate entities out of shapeless chaos, and making these entities be and function in a vital and dynamic way.[1]

As Blake wrote of his art, "I copy Imagination . . . Copiers of Nature {are} Incorrect while Copiers of Imagination are Correct" (*PA* 574–75).

Boehme's work speaks of a dynamic inner drama that takes place within God; a "living: self-moving" drama that illuminates man's relationship to God and which is realized within man. He asks, "Where will you seek God? In the Deep above the Stars? You will not be able to find him there. Seek him in your Heart." This "Birth must be done within you: The Heart, or the Son of God must arise in the Birth of your Life; and then the Saviour Christ is your faithful Shepherd, and you are in Him, and He in you" (*TP* 4.8–9). The "Saviour Christ" declares at the beginning of *Jerusalem*: "I am not a God afar off, I am a brother and a friend; / Within your bosom I reside, and you reside in me" (146, pl. 4, ll. 18–19). As touched upon earlier, Boehme asks "How then should you not have Power and Authority to speak of God, who is your Father, of whose Essence you are?" (*TP* 4.7):

> though we speak of the Creation of the World, as if we had been by as present, and had seen it, none ought to marvel at it, nor hold it for impossible. For the Spirit that is in us, which one Man inherits from the other, that was breathed out of the Eternity into *Adam*, that same Spirit has seen it all, and in the Light of God it sees it still; and there is nothing that is far off, or unsearchable. . . .
>
> So that when the Heaven, and the Birth of the Elements are spoken of, it is not a Thing afar off, or that is distant from us, that is spoken of; but we speak of Things that are done in our Body and Soul; and there is nothing nearer us than this Birth, for we live and move therein, as in the House of our Mother; and when we speak of Heaven, we speak of our native Country. (*TP* 7.6–7)

Blake wrote out of this "Country":

> in your own Bosom you bear your Heaven
> And Earth, and all you behold, tho it appears Without it is Within
> In your Imagination of which this World of Mortality is but a Shadow.
> (*Jer* 225, pl. 71, ll. 17–19)

While the theogonic movements from the *Ungrund* to the Last Judgment are set out to an extent in linear terms in Part II, as if one movement followed on from and as a consequence of another, they occur simultaneously, in an eternal moment in which each moves as a similitude of Boehme's wheel of God, "*one in another*, upwards, downwards, crossways, and yet . . . continually . . . together." The movement that underlies Part II may thus be seen as one that is both progressive and intricately cyclic, in which each aspect of Boehme's scheme that is discussed in turn, both returns to and develops upon those preceding it. For example, the discussion of the three principles speaks from the same ground as and expands upon the preceding discussions concerning God's movement out of the *Ungrund,* and the seven properties. It is this ongoing interaction of parts that opens up such imaginative and creative possibilities in Boehme's theogonic system.

In accord with the understanding that Boehme's vision should be apprehended in eternal as opposed to temporal terms, his works do not propose a beginning of God, but rather that the movement out of the *Ungrund*—the fathomless Nothing—is "the eternal beginning of *the manifestation of God*" (*MM* 4.7). The "whole creation is nothing else but a manifestation of the all-essential, unsearchable God; all whatever he is in his eternal unbeginning generation and dominion, of that is also the creation." He adds, "not that this joy first began with the creation, no, for it was from eternity in the great mystery" (*SR* 16.1–2). As comprehended in the creative interactions of his system, the eternal is not something that is finally completed and thus fixed; it does not propose a predetermined scheme as such. The eternal embraces possibility. By contrast, predetermination imposes a temporal view of the eternal, by setting the determining activities of the eternal *before* the unfolding of time. Accordingly, as apprehended in God's "living: self-moving" inner drama, the theogonic movements of Boehme's mythological vision do not occur at some point *before* the Fall, but are eternal movements, present in every moment.

THE *UNGRUND*

Boehme conceived his vision of the *Ungrund,* the eternal Nothing, in order to come to terms with the existence of evil and the contrariety between God's love and wrath, Yes and No, and light and darkness. While Blake disregarded much that is involved in the vision of the *Ungrund,* as in Boehme's proposal that man should sink in total resignation of self into its stillness and silence, the problems and mysteries which it addresses might well have held a significant degree of resonance for the poet. Moreover, the *Ungrund* casts light on the nature of freedom and has affirmative implications that may certainly be seen to have correspondences in Blake's work.

To begin to describe that which Boehme himself understood to be finally inexpressible, it may be said that the *Ungrund* is the "eternal stillness and rest" (*SR* 2.8), the eternal silence of the abyss—as the Law edition translates the word—out of which the whole of creation comes forth. It is unfathomable: "without nature God is a mystery, understand in the nothing, for without nature is the nothing" (*SR* 3.2). "And it is . . . called a nothing (though it is God Himself) because it is inconceivable and inexpressible" (*TQ* 2.13):[2]

> before . . . this world there was *nothing but God* from Eternity; and after this world, there will be *nothing but God* in Eternity; but the cause why we comprehend not this, is because there is no comprehensibility in God. For where there is a Comprehensibility . . . there is beginning and end. (*TLM* 6.45)

Not only is the *Ungrund* unknowable and unmanifest, it is also unknown to God Himself, for He is not as yet conscious of Himself. As will become clearer, this absence of self-consciousness is so because the *Ungrund* is an eternal indivisible unity without limit. As Boehme writes of God in the *Mysterium Magnum*:

> When I consider what God is, then, I say, he is the *One*; in reference to the *Creature* as an Eternal Nothing. He has neither Foundation, Beginning, or Abode. . . . he is in himself only one; he needs neither *Space*, or *Place*. . . . He is neither like or resembles *any thing* and has no peculiar Place where he dwells. (*[L]* 1.2)

The *Ungrund* is, as the word suggests, groundless, and as such cannot be determined by anything. It is beyond reason and causality.[3]

The *Ungrund* is, significantly, irrational. Beyond the grasp of rational thought, it can only be approached in mythological and symbolic terms. Moreover, as Boehme envisages the *Ungrund* as irrational and groundless, as God has "nothing that can generate him" (*EOG* 1.8), his vision proposes a primary freedom;[4] a freedom that is so by the very fact that it is determined by nothing. To clarify, this "Liberty . . . beyond nature" (*TLM* 4.27) is not derived from being, that is, from that which has a ground. It is not created and is beyond good and evil. Brinton argues that such a conception of freedom must remain a mystery in the face of rationalization, for "the rationalist cannot conceive of a free act. Every effect has its cause and every act is a link in a long chain of cause and effect. A free and undetermined will cannot exist in a universe where there is a reason for everything. Accordingly the rationalist denies freedom."[5]

In this it may already be seen that while Blake might have largely discarded the apophatic aspect of Boehme's work, the free, irrational principle at the core of the German mystic's vision might well have appeared to him as a welcome antidote to the mechanistic, rationalized universe of "Newtons Pantocrator" (*Milton* 98, pl. 4, l. 11). As might also have been of resonance to Blake, not least on account of the significance it proposes for creativity, the "nothingness" of Boehme's *Ungrund* may be understood in terms of potentiality. Berdyaev casts light on this in his view of the *meonic* freedom of the *Ungrund*, the *meonic* being the realm of potentiality, possibility:

> The process of becoming, and the dialectic of world development are possibilities only because non-being exists. If we concede being only, there will be no becoming or development of any sort. Newness in the process of becoming emerges from the heart of non-being. . . .
>
> . . . in the heart of potency, which is not being, and which we are constrained apophatically to call non-being, is lodged that primordial freedom which precedes being, and without which there can be no creation of what is new, of what has not been before.[6]

The possibility inherent in the eternal gives a sense of the dialectic that underlies Boehme's vision, between the Something and the Nothing. As Tillich writes of the "*me on*" which "is the 'nothing' which has a dialectical relation to being":

> everything which can be conceptualized must have being and . . . there is no being without form. Dynamics, therefore, cannot be thought of as something that is; nor can it be thought as something that is not. It is the *me on*, the potentiality of being, which is nonbeing in contrast to things that have form, and the power of being in contrast to pure nonbeing.[7]

The nothingness of the *Ungrund* cannot be conceived as simply nothing. Boehme's God "is the *Nothing and All-Things*, and is one only Will, in which lie the World and the whole creation" (*EOG* 1.8).[8] This *meonic* aspect distinguishes Boehme from the mystics of the *via negativa*. In accord with the irrational principle at the heart of the *Ungrund*, Stoudt has suggested that "an antinomy appeared" in Boehme's works":

> the Source is no-thing, yet all. . . . Two roads present themselves: a positive way and a negative way. Two theologies result: apophatic and cataphatic. The former subordinates affirmation to negation; the latter subordinates negation to affirmation. If the source is all then by affirming creation's multiplicity it may be reached; if the Source is no-thing then by denying created reality it may be reached. Boehme's significance was his combining of both theologies in one comprehending system of thought.[9]

Rufus Jones has highlighted the affirmative aspect resultant of this combination:

> no manifestation, no created universe, no expression, is the ultimate Reality itself. The manifested universe has come out of more than itself. The Abyss is more than anything, or all, that comes out of it, or can come out of it, and it

> lies with its infinite depth beneath everything which appears, as a man's entire life, conscious and unconscious, is in and yet lies behind every act of will, though we can "talk about" only what is voice or expressed.[10]

Understanding that God "is the *Nothing*," and that his "Creation, revelation, manifestation" is also, as Jones puts it, "a dateless and eternal fact,"[11] Boehme did not regard the Creation as having been made out of nothing. Drawing a contrast with Paracelsus, who proposed that "The elements are created out of nothing and long to return again to nothing," Howard Brinton points to Boehme's statement that "Many authors have written that heaven and earth were created out of nothing. Now where nothing is, nothing can come to be" (*Aur* 19.67).[12] In *The Three Principles* Boehme argued:

> you will say, this is . . . God, and he is a Spirit, and has created all Things out of nothing. It is very true, he is a Spirit, *and in our Sight he is as nothing*: And if we had not some Knowledge of him by the Creation, we should know nothing of him at all. And if he himself had not been from all Eternity, there could nothing have ever been. (4.31; emphasis added)

In this, Boehme anticipates Blake's own view, as expressed in *A Vision of the Last Judgment*, where the poet reiterates that in eternity everything exists simultaneously, that in God there is, to cite Jones again, "no 'before'":[13]

> Many suppose that before <the Creation> All was Solitude and Chaos This is the most pernicious Idea that can enter the Mind as it takes away all sublimity from the Bible and Limits All Existence to Creation and to Chaos To the Time and Space fixed by the Corporeal Vegetative Eye and leaves the Man who entertains such an Idea the habitation of Unbelieving Demons Eternity Exists and All things in Eternity Independent of Creation which was an act of Mercy. (563)

Again, the irrational *meonic* freedom, that which is undetermined by—that is, "Independent of"—the "Vegetative" "Creation," is opposed to predestination. Through this dynamic opposition to a "fixed . . . Corporeal" existence, the significance that Boehme's vision of the *Ungrund* offered to Blake becomes apparent, not least in terms of its appreciation of the potency of eternal life.[14]

SEPARATION, CONTRARIETY, AND FIRE

The movement from the *Ungrund* to divine consciousness and creation is reflected and re-embodied in each aspect or stage of Boehme's visionary scheme. To begin to give an overview of this, while God is unknown and unmanifest to Himself in the *Ungrund*, Boehme also speaks of Him as "the Will of the Abyss" (*MM[L]* 1.2), that is, of a will that is groundless and indeterminate, "one only Will," a "Unity" (*Clavis* 30) that is "unsearchable, inconceiveable . . . as nothing" (*EOG* 1.10). As such God is unknown and unmanifest to himself for "Nothing without contrariety can become manifest to itself" (*SP* "Theoscopia," 1.8). The Nothing needs Something that is set over against it to manifest it: "we understand that an eternal will arises in the nothing, to introduce the nothing into something, that the will might find, feel, and behold itself" (*SR* 2:8). The will "seeks itself, and finds itself in itself, and its seeking is a desire, and its finding is the essence of the desire, wherein the will finds itself" (*SR* 2:9). That is, "finding nothing but itself, it desires itself" (*FQ* 1.22):

> It finds nothing except only the property of the hunger, which is itself, which it draws into itself, that is, draws itself into itself, and finds itself in itself; and its attraction into itself makes an overshadowing or darkness in it, which is not in the liberty . . . desire makes essence. (*SR* 2.10)

In the "overshadowing" the contrariety necessary for manifestation is first found, a contrariety in which will and desire are interdependent:

> that the will must be in the darkness is its contrariety. . .
>
> . . . the will may not be nothing, for it desires to manifest in the nothing; and yet no manifestation can be effected, except only through the essence of the desire; and the more the . . . will desires manifestation, the more strongly and eagerly the desire draws into itself. (*SR* 2.11–12)

At this stage in Boehme's theogony, however, the Something that is found is only vague, the first contrast of will and desire being only the beginning or germ of God's manifestation and creation and the contrariety between the two only potential.

This as yet unified opposition is directed outward for the furtherance of God's manifestation. Boehme speaks of this movement in terms of the Word which is breathed forth by God as "the flowing-out of the divine will or the divine knowledge. . . . It is a revelation of the Eternal One" (*WC* "On Divine Contemplation," 3.1). The outflowing Word speaks of the Trinity, the Father, mute in Himself, being the speaker of the Word, the Son the Word that gives voice to the Father, and the Spirit the energy or drive through which the Word "goes forth . . . out of the Mouth of God" (*TP* 14.85). Through the Word "the one only God . . . introduces himself into a Trinity, *viz.* into a *Comprehensibility* of himself" (*EOG* 1.29) in which "the Abyss possesses itself in a Ground" (*EOG* 1.30). While the *Ungrund* is "inconceivable . . . having nothing before, nor after it" (*EOG* 1.10), the "Ground" may be conceived in terms of before and after. In this "Ground" the first will finds "its innate or only begotten Will or Son" (*EOG* 1.33), the second person of the Trinity. The "Place" (*EOG* 1.32) in which the second will is found "is the Ground and Beginning of every Being" (*EOG* 1.34). All the same, while God has attained self-consciousness here, He is not known beyond Himself, and the Creation remains within Himself. Through the third person of the Trinity God moves beyond self-consciousness. The Holy Spirit is the means of creation, "the Former, Framer and Fashioner" (*TP* 4.59) that goes forth and "makes a form" (*SR* 3.3).

The form that the Spirit makes "is the eternal wisdom of the Deity" (*SR* 3.4), "wherein the Spirit of God, which rises out of the Powers with the out-breathed Powers . . . plays with itself" (*EOG* 1.43). This is the "love-play" (*MM* 5.3) of God. Wisdom is "a Subject and Resemblance of the infinite and unsearchable Unity; a Substance wherein the Holy Ghost works, forms and models . . . the Divine understanding in the Wisdom" (*Clavis* 41). She is thus a mirror, "an *Image* of the Holy Number Three . . . a similitude of God" (*TLM* 5.41) in which God is self-revealed. As a mirror she, Sophia, is passive and "generateth nothing" (*TLM* 5.41) and is the "chaste Virgin" (*TP* 14.85). The Spirit "frames" in the mirror of Sophia all that could be, the eternal possibilities of being and creation. The *meonic* freedom of the *Ungrund* is therefore realized through Wisdom. Indeed, "The Form of this world was from Eternity in the Nature of God, but invisible and immaterial" (*TLM* 5.83). It is in the "Delight" of this image that the "spirit of God . . . plays with itself," for "this is now God's Companion to the Honour and Joy of God" (*TP* 14.86). The Word is spoken in Wisdom, and she is that from which "the Creation has taken its Beginning and Original" (*EOG* 1.45).

As comprehended in the *meonic* aspect revealed in Wisdom, the theogonic process has not yet brought God to an essential existence. His "Play" is as yet only within Himself, and He is far from being the revealed, living God. Similarly, the creation is not as yet realized, but merely potential or ideal. It is at this point in Boehme's visionary scheme that the necessity of contrariety is more fully realized:

> The reader is to know that in Yes and No consist all things, be they divine, diabolic, terrestrial, or however they may be named. . . . The No is a counter-stroke of the Yes or the truth, in order that the truth may be manifest and a something. (TQ 3.2)

To attain essence and life God must realize that which is contrary to or other than Himself, his counterstroke, and enter into contention with it. This is brought about by the *Mysterium Magnum*, the great mystery as to why and how the contrariety and multiplicity of creation came into being. Boehme approaches this separative activity in terms of that envisaged by alchemy in the property of fire. In "the Eternal Speaking" of the Word "the Separation or Distinction into Love and Anger, *viz.* into Fire and Light" appears (*EOG* 8.6). In the eternal moment in which God beholds in Wisdom the *meonic* "wonders" (*FQ* 1.75) of all that "lies hid," the fire has its origin.

For the sake of essence and life there must be darkness as well as light. The darkness finds its "Original" in the "overshadowing" of "the will of liberty" by desire. As desire "makes essence" and God's will would "flow out" into an essential reality, desire kindles for that reality in the mirror of Wisdom. Where the "eternal will" is "the *lubet* of liberty" (*lubet* being, roughly, a joyful longing), and is "emanent from itself" (*ToI* 2.5.6) in an expansive and generous "driving forth" (*SR* 3.12), the desire "attracts eagerly and hardly into itself" (*SR* 3.11), drawing "that which the Will Desires" into itself (*TP* 14.61). Where the Will moves toward the objectification of itself, desire is by contrast "self-conceiving, self-overshadowing" (*MM* 3.9), a seeking to satisfy itself. With this the conjunction of will and desire "severs itself into two properties, viz. into joy and sorrow, light and darkness; for it makes two worlds. viz. a dark fire-world . . . and a light fire-world . . . in the shining of the fire in the original the Deity is understood, and in the dark fire . . . the original of nature is understood" (*SR* 2.17). While will and desire are interdependent, bound in an "indissoluble Band" in which "the one always generates the other" (*TP* 14.62), they are also a necessary aspect of the dialectic of Yes and No.

Contrariety is actualized in the separation of will into negative and affirmative wills: "a wrathful [will], according to the nature of the fire and of the darkness, and a good love-will, according to the nature and quality of the light" (*MM* 29.7). While the free will "is the unity of God, that is, the Divine Power and Virtue, the outflowing Wisdom," the wrathful will is a will to nature, a "*Self*-Will" (*EOG* 9.37) which "desires to be a something, and {therefore} does not make itself one with the unity" (*TQ* 3.5). Drawing into itself, it is Nay-saying. Set against this is the affirmative will that is in itself "*free* from Nature" (*TLM* 3.20). However, as "God's *holy* Life would not be manifested without Nature" this "will is set or directed towards the *centrum naturae*, for through Nature must the splendour of Majesty arise" (*SP* "Six Theosophic Points," 1.50). It is thus an outgoing "love-will" from the will of the Father, and expresses the Yes. It enters into "the Comprehensibility or Compaction, *viz.* the self-comprised or compacted Will" (EOG 9.41) of the desire of nature. With this the "comprehensible . . . has inclosed the Will" (*TP* 14.62) and the "one only Will"

> finds itself now out of the nothing in the something, and the something is yet its contrary will, for it is an unquietness, and the free-will is a stillness.
>
> This is now the original of enmity, that nature opposes the free-will, and a thing is at enmity in itself. (*SR* 2.14–15)

In this contention there "now comes the Anxiety, because the Will is shut up in the Darkness" (*TP* 14.63). In reaction to this "the Will . . . sets its Purpose to fly away out of the Darkness," out of the "Source" of "Anxiety" and into the "Source of Meekness" (*TP* 14.63–64). To do this "the Mind generates . . . a Will to live in the Meekness; and the Originality of this Will arises out of the first Will, out of the anguishing Mind, out of the dark" (*TP* 14.65). This "reconceived" will is thus "the first will's son" (*SR* 3.3). Set against the will to nature it is the will to liberty.

Boehme draws a distinction between the two wills. While the "re-conceived will . . . desireth the free lubet of God . . . now it hath taken into itself the horrible astringent hard compunctive sharpness" of the will to nature "and the free lubet is a great meekness." Both wills

> dash together in one another. The sharp will eagerly and mightily desireth the free lubet, and the lubet desireth the austere will; and as they enter into and feel each other, a great flagrat {terror, shriek or crack} is made, like a flash of lightning, in manner as the fire or lightning is enkindled in the firmament. (*MM* 3.25–26)

This is again the point of separation into darkness and light. Moreover,

> when the dark anguish, as the very fervent, stern being, receives freedom in itself, it is transformed in the terror {shriek or crack}, in freedom, into a flash, and the flash embraces freedom or gentleness. Then the sting of death is broken; and there rises in Nature the other will of the Father, which he drew prior to Nature in the mirror of wisdom, viz. his heart of love, the desire of love, the kingdom of joy. (*SP* "Six Theosophic Points," 1.57)

This "Transmutation" is "the allaying, or mitigating" of the No by the Yes, in which "the holy incomprehensible Life" is "*manifested* in the Word" (*EOG* 9.49–51). Where the will to nature is a "*Self*-Will," the affirmative will is generous and giving, "For in the Father's will fire is . . . generated, to which the other will gives the power of gentleness and love. The fire takes the love quality into its essence, and that is now its food, so that it burns, and gives from the consumption, from the terror, the joyous spirit" (*SP* "Six Theosophic Points," 1.58).

This "Transmutation" of the No into the Yes is the goal of all that springs from the Creation. The fact that the two wills are at once distinct and interdependent highlights the sublime paradox that gives shape to Boehme's vision. Brinton captures this, underlining the necessity of viewing "the process from an eternal, not a temporal, standpoint," in which cause and effect are coexistent, simultaneous, and interchangeable:

> Mysticism, for Boehme, is not alone a mysticism of the Father, the dark transcendental background of all things, nor solely a mysticism of the Son, the luminous goal of nature, but above all a mysticism of the Spirit, the *life* which eternally pours from one into the other and again returns from whence it came. . . .
>
> . . . each of our two wills is the "matter" or unmanifested substratum of the other and cannot exist by itself. Each also, by going far enough, passes through a mystical stage which transforms it into the other.[15]

The free will must pass through the fire of the "anguish-source," and the "will arising out of the anguishing Mind" can only attain "true understanding" (*MM* 5.14), self-consciousness, and personality through the "lustre of liberty." Although the "light-world . . . dwells in freedom in the unground, out of Nature," it "proceeds from the fire-world. It receives its life and sensibility from the fire" (*SP* "Six Theosophical Points," 2.34). This is the "unbeginning and indissoluble Band" (*TP* 14.62) in which "The gentleness gives and the fire takes. The gentleness is emanent from itself, and gives a substance that is like itself . . . and the fire swallows this up, but out of it produces light" (*ToI* 2.5.6). This "Band" of giving and taking, of feeding, swallowing, and manifestation may be conceived in terms of impregnation and birth. This takes place in Wisdom. As seen, the "eternal will . . . brings itself into a desire" for that which it beholds in Wisdom: this "desire is an impressing, a conceiving {of} itself," or an impregnation (*MM* 1.6). In other words, Boehme perceived the "overshadowing" effected by desire as synonymous with its impregnation. As his work developed he came to regard this "overshadowing" and impregnation as the work of the imagination, of an outgoing and creative faculty that, through the mirror of Wisdom, acts as a bridge between the Nothing and the Something. The seven properties of Eternal Nature give form to this bridge.

THE SEVEN PROPERTIES

The "will of freedom, which is called Father, desires to manifest itself." This "it cannot do without properties" (*SP* "Six Theosophic Points," 1.52–53). Before discussing each of the seven natural properties it is necessary to comment on them as a whole. It is through them that the No arises and is allayed by and "Transmuted" into the Yes. Likewise, it is the seven properties that bring about the objectification of the one eternal will. The process of becoming that lies at the heart of Boehme's work is given shape by the seven. They realize the *meonic* aspect of existence. Out "of the Properties the Creation, *viz.* all Creatures *exist*" (*EOG* 9.38), eternally and temporally. The seven natural properties explore the means by which the "separable Things" that constitute Eternal Nature arise out of the original unity.

As is apparent in much of the spiritual tradition, the number seven is one that is resonant. In Boehme's writings, the seven properties correspond with the seven days of the week. As will take on significance, "God has appointed six days for man to work, and the seventh day is the perfection wherein the six do rest" (*SR* 9.2). They are also understood in terms of the seven days of Creation. As the seven properties and the Creation are to be perceived as activities that are present and working in an eternal moment, they speak of the millenarian world week, of the six millennia that find their "rest" in the Sabbath of the seventh: "one day *is* with the Lord as a thousand years, and a thousand years as one day."[16] This is echoed in Blake: "I walk up and down in Six Thousand Years: their Events are present before me" (*Jer* 229, pl. 74, l. 19): "The ancient tradition that the world will be consumed in fire at the end of six thousand years is true" (*MHH* 39, pl. 14). Accordingly, Boehme's properties draw upon *Revelation*: "the *seven* Forms of the Eternal Nature . . . *are the seven seals of the Son of God, as the Apocalypse witnesseth*": "the *six* seals are the *Birth* of the Eternal Nature" (*TLM* 3.21, 44). Just as Blake drew upon *Revelation* for the Seven Angels of the Presence and the Seven Eyes of God, Boehme's properties correspond to "the seven eyes, which are the seven Spirits of God sent forth unto all the earth," to the "seven lamps of fire burning before the throne, which are the seven Spirits of God," and to the "seven stars . . . and the seven golden candlesticks" (*TLM* 3.41–44).[17] Furthermore, "The ancient philosophers have given names to the seven planets according to the seven forms of nature; but they have understood thereby another thing, not only the seven stars, but the sevenfold properties in the generation of all essences" (*SR* 9.8). Each of the properties is linked to the astrological character of one of the seven planets (*TLM* 9.63–116).[18]

In harmony the seven properties form Eternal Nature, in discord temporal nature. To speak primarily of the Eternal Nature for the moment, they act as the illumination of divine mystery. As Evelyn Underhill suggests, the Eternal Nature may be seen as the "Archetypal" or "Perfect" world, comparable to such realms in Indian, Greek, Egyptian, Celtic, and Jewish thought.[19] It realizes the possibilities revealed in the mirror of Wisdom. That is, that which is *meonic* in the virgin Sophia becomes actual and living in Eternal Nature. However, from the perspective of the temporal world, the actualized and living "wonders" appear *meonic*. They are, in Blake's words,

"Shadowy to those who dwell not in them, mere possibilities: / But to those who enter into them they seem the only substances" (*Jer* 158, pl. 13, ll. 64–65). To gain a clearer understanding of Eternal Nature, one may look very briefly at its relationship to temporal nature. The seven properties that give form to "external nature . . . proceed from the eternal" (*SR* 9.8). The temporal "world, with all that belongs to it, as well as man, is *created* as an Out-birth, out of the Eternal Nature; understand, out of the seven Seals of the Eternal Nature" (*TLM* 3.40). As Blake wrote of "Heavenly Canaan," the difference between eternal and temporal nature is "As the Substance is to the Shadow" (*Jer* 224, pl. 71, ll. 1–2):

> The Nature of Visionary Fancy or Imagination is very little Known and the Eternal nature and permanence of its ever Existent Images is considerd as less permanent than the things of Vegetative and Generated Nature yet the Oak dies as well as the Lettuce but its Eternal Image and Individuality never dies. but renews by its seed. (*VLJ* 555)

By contrast with temporal nature, the Eternal Nature is "an eternal Generating" that "renews by its seed," "an unbeginning Birth, and it has neither Number nor End, and its Depth is bottomless" (*TP* 4.18). However, while it is without beginning, it is in its "seed" eternally present within temporal nature as a "Center": "The Eternal Center, and the Birth of Life . . . are every where. If you make a small Circle, as small as a little Grain, [or Kernel of Seed,] there is the whole Birth of the Eternal Nature" (*TLM* 6.43).

As Eternal Nature expresses a process of becoming, it is creatively dynamic. Franklin perceptively observes that the significance of the seven properties lies not in what they are but in what they do: "meaning is found in activity and relationships, the search for identity, and not in circumscription."[20] Boehme describes a property—or quality, as he also refers to it—as "the mobility, boiling, springing and driving of a thing" (*Aur* 1.4). He apprehends within the properties a painful goad to activity, and that the conflict of the properties is essential:[21]

> in Nature there is one Thing always set opposite to another, the one to be the Enemy to the other.
>
> Yet not to *that End* to be at Enmity one against another, but that in the Strife one should stir up the other, and manifest it . . . and be an Exulting and Joyfulness in the eternal ONE. (*EOG* 2.69–70)

As Blake wrote, suggesting the "garment" of God's "corporeal essence":

> Joy and Woe are woven fine
> A Clothing for the soul divine

Under every grief and pine
Runs a joy with silken twine.

(*AoI* 491, ll. 59–62)

This view is in part echoed in Swedenborg, who perceived a "spiritual equilibrium which . . . may be compared to a balance, in each scale of which equal weights are placed; if then a little be added to the scale of one side the tongue of the balance above vibrates."[22] However, while this view suggests a necessary tension, it is far from the dynamic pain and conflict that gives substance and life to Boehme's vision. Swedenborg argued that "An Equilibrium is necessary to the existence and subsistence of all things, and consists in the equality of action and re-action between two opposite powers, producing Rest or Equilibrium. . . . Thus there exists a spiritual Equilibrium or Liberty betwixt good and evil, by the action of one, and the re-action of the other."[23] Paley proposes that Blake's view of Swedenborg's "Rest or Equilibrium" is "a static view in which there is no 'progression' but the maintenance of an existing order. The two forces are not contraries in Blake's sense, but negations."[24] As the poet wrote in *Jerusalem*:

this is the manner of the Sons of Albion in their strength
They take the Two Contraries which are called Qualities, with which
Every Substance is clothed, they name them Good and Evil
From them they make an Abstract, which is a Negation
Not only of the Substance from which it is derived
A murderer of its own Body: but also a murderer
Of every Divine Member: it is the Reasoning Power
An Abstract objecting power, that Negatives every thing.

(*Jer* 152–53, pl. 10, ll. 7–14)

By contrast, where Swedenborg declared that there is "no relation or progression of good to evil . . . for in each and all respects they are opposites,"[25] Boehme perceived that the "Two Contraries" are "woven fine" and together clothe the living—as opposed to abstract—"Substance" of the seven properties or "Divine Members," that there

> are found *two qualities*, a *good* one and an *evil* one, which are in each other as one thing in this world, in all powers, in the stars and elements, as also in all the creatures; and no creature in the flesh, in the natural life, can subsist, unless it hath the two qualities. (*Aur* 1.3)

To look more closely now at the relationship and movements between the seven properties, Boehme states in *Mysterium Magnum* that it is not "as if the seven Properties were *divided*, and one were near by another, or sooner manifest than another. All seven are but *as one*; and none is the first, second, or last; for the last is again the first" (6.22). One property "generateth another" and they "are in one another as one" (*TLM* 6.45; *SR* 2.39). In this, as several critics have noted,[26] parallels may be drawn with Los's furnaces, which are also "Seven-fold each within other" (*Jer* 202, pl. 53, l. 10), and which are similarly agents of an often painful, form-giving process. Where Boehme understood that the "syderial and elementary spirit cannot discern . . . much less comprehend" the eternal generation of Eternal Nature (*TP* 4.18), Los's furnaces are "incomprehensible / To the Vegetated Mortal Eye's perverted and single vision" (*Jer* 202, pl. 53, ll. 10–11). Likewise, Blake's Seven Eyes of God, which correspond to the "seven-fold" furnaces, are also "one within the other" (*FZ* 312, Night 1, l. 555). In brief, the activities of the seven properties point once more to Boehme's wheel of God "wherein many wheels are made *one in another*, upwards, downwards, crossways, and yet they continually turn, all of them together" (*Aur* 21.64). The possibilities of their interactions, and of that to which they give form are limitless: "The Birth of the eternal Nature is like the [Thoughts or] Senses in Man, as when a [Thought or] Sense is generated by something, and afterwards propagates itself into infinite many [Thoughts]" (*TP* 3.9). The seven are active in that "proper sphere" that Blake regards as the realm of the Arts, namely "invention and visionary conception" (*DC* 541). They positively nurture vision and require active participation: they rouse "the faculties to act."

Certain aspects of Blake's work are suggestive of and cast light on the significance and potency of the seven. It may be said that Blake, like his Milton, "oft conversed / In vision and dream beatific with the Seven Angels of the Presence" (*Milton* 131, pl. 32, ll. 1–2). Just as Boehme's properties correspond to the seven days, and create time and space, as they generate forms through which the "desirous Reader" can work, and as they are "in one another," active in an eternal moment,

> There is a Moment in each Day that Satan cannot find
> Nor can his Watch Fiends find it, but the Industrious find
> This Moment and it multiply. and when it once is found
> It renovates every Moment of the Day.
>
> (*Milton* 136, pl. 35, ll. 42–45)

Drawing significant parallels between divine creation and that of the individual, Blake also wrote that

> every Seven Ages is Incircled with a Flaming Fire . . .
> . . . .
> Every Time less than a pulsation of the artery

> Is equal in its period and value to Six Thousand Years.
>
> For in this Period the Poets Work is Done: and all the Great
> Events of Time start forth and are conceivd in such a Period
> Within a Moment.
>
> (*Milton* 127, pl. 28, ll. 58–63, pl. 29, ll. 1–3)

This "Moment" is found in the "seed" or "Center" of Eternal Nature. Similarly, "Los's Halls" are suggestive of the *meonic* creativity of Eternal Nature:

> All things acted on Earth are seen in the bright Sculptures of
> Los's Halls and every Age renews its powers from these Works
> With every pathetic story possible to happen from Hate or
> Wayward Love and every sorrow and distress is carved here
> Every Affinity of Parents Marriages and Friendships are here
> In all their various combinations wrought with wondrous Art
> All that can happen to Man in his pilgrimage of seventy years.
>
> (*Jer* 161, pl. 16, ll. 61–67)

The seven properties thus forge an imaginative bridge between human and divine creativity.

As noted, in harmony the seven properties form Eternal Nature. Boehme speaks of the relationship between the "divine understanding" and that which is manifested by the seven in terms of play. This play is the harmony of the seven properties which, like Blake's wheels of Eden, "Wheel within Wheel in freedom revolve in harmony and peace" (*Jer* 159, pl. 15, l. 20). The properties are "*distinct spirits,*" the "Voices" of God's "eternal pregnant Harmony. . . . they are God's Instrument, in which the spirit of God *melodizes* in his Kingdom of Joy" (*MM[L]* 8.2). They are "his Strings in the *All-Essential Speaking*, and are all of them tuned for the great *Harmony* of his Eternal Speaking Word; so that . . . the Voice of the unsearchable God is manifest and made known" (*MM[L]* 8.31). These "Voices" find expression in Blake. When the "Starry Seven" appear toward the end of *Milton,*

> there went forth from the Starry limbs of the Seven: Forms
> Human; with Trumpets innumerable, sounding articulate
> As the Seven spake . . .
> . . . .
>
> Then loud the Furnaces of Los were heard!
>
> (140, pl. 39, ll. 3–15)

Boehme speaks of the "articulate" harmony of the seven in terms of the temperature, a harmonious mixture and balance. As will be developed, when the temperature is disrupted, the seven properties are at variance with one another and give voice to the strife of the fallen world, a strife reflected in that of Blake's fallen Zoas.[27] At the same time, when the seven are in "equal concord and harmony," they give form to the conflict that is necessary to "Joy" (*MM* 11.16). Their harmony is envisioned as an "incessant and lasting enjoyment and labour" (*SR* 16.14). This points again to Blake's exhortation to "Mental Fight":

> Our wars are wars of life, and wounds of love,
> With intellectual spears, and long winged arrows of thought:
> Mutual in one anothers love and wrath all renewing
> We live as One Man.
>
> (*Jer* 180, pl. 34, ll. 14–17)

In this it may be proposed in passing that the tense and generative activities of the seven properties were alive and working between Blake and Boehme in their "converse in the spirit."

Boehme conveys the vitality of the "labour" of the seven by speaking of it as "a continual love-combat or wrestling delight" (*SR* 16.15), a love-play in which each property "embraceth the other with friendly desire" (*TLM* 3.13). The properties "all jointly desire to enter again into . . . the one. And there . . . one tasteth, smelleth, feeleth, heareth and seeth the other" (*MM* 5.14). This "harmony of hearing, seeing, feeling, tasting and smelling is the true intellective life" (*MM* 5.14). While the seven properties are, in harmony, interdependent and unified, they are nonetheless differentiated. By contrast with many in the spiritual tradition, both visionaries placed great importance on the activities of the senses. In Blake's terms, "General Forms have their vitality in Particulars" (*Jer* 251, pl. 91, l. 29). At the culmination of *Jerusalem*, the "Four Living Creatures" are united in a "mutual intercourse and entrance into each other" (*MM* 3.13), restoring the divine temperature and realizing the "true intellective life":

> they conversed together in Visionary forms dramatic which bright
> Redounded from their Tongues in thunderous majesty, in Visions
> In new Expanses, creating exemplars of Memory and of Intellect
> Creating Space, Creating Time according to the wonders Divine
> Of Human Imagination . . .
> . . . .
> . . . such was the variation of Time and Space
> Which vary according as the Organs of Perception vary and they walked
> To and fro in Eternity as One Man reflecting each in each and clearly seen
> And seeing: according to fitness and order.
>
> (257–58, pl. 98, ll. 28–40)

Frosch's view of this passage may equally be applied to Boehme's apprehension of the "true intellective life":

> What Blake implies is not a fusion of the faculties into one undifferentiated organic sense. The effect of synaesthesia here . . . is not to erase distinctions between kinds of sensation but to play them off against one another, setting up a rich and mutually heightening interaction. Blake's risen body is founded not on a return to non-individuation but on the individuality of minute particulars, and its character, in all respects, is dialectical.[28]

While the seven properties interact "one in another" it is necessary to differentiate between them.

7
The First Four Properties

THE FIRST AND SECOND PROPERTIES

Boehme's first property of Eternal Nature "is astringent, harsh, impressing, self-conceiving, self-overshadowing; and it maketh . . . the great darkness of the abyss" (*MM* 3.9). That is, it is born out of the eternal will that "arises in the nothing, to introduce the nothing into something" (*SR* 2.8). It is the overshadowing and darkening of "the desire of the eternal Word, which is God," and "is the beginning of the eternal nature" (*MM* 6.14). Accordingly, the first property is the realization of desire:

> the will seeks itself and finds itself in itself, and its seeking is a desire, and its finding is the essence of the desire, wherein the will finds itself.
>
> It finds nothing except only the property of the hunger, which is itself, which it draws into itself, that is, draws itself into itself, and finds itself in itself. (*SR* 2.9–10)

The first property is thus "the beginning of perceivancy" (*MM* 3.9). Moreover, as the "astringent desire conceiveth itself, and draweth into itself" (*MM* 3.15), it expresses the *Self*-Will." In this, as certain students of Blake and Boehme have noted,[1] the first property may be seen to be elucidated in the "self-contemplating shadow" of the "solitary" Urizen, who similarly draws into himself, "into a deep world within: / . . .wild dark and deep, / . . . Where nothing was" (*BU* 71, pl. 3, l. 21; 72, pl.4, ll. 15–17). As Boehme's will "finds nothing except only the property of the hunger, which is itself," Urizen is "consum'd inwards" (*BU* 72, pl. 4, ll. 14–15):

> Lo, a shadow of horror is risen
> In Eternity! Unknown, unprolific!
> Self-closd, all-repelling: what Demon
> Hath form'd this abdominable void?
>
> (*BU* 70, pl. 3, ll. 1–4)

As the activity of the first property is an "attraction into itself" (*SR* 2.10), it is a "compaction," a "coagulation, or impression" (*MM* 3.6). In this "impression" the first property is "the Desire which belongs to God the Father, yet it is only a Spirit" (*Clavis* 127), that is, the germ or seed of substance, rather than substance itself. In itself it is akin to the "solitude" which Blake's Oothoon speaks of, "Where the horrible darkness is impressed with reflections of desire" (*VDA* 50, pl. 7, l. 11). As the "beginning of the eternal nature" and "a cause of . . . all corporality" (*SR* 4.5) it is, however, the alchemical "*Prima Materia*, or first Matter" (*TP* 1.9), the "first mother of all things" (*SR* 4.4) from which the other properties spring. In the light of this, it is interesting to note that Urizen's "deep world within" is described as "Natures wide womb . . . condensing," and that Urizen himself is seen as "a clod of clay" (*BU* 72, pl. 4, l. 17; 74, pl. 6, l. 10), a traditional association of the *Prima Materia*. In addition, the first property "maketh itself substantial in a spiritual manner, wholly rough, harsh, hard and thick" (*MM* 3.9). Again, parallels may and have been drawn with Blake. As Aubrey suggests,[2] as the first property is a "power" that "encloses and makes hard, cold and dark" (*SR* 9.9), it may be seen to be given expression in, for example, *The Book of Urizen* and *Jerusalem*: in, among others, the "petrific abdominable chaos," the "cold horrors," "dim rocks," "hills of stor'd snows," and "mountains of hail and ice"; in the "petrific hardness" of Albion who is "darkening, cold," and in the "bones of solidness" formed in the first of the seven days of the creation of Urizen (*BU* 71–72, pl. 3–4; 75, pl. 10; *Jer* 147, pl. 4, l. 35; 179, pl. 34, ll. 1–8).

As the significance of the properties lies in their activities, the second property arises in reaction to the first. As the first is a "dark astringent hardness" that "encloses," the "impression" longs to be free of it and "conceives in itself another will to go out from the darkness again into the liberty" (*SR* 2.11). Where the first property is a force of contraction, the second is one of expansion, a "compunction," that is, "the beginning of motion, stirring and life" (*MM* 3.10). Accordingly,

> here ariseth the first enmity between the astringency or hardness, and the compunction . . . of stirring . . .
>
> . . . in the dark desire it is the original of enmity, pain and torment; and of the eternal original of God's anger, and of all unquietness. (*MM* 3.10–11)

The "compunction" of the second property acts as a "Sting or Prickle," a "Sharpness" and "Bitterness," as a "poisonous or venemous, hostile . . . Thing" (*TP* 1.10, 13; *SR* 14.10), and is a goad to "motion, stirring and life." In this, Boehme perceived the second property as "the true original of the Mercurial life" (*MM* 3.10). In the "dark desire" Mercury's "motion and hunger is a pricking, adverse and . . . bitter pain and woe . . . a poison-source" (*SR* 9.19). As the first property is the germ or seed of substance, so too in the second property "you must understand hereby no *Materia*, Matter, or comprehensible Thing; but all no other than Spirit, and the Source of the original Nature" (*TP* 1.10). However, while the "Mercurial life" that springs from the second property is like the Holy Spirit in that it too is a "Former, Framer and Fashioner" that goes forth "and makes forms and shapes " (*TP* 4.59; *SR* 4.36), it cannot as yet be identified in terms of the third person of the Trinity, on account of the painful and poisonous bitterness of the "compunction." Likewise, while Mercury is "the outflown Natural working word of God, which has been the Separator, Divider, and Former of every substance" (*Clavis* 115), and while the second property is thus the origin of "sound in the spirit, understand, the separator of the sound, viz. of the tone; also of all pronunciations of speeches" (*SR* 9.20), the Word of God is not as yet articulate. At this point in the properties, there is "only a noise from the hardness," "the cursing and awakening of the opposite will of the bitter poisonful enmity," "the greatest unquietness . . . like a raging madness" (*SR* 14.13, 9.22; *MM* 3.16). In the second property "the separator of the powers and virtues" "makes stinging, breaking, and dividing of the hardness; it cuts asunder the attracted desire, and brings it into multiplicity and variety" (*Clavis* 162, 161). As the contrariety of division is necessary to existence, perception, and understanding, as seen, so the second property is "a cause . . . of the senses" (*MM* 6.15). Mercury "distinguishes and dissipates the hardness" of the "enclosed" first property "and opens it to life" (*SR* 4.36).

The first two properties thus give shape to the contrariety on which existence is dependent. The "hardness is retentive, the attraction {or compunction} is fugitive: the one will into itself, the other will out of itself" (*MM* 3.15). In other words, the first reiterates the will to nature, the second the will to liberty: "Hence arises the first enmity and opposition; for the two forms, which yet are but one, make themselves their own enemies; and yet if this were not, there would not be any essence, neither body nor spirit, also no manifestation of the eternity of the abyss" (*SR* 14.19). The first two properties are therefore bound together in an "indissoluble Band" of opposition: "For . . . before the desire is the liberty, viz. the nothing, and the will may not be a nothing, for it desires to manifest in the nothing; and yet no manifestation can be effected, except only through the essence of the desire" (*SR* 2.12). In this,

> It is even here as father and son; the father would be still, and hard, and the compunction, viz. his son, stirreth in the father, and causeth unquietness, and this the father, viz. the astringency, cannot endure; and therefore he attracteth the more eagerly and earnestly in the desire, to hold and shut in the disobedient son; whereby the son groweth only more strong in the compunction. (*MM* 3.11)

To regard this another way, the second property introduces "a bitter stinging which the hardness cannot endure; for it would be still, and thereupon it does more vehemently impress itself to withhold the sting, and yet the sting does thereby only grow the greater" (*SR* 14.19).

It is now possible to focus a little more on Blake, to illuminate the activities, significance, and vital energies of the seven properties and suggest forms to which they might give birth, to give flesh and life, as it were, to the properties, to dramatize them as Blake did. As suggested in Part I, there are aspects of Blake's work that present obvious similarities with Boehme. One such passage appears in *The Book of Los.* As Urizen may be seen to give form to the constrictive character of the first property, Los may be seen in terms of the expansive and raging "Mercurial Life" of the second property:

> Coldness, darkness, obstruction, a Solid
> Without fluctuation, hard as adamant
> Black as marble of Egypt; impenetrable
> Bound in the fierce raging Immortal.
> ....
> Bound in his expanding clear senses
>
> The Immortal stood frozen amidst
> The vast rock of eternity; times
> And times; a night of vast durance:
> Impatient, stifled, stiffend, hardned.
>
> Till impatience no longer could bear
> The hard bondage, rent: rent, the vast solid
> With a crash from immense to immense
>
> Crack'd across into numberless fragments.
> (91–92, pl. 4, ll. 4–18)

As both the properties and the Zoas act "one within the other" in a vital and dynamic interrelationship, each Zoa cannot be seen in terms of only one of the properties. Los himself also acts as a constrictive force, "forging chains" for Urizen's "bones of solidness" (*BU* 75, pl. 10, ll. 15–41), and, as in *The Four Zoas*, nailing and binding down his son Orc, "the howling fiend" (*FZ* 341, Night 5, ll. 97–112). In this, particularly in the latter example, Blake gives imaginative form to the forces that Boehme presents as "father and son," to the father who would "hold and shut in the disobedient son." Moreover, regarding Orc with "Jealousy" and "Grief," Los experiences the painfully relentless and "indissoluble Band" of contraction, expansion, and division within himself:

a tightening girdle grew
Around his bosom like a bloody cord. in secret sobs
He burst it, but next morn another girdle succeeds
Around his bosom. Every day he viewd the fiery youth
With silent fear and his immortal cheeks grew deadly pale
Till many a morn and many a night passd over in dire woe
Forming a girdle in the day and bursting it at night.
(*FZ* E340–41, Night 5, ll. 83–89)

Orc and Urizen similarly cast light on the first two properties, Orc's rage at the latter echoing the raging "curse" of the sting of the second property, the bitterness and pain, the "compunction," and the process wherein the "hardness . . . does more vehemently impress itself to withhold the sting, and yet the sting does only thereby grow the greater": "Curse thy Cold hypocrisy . . . / . . . Now When I rage my fetters bind me more / O torment O torment A Worm compelld . . . / Art thou the cold attractive power that holds me in this chain" (*FZ* 356, Night 7, ll. 135–46). Finally, as the first property is the *Prima Materia*, the "mother of all things," and the second the beginning of "motion, stirring and life," the two may be heard and felt at the beginning of the fifth Night of *The Four Zoas*, through the pregnant Enitharmon and the birth of Luvah-Orc:

Enitharmon stretchd on the dreary Earth
Felt her immortal limbs freeze stiffning pale inflexible
. . . .
The groans of Enitharmon shake the skies the labring Earth
Till from her heart rending his way a terrible Child sprang forth
In thunder smoke and sullen flames and howlings and fury and blood

Soon as his burning Eyes were opend in the Abyss
The horrid trumpets of the deep bellowd with bitter blasts
. . . .
Discord began then yells and cries shook the wide firma[m]ent.
(*FZ* 339, Night 5, ll. 5–45)

THE THIRD PROPERTY

As the first two properties "cannot sever and part asunder one from the other," as suggested, "they remain in each other as a rotating wheel: the one will ascend, the other descend" (*MM* 3.15). This wheel, "the first Mobility" (*TP* 1.10), is the third property, "which runs into itself as an horrible essence, where both properties are known only as one, and yet each remains in itself unaltered" (*SR* 14.20). In this property there arises a conflict of desires which "makes a continual confusion and contrition" (*SR* 2.13). The "third form is the anxiousness which arises in nature from the first and second form, and is the upholder or preserver of the first and second" (*SR* 2.30). It is a state of anguish "by reason of the raging in the impression, where the impressed hardness falls into a tearing anguish and pain by reason of the sting" (*SR* 14.10). By reason of the conflict of desires and the resultant anguish, the third property is "the cause of feeling" (*SR* 9.11) and of "the mind, wherein the senses become active" (*MM* 6.16). The two contrary properties desire rest and release from the whirling anguish, but they "cannot go any wither" (*MM* 3.16); "there is no separating or departing" (*SR* 14.20), "no Rest there, and . . . the turning Wheel runs as fast as a swift Thought, for the Prickle drivest so fast" (*TP* 1.11). The desire to be free from the pain of the anguish only increases it: "the Anguish . . . generates again the Anguish" (*TP* 10.43). Blake understood this well: "If any desire what he is incapable of possessing, despair must be his eternal lot" (*NNR* 2).

Blake's work speaks again and again of the revolving anguish:

> O that I had not seen the day then should I be at rest
> Nor felt the stings of desire nor longings after life.
> (*FZ* 357, Night 7, ll. 202–3)

In *The Book of Urizen* the contentions of Urizen and Los express powerfully the restlessly stinging pain and anguish realized in the third property:

> In fierce anguish and quenchless flames
> To the desarts and rocks He {Urizen} ran raging
> To hide, but He could not: combining
> He dug mountains and hills in vast strength,
> He piled them in incessant labour,
> In howlings and pangs and fierce madness
> . . . .
>
> On ages roll'd ages in ghastly
> Sick torment; around him in whirlwinds
> Of darkness the eternal Prophet howl'd
> Beating still on his rivets . . .
> . . . .
>
> And Urizen (so his eternal name)
> His prolific delight obscurd more and more
> In dark secrecy . . .
> . . . .
>
> The eternal mind bounded began to roll

Eddies of wrath ceaseless round and round
. . . .

Restless turnd the immortal inchain'd
Heaving dolorous! anguish'd! unbearable.
(73, pl. 5, ll. 19–24; 74–75, pl. 10, ll. 5–32)

In *The Four Zoas* Los's endeavors give energetic form to the ceaseless contention of the Creation:

Terrified Los beheld the ruins of Urizen beneath
A horrible Chaos to his eyes. a formless unmeasurable Death
Whirling up broken rocks on high into the dismal air
And fluctuating all beneath in Eddies of molten fluid

Then Los with terrible hands siezd on the Ruind Furnaces
Of Urizen. Enormous work: he builded them anew
Labour of Ages in the Darkness . . .
. . . .

But Urizen slept in a stoned stupor in the nether Abyss
A dreamful horrible State in tossings on his icy bed
Freezing to solid all beneath . . .
. . . .

. . . Round him Los rolld furious
His thunderous wheels from furnace to furnace . . .
. . . .

. . . mills he formd and works
Of many wheels.
(335, Night 4, ll. 161–83)

With the third property nature has arisen out of the *Ungrund* to the extent where the Light is a possibility, but not as yet realized. As suggested in the understanding that each of the three properties "is only a Spirit," their activities are as yet unconscious.[3] While the senses arise in the first three properties, "no right feeling is perceived" as yet (*MM* 3.16); that is, life is not as yet realized or substantial. The anguish of the whirling wheel may be understood as the struggle of the mind (divine, and by association human) in the darkness to bring itself out of unconsciousness, and into existence and substance. At this point, however, the properties have reached a condition comparable to that of which Los's Spectre laments:

my griefs advance . . . forever and ever without end
O that I could cease to be! Despair! I am Despair
Created to be the great example of horror and agony . . .
. . . .
. . . the Almighty hath made me his Contrary
To be all evil, all reversed and forever dead: knowing
And seeing life, yet living not.

(*Jer* 153–54, pl. 10, ll. 50–58)

As with the properties, the Spectre cannot "cease to be" and thus "every moment" his "Despair" "accumulates more and more" (*Jer* 153, pl. 10, l. 45). In the same spirit Blake writes in *Jerusalem* of "the Spectres / Of all the inhabitants of Earth wailing to be Created" (158, pl. 13, ll. 62–63). Franklin compares the struggle of the mind in the darkness to *The Book of Urizen*, where the protagonist is portrayed in a state anterior to consciousness and identity:

unknown, abstracted
Brooding secret, the dark power hid.

. . . .
. . . he strove in battles dire
In unseen conflictions with shapes
Bred from his forsaken wilderness
. . . .

Dark revolving in silent activity:
Unseen in tormenting passions;
An activity unknown and horrible;
A self-contemplating shadow,
In enormous labours occupied.

(70–71, pl. 3, ll. 6–22)[4]

As with Los's Spectre, contrariety arises because while Boehme's dark mind would be free of itself it would also be itself:

with the seeking in itself it makes the centre of nature: For it is like a poison, a will of dreadful aspiring . . . for this desire desires only anguish, and to be horrible, to find itself in itself, out of the nothing in the something. . . .

And we understand by the centre in itself, with the aspiring wrathfulness, with the wrathful will to nature, the dark world. (*SR* 2.33–34)

In *Jerusalem* Albion's Spectre has "a white Dot calld a Center from which branches out / A Circle in continual gyrations." The "unfortunate contemplator / . . . becomes his food[:] such is the way of the Devouring Power" (*Jer*

175, pl. 29, ll. 19–24). That is, the "desire of the dark world is after the manifestation, viz. after the outward world, to attract and draw the same essentiality into it, and thereby to satisfy its wrathful hunger" (*SR* 2.35). This hunger underlies all existence, and is at the same time, in the wrathful aspect of God, an "Eternal Death" (*TLM* 8.38), a phrase that appears repeatedly in Boehme. Blake gives voice to this "anguish-source":

> A murderous Providence! A Creation that groans, living on Death.
> Where Fish and Bird and Beast and Man and Tree and Metal and Stone
> Live by Devouring, going into Eternal Death continually.
>
> (*Jer* 199, pl. 50, ll. 5–7)

When Los endeavors to labor,

> still the Spectre divided, and still his pain increas'd!
>
> In pain the Spectre divided: in pain of hunger and thirst:
> To devour Los' Human Perfection.
>
> (*Jer* 149, pl. 6, ll. 10–14)

The twelve Sons of Albion

> Revolve upon his mountain groaning in pain: beneath
> The dark incessant sky, seeking for rest and finding none:
> Raging against their Human natures, ravning to gormandize.
>
> (*Jer* 164, pl. 19, ll. 20–23)

As is comprehended in this, as there is no substance or "essentiality" in the first three properties in themselves, there is nothing—neither from the "outward world" nor from the Light—for the hunger to feed upon but itself. Again, "the Anguish . . . generates . . . the Anguish," "desires only Anguish." As Blake contrasts the Devourer and the Prolific in *The Marriage* (40, pl. 16), Boehme's

> Anguish . . . is the eternal Worm which generates and eats itself, and in its own Fierceness in itself lives in the Darkness which itself makes . . . generating in itself, and gnawing [eating or devouring] in it, and yet consuming nothing, neither multiplying nor lessening. (*TP* 14.64)

Aubrey compares this to the "Worm," which, as quoted above, Orc is "compelld" to become, "A Self consuming dark devourer" (*FZ* 356, Night 7, l. 156).[5] The dark will of the first three properties is dependent on something beyond or higher than itself to release it from the blindly whirling wheel of itself, as Los realizes:

These Spectres have no [*Counter*(parts)] therefore they ravin
Without the food of life Let us Create them Count[erparts]
For without a Created body the Spectre is Eternal Death.
(*FZ* 369, Night 7, ll. 408–10)

THE FOURTH PROPERTY

In the fourth property fire springs to life. It has its origin out of both the dark and light worlds. In the anguish of the first three properties desire arises for the liberty of the light. At the same time, so to speak, the liberty desires to be manifest, and to achieve this it enters into the dark world. The sharp will and free will thus desire each other and "dash together . . . and as they enter into and feel each other, a great flagrat {terror, shriek or crack} is made, like a flash of lightning . . . And in this flagrat the fire is enkindled" (*MM* 3.25–26). With this the fire "becomes shining" (*TP* 10.47) and manifests the light. This manifestation in the fourth is equated with the sun and "is called Sol, viz. the light of nature" (*SR* 9.12). As Blake's Los has often been regarded as an anagram of Sol, and as he appears as "a terrible flaming Sun" (*Milton* 116, pl. 22, l. 6), it is not surprising that parallels have been drawn between the "Eternal Prophet," "the fourth immortal starry one" (*FZ* 301, Night 1, l. 14), and Boehme's fourth form of Eternal Nature.[6] Indeed, just as Los's furnaces bring about a separative activity, Boehme's fire separates the dark and light worlds. The "flagrat in the darkness is God's anger," while in the light it becomes a "triumphant divine kingdom of joy" (*MM* 4.6). In other words, "we are to understand by the enkindling of the fire, a two-fold fire" (*MM* 4.8). Viewing the life of the properties eternally, in the moment in which each acts within the other, the *flagrat* does not only give rise to the light world:

> in this flagrat . . . the astringent harsh darkness, which is cold, is dismayed at the light and great meekness . . . and becomes in itself a flagrat of death, where the wrathfulness and cold property retireth back into itself, and closeth up itself as a death. For in the flagrat the dark mind becomes essential; it sadly betakes itself into itself, as an ownness, as a great fear before the light, or as an enmity of the light. (*MM* 3.26)

The light may be seen as a cause of the anguish of the darkness.

Blake gives form to the movement through which the "dark mind . . . betakes itself into itself" in *Jerusalem.* The Cities of Albion rise "With one accord in love sublime" and attempt "with kindest violence to bear him back / Against his will thro' Los's Gate to Eden," "his native home":

but Albion dark,
Repugnant; rolld his Wheels backward into Non-Entity
Loud roll the Starry Wheels of Albion into the World of Death
And all the Gate of Los, clouded with clouds redounding from
Albions dread Wheels . . .
. . . every little particle of light and air, became Opake
Black and immense, a Rock of difficulty and a Cliff
Of Black Despair.

(*Jer* 186, pl. 39, ll. 1–12)

Ahania's fall in *The Four Zoas* conveys powerfully the fierce "Terror" of the "Fire-flash":

A crash ran through the immense The bounds of Destiny were broken
The bounds of Destiny crashed direful and the swelling Sea
Burst from its bonds in whirlpools fierce . . .
. . . .

Down from the dismal North the Prince in thunders and thick clouds

As when the thunderbolt down falleth on the appointed place
Fell down down rushing ruining thundering shuddering
Into the Caverns of the Grave and places of Human Seed
Where the impressions of Despair and Hope enroot forever
A world of Darkness. Ahania fell far into Non Entity.

(329, Night 3, ll. 135–44)

The "Dark virgin" speaks to Orc of the "impressions of Despair" in *America*:

O what limb rending pains I feel. thy fire and my frost
Mingle in howling pains, in furrows by thy lightnings rent;
This is eternal death.

(52, pl. 2, ll. 15–17)

In *The Book of Los* Blake casts light on the dark aspect of the "two-fold fire":

Wide apart stood the fires: Los remain'd
In the void between fire and fire[.]
In trembling and horror they beheld him
They stood wide apart, driv'n by his hands
And his feet which the nether abyss
Stamp'd in fury and hot indignation

But no light from the fires all was
Darkness round Los.

(91, pl. 3, ll. 43–49, pl. 4, l. 1)

The separation made in the fourth property is that in which the dark and light worlds are interdependent yet discrete. It realizes the contrariety necessary to overcome the "Eternal Death" of the first three properties in themselves. Blake's Milton speaks of this:

> All that can be annihilated must be annihilated
> That the Children of Jerusalem may be saved from slavery
> There is a Negation, and there is a Contrary
> The Negation must be destroyed to redeem the Contraries
> The Negation is the Spectre.
>
> (*Milton* 142, pl. 40, ll. 30–34)

The fourth property is therefore "the dividing Mark or bound" (*Clavis* 126): "the Deep of the Darkness is as great as the Habitation of the Light; and they stand not one distant from the other, but together in one another" (*TP* 14.76). They are, however, separated by a "Limit" or "Bar," and the maintenance of this is an act of mercy. Los declares in *Milton:*

> We were placed here by the Universal Brotherhood and Mercy
> With powers fitted to circumscribe this dark Satanic death
> And that that Seven Eyes of God may have space for Redemption.
>
> (119, pl. 23, ll. 50–52)

The fourth property is a point of "sharp Regeneration" (*TLM* 14.76), one of transition and transformation. Pivotal, it may be understood as the hub of the whole wheel of the seven properties. As "soon as the stroke is given the astringent chamber is opened, and . . . the forms of nature are awakened, and are as a turning wheel" (*SR* 2.40). This moment of transformation may be compared to the point in *The Four Zoas* where Los, at his furnaces, awakens to his task: "look[!] my flames enlume afresh / Before my face ascending with delight as in ancient times" (370, Night 7, ll. 444–45).[7] In this wakening or opening the fourth property forms a center through which the mind, divine and human, may ascend or descend. It is through this center that God moves—or looks—into desire and will, and all that follows therefrom. Similarly, man's "Soul is an Eye in the Eternal Abyss" (*FQ* "Appendix," par. 1), and is placed in the fourth between light and darkness, Heaven and Hell. The fourth property, the limit, is both the point of temptation and redemption. This point or center can be seen in *Milton*:

> Now Albions sleeping Humanity began to turn upon his Couch;
> Feeling the electric flame of Miltons awful precipitate descent.
> Seest thou the little winged fly, smaller than a grain of sand?
> It has a heart like thee; a brain open to heaven and hell,

Withinside wondrous and expansive; its gates are not clos'd,
I hope thine are not . . .
. . . .
Seek not thy heavenly father then beyond the skies:
There Chaos dwells and ancient Night and Og and Anak old:
For every human heart has gates of brass and bars adamant,
Which few dare unbar because dread Og and Anak guard the gates
Terrific . . .
. . . .

Thus Milton fell thro Albions heart.

(114, pl. 20, ll. 25–41)

Imagination, divine and human, may look—or move—into the lower, dark world, or the higher, light world. What it sees it makes: "as the spirit is, so is the essence" (*MM* 4.8). What is seen is dependent on the beholder and the limit, the "Bar" that separates the light and dark worlds:

There is a Grain of Sand in Lambeth that Satan cannot find
Nor can his Watch Fiends find it: tis translucent and has many Angles
But he who finds it will find Oothoons palace, for within
Opening into Beulah every angle is a lovely heaven
But should the Watch Fiends find it, they would call it Sin
And lay its Heavens and their inhabitants in blood of punishment.

(*Jer* 183, pl. 37, ll. 15–20)

The limit was apparent to Blake in *The Marriage*: "I was walking among the fires of hell, delighted with the enjoyments of Genius; which to Angels look like torment and insanity" (35, pl. 6). The limit appears again in *Jerusalem*:

those in Great Eternity who contemplate on Death
Said thus. What seems to Be: Is: To those to whom
It seems to Be, and is productive of the most dreadful
Consequences to those to whom it seems to Be: even of
Torments, Despair, Eternal Death.

(179, pl. 32, ll. 50–54)

Boehme placed equal importance on the role of the imagination, a role that marks them out as kindred spirits: "Imagination . . . maketh Substance" (*ToI* 2. 2.23).

Where the first three properties are unrealized in themselves, in the fourth property, "in the Fire is the Substance and Essentiality generated" (*TP* 10.43) and with them "corporality and multiplication begin" (*SR* 4.8). The separation in the fourth property is, again, the "eternal beginning of *the manifestation of God*" (*MM* 4.7). Through it consciousness arises, as do the "intellective life" and "understanding . . . viz. a spirit which knows what itself is in the properties" (*MM* 3.18). Boehme's enkindled fire springs to life again in Blake's "Mental Fires":

> when all Tyranny was cut off from the face of Earth
> Around the Dragon form of Urizen and round his stony form
> The flames rolling intense thro the wide Universe
> Began to Enter the Holy City Entring the dismal clouds
> In furrowd lightnings break their way the wild flames li[c]king up
> The Bloody Deluge living flames winged with intellect
> And Reason . . .
> From the clotted gore and from the hollow den
> Start forth the trembling millions into flames of mental fire
> Bathing their Limbs in the bright visions of Eternity.
>
> (*FZ* 388, Night 9, ll. 80–89)

As the realization of that which is perceived, "the fire causeth the feeling [or sensibility] in the sharpness of the dead Corporeity: for without fire there is *no body,* that hath sensibility [or feeling]" (*TLM* 4.15).

Through Ahania's fall in *The Four Zoas* Blake suggests the consequences of the dark mind's falling back into essence:

> She Continued falling. Loud the Crash continud loud and Hoarse
> From the Crash roared a flame of blue sulphureous fire from the flame
> A dolorous groan . . .
> . . . .
> . . . from the Dolorous Groan one like a shadow of smoke appeard
> And human bones rattling together in the smoke and stamping
> The nether Abyss and gnasshing {*sic*}in fierce despair. panting in sobs
> Thick short incessant bursting sobbing. deep despairing stamping struggling
> Struggling to utter the voice of Man struggling to take the features of Man struggling
> To take the limbs of Man.
>
> (329–30, Night 3, ll. 145–58)

By contrast, in the climax of *The Four Zoas* Blake recalls the "Shriek" of Boehme's *flagrat* and the birth of the essence of the light:

> And when Morning began to dawn upon the distant hills
> a whirlwind rose up in the Center and in the Whirlwind a shriek
> And in the Shriek a rattling of bones and in the rattling of bones
> A dolorous groan and from the dolorous groan in tears
> Rose Enion like a gentle light.
>
> (400, Night 9, ll. 590–94)

Boehme speaks of the beginning of essence in the fourth property as a "Cross-Birth," in which the essence of "God in love and anger" and "heaven and hell" arises (*SR* 14.32). The center of the fourth property is the center of the cross, which acts as a "Bar" or limit, separating the dark from the light world. It "is as *a Growing Tree* . . . out of which the Essences of the desiring spring forth, like a Tree or Sprout" (*TLM* 4.16). The essence that arises from the cross-birth in the dark world is given form in Albion's Spectre's "desiring":

> the Spectre . . . is the Great Selfhood
> Satan: Worshipd as God by the Mighty Ones of the Earth
> Having a white Dot calld a Center from which branches out
> A Circle in continual gyrations. this became a Heart
> From which sprang numerous branches varying their motions
> Producing many Heads three or seven or ten, and hands and feet
> Innumerable at will.
>
> (*Jer* 175, pl. 29, ll. 17–23)

This dark essence inverts the meaning of the crucifiction: "The Modern Church Crucifies Christ with the Head Downwards" (*VLJ* 564). By contrast, when Enion arises "like a gentle light" in *The Four Zoas* Blake gives expression to the liberating essence of the cross-birth:

> The roots shoot thick thro the solid rocks bursting their way
> They cry out in joys of existence. the broad stems
> Rear on the mountains stem after stem . . .
> . . . .
>
> Joy thrilld thro all the Furious form of Tharmas humanizing
> Mild he Embracd her whom he sought.
>
> (401, Night 9, ll. 604–14)

As suggested, the goal of the properties is the manifestation of the Light of Christ. The crucifixion is the birth of this Light *through* death, as Jesus tells Albion:

> Fear not Albion unless I die thou canst not live
> But if I die I shall arise again and thou with me
> . . . .
>
> if God dieth not for Man and giveth not himself
> Eternally for Man Man could not exist. for Man is Love:
> As God is Love.
>
> (*Jer* 255–56, pl. 96, ll. 14–15, 25–28)

As the "Great Selfhood" finds essence when the cross is turned "Head Downwards," it must be cast off on the cross:

> Like as the candle dies in the fire, and out of that death the light and power proceed, viz. the great painless life; so out of Christ's dying and death the eternal divine sun should and must arise in the human property; but the selfishness of the human property, viz. the soul's own self-will to live in the fire's might must here die and be drowned in the image of love, and the image of love must also resign and give itself in unto the wrath of death, that so all might fall down into death, and arise in God's will and mercy through death. (*SR* 11.84)

Addressing the Deists as perpetrators of the Satanic cross, Blake wrote that "Man is born a Spectre or Satan and is altogether an Evil, and requires a New Selfhood continually and must continually be changed into his direct Contrary" (*Jer* 200, pl. 52, "To the Deists"). Blake understood with Boehme that "All that can be annihilated must be annihilated." The will to liberty takes hold of the essence in the darkness "and brings it forth through the fire, where the grossness, viz. the rawness, does then die in the fire" (*SR* 14.30). Fire purifies. Everything must pass through this fire, just as the free will must pass through nature, "through darkness, so that the light might be made known and manifest" (*SR* 14.23). This yet again stresses the necessity of contrariety, for there must be Eternal Death as well as Eternal Life. The "Man . . . seen in the Furnaces" in *Jerusalem* understands this:

> Albion goes to Eternal Death: In me all Eternity.
> Must pass thro' condemnation, and awake beyond the Grave!
> . . . .
> Albion hath enterd the State Satan! Be permanent O State!
> And be thou for ever accursed! that Albion may arise again:
> And be thou created into a State! I go forth to Create
> States: to deliver Individuals evermore! Amen.
>
> So spoke the voice from the Furnaces, descending into Non-Entity.
> (177–78, pl. 31, ll. 5–17)

The State maintains the merciful limit. Los recalls the pain and difficulty of the process or passage:

> I took the sighs and tears, and bitter groans:
> I lifted them into my Furnaces; to form the spiritual sword.
> That lays open the hidden heart: I drew forth the pang
> Of sorrow red hot: I workd it on my resolute anvil:

I heated it in the flames . . .
. . . .
Loud roar my Furnaces and loud my hammer is heard:
I labour day and night, I behold the soft affections
Condense beneath my hammer into forms of cruelty
But still I labour in hope.

(*Jer* 152, pl. 9, ll. 17–27)

Hope comes through the light world. Through the cross-birth the destructive becomes creative. The "spiritual sword" separates the darkness from the light and, falling and rising respectively, the two roll apart, revolving one against the other. Blake saw this:

I stood among my valleys of the south
And saw a flame of fire, even as a Wheel
Of fire surrounding all the heavens: it went
From west to east against the current of
Creation and devourd all things in its loud
Fury and thundering course . . .
. . . .
. . . I asked a Watcher and a Holy-One
Its Name? He answerd. It is the Wheel of Religion
I wept and said. Is this the law of Jesus
This terrible devouring sword turning every way
He answerd; Jesus died because he strove
Against the current of this Wheel . . .
. . . .
. . . Jesus is the bright Preacher of Life
Creating Nature from this fiery Law,
By self-denial and forgiveness of Sin.
Go therefore, cast out devils in Christs name
. . . .
For Hell is opend to Heaven.

(*Jer* 232–33, pl. 77, ll. 1–35)

At the opening of *Jerusalem*, Blake writes "Of the Sleep of Ulro! and of the passage through / Eternal Death! and of the awaking to Eternal Life" (146, pl. 4, ll. 1–2). As the first three properties can reach no further than the fire, the passage through the fourth into the higher ternary is the satiating of the hunger of anxiety and the entrance into "Eternal Life." Blake's "Veil of Vala" closes off the possibility of light. The *flagrat* that opens the light world "rent in twain the veil . . . which hung before the clear face of God" (*SR* 11.70). This rending may be seen in *Milton*:

> These are the Sexual Garments, the Abomination of Desolation
> Hiding the Human Lineaments as with an Ark and Curtains
> Which Jesus rent: and now shall wholly purge away with Fire
> Till Generation is swallowed up in Regeneration.
>
> (142–43, pl. 41, ll. 25–28)

With the purgative action of fire

> the very fervent, stern being, receives freedom in itself, it is transformed in the terror, in freedom, into a flash, and the flash embraces freedom or gentleness. Then the sting of death is broken; and there arises in Nature the other will of the Father, which he drew prior to Nature in the mirror of wisdom, viz. his heart of love, the desire of love, the kingdom of joy. (*SP* "Six Theosophic Points," 1.57)

Los anticipates this moment,

> When all Albions injuries shall cease, and when we shall
> Embrace him tenfold bright, rising from his tomb in immortality.
> They have divided themselves by Wrath. they must be united by
> Pity: let us therefore take example and warning O my Spectre.
> O that I could abstain from wrath! O that the Lamb
> Of God would look upon me and pity me in my fury.
> In anguish of regeneration! in terrors of self annihilation.
>
> (*Jer* 150, pl. 7, ll. 55–61)

This is Boehme's point of "sharp Regeneration" in the fourth property:

> O holy Generation! [*Image*] of regeneration!
> O point of mutual forgiveness between Enemies!
> Birthplace of the Lamb of God incomprehensible!
>
> (150, pl. 7, ll. 65–67)

Los declares to his Spectre, his blindly driving attendant selfhood,

> I know thy deceit and thy revenges, and unless thou desist
> I will certainly create an eternal Hell for thee. Listen!
> Be attentive! be obedient! Lo the Furnaces are ready to receive thee.
> I will break thee into shivers! and melt thee in the furnaces of death;
> I will cast thee into forms of abhorence and torment if thou
> Desist not from thine own will, and obey not my stern command!
> ....
> I will compel thee to assist me in my terrible labours. To beat
> These hypocritic Selfhoods on the Anvils of bitter Death.
>
> (*Jer* 151, pl. 8, ll. 7–17)

This assertion of Los's will against the Spectre's can be heard in Boehme's Christ on the Cross:

> "Death! Where is thy sting" . . . "Hell! Where is now thy victory" . . . O death, I am to thee a death; Hell! I am to thee a conqueror; thou must serve me for the kingdom of joy: Thou shalt be my servant and minister to the kingdom of joy; thou shalt enkindle the flames of love with thy wrath, and be a cause of the spring in paradise. (*SR* 11.72)

In the enkindling of Boehme's fire the essence of desire in the dark world "is consumed in the fire-flagrat; that is, it doth, as 'twere, die to its selfhood" (*MM* 4.18). Death is consumed by life. At the same time, perpetuating the cycles, "The fire takes the love-quality into its essence, and that is now its food, so that it burns, and gives from the consumption, from the terror, the joyous spirit" (*SP* "Six Theosophic Points," 1.58). Through the cross-birth, "the hunger unto death was made a hunger to life; for the love tinctured the anger, that the fire-desire to the dark impression became a desire of life" (*SR* 11.67). Addressing Los, the Spectre gives voice to the necessity of this transformation:

> Thou never canst embrace sweet Enitharmon . . . Till
> Thou art united with thy Spectre Consummating by pains and labours
> That mortal body and by Self annihilation back returning
> To Life Eternal be assurd I am thy real Self
> Tho thus divided from thee and the Slave of Every passion
> Of thy fierce Soul Unbar the Gates of Memory look upon me
> . . . .
>
> If we unite in one[,] another better world will be
> Opend within your heart and loins and wondrous brain
> Threefold as it was in Eternity and this the fourth Universe
> Will be Renewd by the three and consummated in Mental fires.
> (*FZ* 368, Night 7, ll. 342–56)

Los answers:

> Even I already feel a World within
> Opening its gates and in it all the real substances
> Of which these in the outward World are shadows which pass away
> Come then into my Bosom.
> (368, Night 7, ll. 364–67)

8

The Fifth and Sixth Properties

THE FIFTH PROPERTY

The birth into the light is realized through rather than by the fourth property. As suggested, it is brought about by the activities of all seven properties. The discussion of the cross-birth, the passage into the light, and the interdependency of the light and dark worlds has therefore already touched on the fifth, sixth, and seventh properties of Eternal Nature. Likewise, the activities of the first three properties—contraction, expansion, and rotation—are also at work in the second three. As the emergence of light is the "allaying, or mitigating" of the No by the Yes, each property in the higher ternary is paired with one in the lower. While dependent on the lower, the higher allays or transforms it through the fire. Equally, the higher *is* the allaying and transformation of the lower. While there is, as seen, no final or absolute fixity of association, "It is especially to be observed, that always the First and the Seventh property are accounted for one; and the Second and Sixth; also the Third and Fifth; and the Fourth is only the dividing Mark or bound" (*Clavis* 126). The pairings correspond to the Trinity. The first and seventh properties are "especially" equated with the Father, the second and sixth with the Son, and the third and fifth with the Holy Ghost (*Clavis* 127–29).

The fifth property is the fulfilling of the anguish of the third. It is the "Place" in which "the Light has its Original" (*TP* 5.10) and in which "the holy generation, and the triumphant kingdom of the great love of God, doth consist, and is manifest" (*MM* 6.18). The fifth is therefore the property "wherein the sprouting forth of Paradise consists" (*TP* 5.25). The light that is born here is "meek, pleasant, lovely," "all . . . is pleasant and chearful, and . . . the soft Light of the Heart of God makes all courteous and chearful" (*MM* 5.1; *TP* 5.13). It is comparable to Blake's Beulah, which is "pleasant" and "lovely," a "place of affection sweet and mild benevolence" (*Milton* 129, pl. 34, ll. 1–7). In it the "mother of all things," the *Prima Materia*, is transformed through the fire into "an eternal, unbeginning soft [or meek] Spirit." The "Spirit which goes forth in the soft Matrix is the Holy Ghost" (*TP* 5.13–14), which in the third property "is only a fiery Spirit; but in the fifth

Property, the great Love is manifested therein" (*Clavis* 129). With the birth of light comes the birth of love. The fifth property is equated with Venus.

Through love, the desire that is repressed and unsatiated in the lower ternary is released and fulfilled. The "fifth form is now the second desire" (*SR* 4.9), namely, the "love-desire." It originates in the free will and is purified through the fire. Boehme speaks of it in terms of a "sweet Water" (*TP* 2.11) that quenches the wrath and anguish. With it there "springs up the sweet Water-Spirit{,} a very sweet pleasant Source or Fountain" (*TP* 2.11). At the same time "an oil . . . ariseth from the love-lubet" (*SR* 8.33) that feeds the fire and sustains the light. Aubrey compares this "Oil . . . sweeter than any sugar," this "pure and transparent" "Pearl," "whiter than any Thing in Nature" (*MM[L]* 10.22–23), to Blake's Ololon: "There is in Eden a Sweet River, of mild and liquid pearl, / Namd Ololon" (*Milton* 115, pl. 21, ll. 15–16).[1] Parallels may similarly be seen in the redemptive "milk and oil" of *The Book of Thel.* Giving voice to the casting off of selfhood, and the transformation of the *Prima Materia*, the "first mother of all things" (associated in the alchemical tradition with clay) into the gentle humility of the "soft Matrix," Blake conveys the sacred quality of the "oil," of the pearl "that none can take away":

> The Clod of Clay heard the Worms voice, and raisd her pitying head;
> She bow'd over the weeping infant, and her life exhal'd
> In milky fondness, then on Thel she fix'd her humble eyes.
>
> O beauty of the vales of Har. we live not for ourselves,
> Thou seest me the meanest thing, and so I am indeed;
> My bosom of itself is cold, and of itself is dark.
>
> But he that loves the lowly, pours his oil upon my head.
> And kisses me, and binds his nuptial bands around my breast.
> And says; Thou mother of my children, I have loved thee.
> And I have given thee a crown that none can take away.
>
> (5, pl. 4, ll. 7–12, pl. 5, ll. 1–4)

At the climax of *Jerusalem*, the fire of the properties is transformed into the "sweet Water" of redemption:

> Self was lost in the contemplation of faith
>
> . . . .
>
> . . . Albion . . . threw himself into the Furnaces of affliction
> All was a Vision, all a Dream: the Furnaces became
> Fountains of Living Waters flowing from the Humanity Divine
>
> (*Jer* 256, pl. 96, ll. 31, 35–43)

With the transformation of the "first Mother" in the fifth property the water is the first substance. As "desire makes essence" and as the fifth property is the "love-desire," the fifth is "the beginning of all corporality" (*SR* 9.15). As seen, the desire in the darkness is in itself restrained and thus insubstantial. Without its active contrary of light it would be merely an "Eternal Death." In *The Marriage of Heaven and Hell*, Blake illuminates this:

> Those who restrain desire, do so because theirs is weak enough to be restrained; and the restrainer or reason usurps its place and governs the unwilling.
>
> And being restraind it by degrees becomes passive till it is only the shadow of desire. (34, pl. 5)

Desire is essential to life. The importance Blake and Boehme place on it again highlights their particular affinities. It is immensely significant that Boehme envisages desire in the higher ternary as well as in the lower. While the first and second desires are separated by the "Mark or bound" of the fourth property, they are by no means unrelated. Through an act of will—as opposed to the "Eternal Death" of Blake's "unwilling"—the second desire is the transformation of the first. Passing through the fourth property, the will transforms the desire into the second. Desire is necessary, as Blake stresses in *The Marriage*, evoking the "Messiah" who "prays to the Father to send the comforter or Desire that Reason may have Ideas to build on, the Jehovah of the Bible being no other than he, who dwells in flaming fire" (35, pl. 6). The mutual dependence, in which the lower and higher desire each give and take, feed and consume, is given expression in Blake's Prolific, which "would cease to be Prolific unless the Devourer as a sea recievd [*sic*] the excess of his delights" (*MHH* 40, pl.16).

With the birth of the light the tincture arises, that is, "the cause of the Shining, or of the Luster." An agent of distinction, it "separates, and brings the Pure and Clear from the Impure" (*TP* 12.25). As it is illuminative, the tincture enables perception. The love-desire of the fifth property first gives birth to the senses, each of which is distinguished in the "water of love," the "water of the desire" (*SR* 14.34). The movements of Boehme's properties lie at the core of visionary activity. The light is a medium in which the senses might act. Their awakening is mirrored at the end of *Jerusalem*, where Blake likewise equates the senses with the "Water of Life." Giving form to the separation of the "Pure and Clear from the Impure" of the cross-birth,

> the dim Chaos brightend beneath, above, around! Eyed as the Peacock
> According to the Human Nerves of Sensation, the Four Rivers of the Water
> of Life

> South stood the Nerves of the Eye. East in Rivers of bliss the Nerves of the
> Expansive Nostrils West, flowd the Parent Sense the Tongue. North stood
> The labyrinthine Ear
> . . . .
> Driving outward the Body of Death in an Eternal Death and Resurrection
> Awaking it to life among the Flowers of Beulah rejoicing in Unity
> In the Four Senses
>
> (*Jer* 257, pl. 98, ll. 14–22)

The fifth sense of "feeling" or touch is comprehended in the arisen and unified "Body" of the "Four Senses." In Boehme's fifth form of Eternal Nature, the properties and senses are also "rejoicing in Unity," entering into "a feeling, tasting, smelling, hearing, seeing essence . . . even then one property entereth mutually into another, for they are all proceeded out of the one, viz. out of the free lubet. Therefore also this free lubet is yet in all, and they all jointly desire to enter again into this free lubet, viz. into the one" (*MM* 5.4). As Brinton notes, the "birth of love, the fifth nature form . . . holds the spiritual universe together."[2]

While the properties desire unity through the fifth, they are at the same moment and of necessity a movement toward multiplicity, a movement that begins to speak of the sixth property. Discussion of the fifth necessarily involves its relationship to the other properties. Unity and distinction and multiplicity are dependent on each other. Each property

> desireth, in this Venus-property, to generate again such a creature as it is in itself. Hence ariseth the strong ardent imagination and fiery desire, that the properties do again desire into one, viz. into the fountain whence they proceeded; for in the same they may generate the assimulate of themselves. (*MM* 15.3)

Through the fifth property "all creatures do desire copulation, each with its own kind; and so they do generate a third, viz. an assimulate . . . a similitude" (*MM* 14.9). Where the contrariety of the first two properties produces only the third, which is painful, unresolved, and unassimilated for want of something substantial to feed upon, assimilation and substance are realized through the love-desire of the fifth. Where the wheel of the lower ternary is one of anguish, in the higher it is "a joyful Wheel in the Birth" (*TP* 2.11). In the unity of the "free lubet," the properties "embrace each other in their holy conjunction, wherein then the real divine kingdom of joy consisteth" (*MM* 5.4).

The desire to generate a similitude anticipates God's creation of man in His image. Through imagination, which "generateth substance," the image becomes substantial. Without the "strong ardent imagination and fiery desire," the image or similitude cannot exist. In *Jerusalem* Blake portrays the "mild . . . Saviour"

> Displaying the Eternal Vision! The Divine Similitude!
> In loves and tears of brothers, sisters, sons, fathers, and friends
> Which if Man ceases to behold, he ceases to exist.
>
> (179–80, pl. 34, ll. 10–13)

The "Divine Similitude" is the affirmation of multiplicity. The similitude is at once something that distinguishes and identifies, a movement that embraces both unity and multiplicity. In the same passage in *Jerusalem* the "Saviour" declares

> Mutual in one anothers love and wrath all renewing
> We live as One Man; for contracting our infinite senses
> We behold multitude; or expanding: we behold as one,
> As One Man all the Universal Family . . .
> . . . .
> Giving, receiving, and forgiving.
>
> (180, pl. 34, ll. 16–22)

At the beginning of *Milton* the poet calls upon the Daughters of Beulah, evoking the Paradise that is "springing forth" in the fifth property. The Daughters

> delight the wanderer and repose
> His burning thirst and freezing hunger! Come into my hand
> By your mild power; descending down the Nerves of my right arm
> From out the Portals of my Brain, where by your ministry
> The Eternal Great Humanity Divine. planted his Paradise,
> And in it caus'd the Spectres of the Dead to take sweet forms
> In likeness of himself.
>
> (96, pl. 2, ll. 4–10)

As seen, Los *recognizes* that "These Spectres have no [*Counter*(parts)] therefore they ravin / Without the food of life Let us Create them coun[terparts]" (*FZ* 369, Night 7, ll. 407–8). He declares in the spirit of "strong ardent imagination and fiery desire," "Stern desire / I feel to fabricate embodied semblances in which the dead / May live before us" (*FZ* 370, Night 7, ll. 439–41). It is at this point in *The Four Zoas* that Los *observes* "look[!] my flames enlume afresh / Before my face ascending with delight as in ancient times" (*FZ* 370, Night 7, ll. 444–45). Enitharmon adds:

> if thou my Los
> Wilt in sweet moderated fury. fabricate forms sublime
> Such as the piteous spectres may assimilate themselves into
> They shall be ransoms for our Souls that we may live.
> (370, Night 7, ll. 452–55)

The "copulation" and "holy conjunction" enacted by the properties speak of the divine love-play that unfolds the infinite possibilities revealed in the mirror of Wisdom: "the eternal understanding . . . gives itself into the something, and again takes the something into itself; and thence brings or gives forth another thing" (*MM* 5.3). For Blake these are "the sports of Wisdom in the Human Imagination / Which is the Divine Body of the Lord Jesus" (*Milton* 96, pl. 3, ll. 3–4). This "mutual intercourse, consent, and qualifying into one another, is the pleasant taste of love" (*MM* 5.12): "And here is nothing but the Kiss of Love, and Wooing, and here the Bridegroom embraces his beloved Bride" (*TP* 2.12). The desire that is restrained in the lower ternary, is fulfilled in the higher. Each property interacts with all of the others through a love-play of each and all of the senses. The great significance accorded to the activities of the senses again distinguishes Boehme and Blake from many other mystics and visionaries. Regarding them as an essential part of God's love-play, Boehme envisions an elevation of the senses that manifests the eternal and the glory of God: God glorying in Himself. The human senses are a similitude of the divine. Isaiah declares in *The Marriage*, "I saw no God. nor heard any, in a finite organical perception; but my senses discover'd the infinite in every thing" (38, pl. 12). Boehme's properties actively explore the possibilities of the senses. The discovery of which Isaiah speaks is the revelation or manifestation of possibility, of what lies in the fertile *meonic* realm. In this, discovery is creative. Boehme himself perceived creativity in the activities of the senses. Just as the seven properties interact and give birth in infinite variations, "when a man beholdeth the *wheel*" of the senses, "he continually seeth somewhat that is more and more wonderful." As touched upon in chapter 6 and elaborated above, Boehme's vision charges the senses with a synesthetic quality that plays "them off against one another, setting up a rich and mutually heightening reaction."[3]

It is in such a spirit that Blake writes of the expansion and contraction of man's "infinite senses," and that he speaks in *The Marriage* of the "enlarged and numerous senses" of the "ancient Poets" (38, pl. 11). Boehme and Blake are visionaries. The "strong ardent" play of perception lies at the core of their works. In both, perception is the imaginative engagement of all senses. It is in part because of this that Boehme uses the sensual imagery—or similitude—of "copulation." For both desire should not be merely repressed, but transformed. The embrace is a spiritual consumption and nourishment:

> The ancient tradition that the world will be consumed in fire at the end of six thousand years is true . . .
>
> This will come to pass by an improvement of sensual enjoyment. (*MHH* 39, pl. 14)

Perception of God's eternal love-play is "sensual enjoyment." As the tincture is "a Thing that separates, and bring the Pure and Clear from the Impure," enabling perception, Blake saw that "If the doors of perception were cleansed every thing would appear to man as it is: infinite" (*MHH* 39, pl. 14). Boehme's properties rouse "the faculties to act" against the sensory diminishment Blake perceived in the fallen world: "man has closed himself up, till he sees all things thro' narrow chinks of his cavern" (*MHH* 39, pl. 14). As seen in the discussion of the fourth, Boehme's properties strive against this closure, revolving around the possibility of opening.

The one divine Will is at work in the properties. As a compelling force, it exerts necessity. When Blake speaks of those who "opend within into Eternity at will" (*FZ* 350, Night 6, l. 282), he is speaking with this necessity in view. The "Will must not be bended but in the day of Divine / Power" "the Will cannot be violated" (*Jer* 186, pl. 39, l. 18; *FZ* 351, Night 6, l. 282). Necessity underlies the embraces enacted by the properties, for if there is no "embracing and acceptable relish," then the "striving contrary will" (*TLM* 3.13) of the "Wrath" comes to the fore; the light becomes dark and love turns to anguish. Love is necessary to the vision of both Boehme and Blake. In plate 66 of *Jerusalem*, Blake depicts the closure of man's possibilities: the senses shrink, as do, accordingly, the "heavens," and the "Divine Vision" becomes, notably, "an awful fiery wheel." Blake then makes his point: "Lo! / He who will not comingle in Love, must be adjoind by Hate" (218–19, ll. 35–56). As will be developed in later chapters, the refusal or failure to embrace the necessity of the one divine Will results for both in a division into an infertile enmity. Appositely, Blake engages with this in his extensive depiction of the war of sexual opposites. When Los and Enitharmon, and also Urizen and Ahania are detached from one another, "Two Wills they had; Two Intellects: and not as in times of old" (*Jer* 245, pl. 86, l. 61; *FZ* 320, Night 2, l. 206). For Blake, as in Boehme, this disunion is an aberration: "In Eternity Woman is the Emanation of Man she has No Will of her own There is no such thing in Eternity as a Female Will" (*VLJ* 562). Without "holy conjunction" man is divided within himself, at the mercy of the shadows of love and desire. Inverting the creative movements of the properties,

> all the Males combined into One Male and every one
> Became a ravening eating Cancer growing in the Female
> A Polypus of Roots of Reasoning Doubt Despair and Death.

Going forth and returning from Albions Rocks to Canaan:
Devouring Jerusalem.

(*Jer* 223, pl. 69, ll. 1–5)

Through this "the Infernal Veil grows in the disobedient Female: / Which Jesus rends and ... removes away / From the Inner Sanctuary" (*Jer* 223, pl. 69, ll. 38–40). The "Veil" is that which Jesus removes in the opening of the fourth property. With a sexual explicitness that would have shocked Boehme, Blake reasserts the necessary relationship of opposites, evoking the passage through the fourth into the light of the fifth: "Embraces are Comminglings: from the Head even to the Feet; / And not a pompous High Priest entering by a Secret Place" (*Jer* 223, pl. 69, ll. 43–44). The "High Priest" is the "Watch Fiend" who cannot find the "Grain" or center of the fourth property. One-eyed, he sees only into the darkness.

In *The Book of Ahania*, Ahania, divided from her "Counterpart" Urizen, recalls the days of their communion, desiring to return to it. Her recollection recalls the movements of Boehme's properties, the joyous and sensual beauty of God's love-play. For instance, she recalls "the sons of eternity, singing / To awake bright Urizen my king! / To arise to the mountain sport, / To the bliss of eternal valleys" (89, pl. 5, ll. 3–7). Desiring the "chambers of love" she remembers how, when Urizen's hand was "full of generous fire," the

eternal births sung around Ahania
In interchange sweet of their joys.
Swelld with ripeness and fat with fatness
Bursting on winds my odors,
My ripe figs and rich pomegranates
In infant joy at thy feet
O Urizen, sported and sang.

(89, pl. 5, ll. 18–34)

This whole passage calls to mind the world of giving and receiving. Where restrained desire breeds the "shadow of desire," the love-desire gives birth to the fulfillment of desire. By contrast with the destructive enmity between the male and female "Two Wills," Blake asks

What is it men in women do require
The lineaments of Gratified Desire

What is it women do in men require
The lineaments of Gratified Desire.

(*SB* 474–75)

By contrast with the "Swelld and bloated General Forms," the satanic inversion of the "lineaments of Gratified Desire" produced by the "Two Wills," he writes of

> the Divine-
> Humanity, who is the Only General and Universal Form
> To which all Lineaments tend and seek with love and sympathy
> All broad and general principles belong to benevolence
> Who protects minute particulars, every one in their own identity.
> (*Jer* 185, pl. 38, ll. 19–23)

Through the movements to unity and multiplicity, the seven properties draw the "lineaments of Gratified Desire." Their desire and "copulation" is fulfilled in the "lineaments" of the "assimulate" or similitude to which they give birth. In part, for Blake the "lineaments of Gratified Desire" are the created work of art. Chapter 5 discussed artistic activity in terms of Boehme's apprehension of similitude. The correspondence between the similitude and creative activity may now be seen more clearly. The seven properties give form to the similitude and thus, as proposed, positively nurture creative activity. The gratified lineaments are those that are given form. They appear through the fifth property, the "beginning of all corporality." As will become clearer in the discussion of the seventh property, the manifestation and love-play of the senses in the fifth and sixth properties bring with it a body: "the Divine Humanity." Blake argued in *The Marriage* that "that calld Body is a portion of Soul discernd by the five Senses" (34, pl. 4). Again, discernment or discovery is creative. Having recognized the "Stern desire / . . . to fabricate embodied semblances" in *The Four Zoas*, Los and Enitharmon set to work. Los begins with the "dividing Mark or bound," the "line of the almighty" discussed in chapter 5, and Enitharmon works through the mildness and gentleness of the tincture:

> first he drew a line upon the walls of shining heaven
> And Enitharmon tincturd it with beams of blushing love
> It remaind permanent a lovely form inspird divinely human
> Dividing into just proportions Los unwearied labourd
> The immortal lines upon the heavens till with sighs of love
> Sweet Enitharmon mild Entrancd breathd forth upon the wind
> The spectrous dead Weeping the Spectres viewd the immortal works
> Of Los Assimilating to those forms Embodied and Lovely
> In youth and beauty in the arms of Enitharmon mild reposing.
> (370–71, Night 7, ll. 466–74)

In Enitharmon's arms lie the forms given birth through Boehme's fifth and sixth properties.

THE SIXTH PROPERTY

While the properties are united through the love-desire of the fifth, they are distinguished by the sixth. They give form to Blake's view in *Milton* that "Every thing in Eternity shines by its own Internal light" (104, pl. 10, l. 16). At the same time they are united in their separate identities as a "six-fold self-subsisting essence" (*TP* 2.12). Just as contrariety is necessary to existence, distinction is essential to the manifestation of eternal unity. Without it, God would not be known to Himself. Equally—and in this the relevance of Boehme's theogonic vision to Blake becomes clearer—without distinction, the "dividing Mark or bound," God would not be known to man. This again underlines the significance of individual identity and "minute particulars" in both Blake and Boehme. Proposing parallels between Boehme's imaginative scheme, in which the properties explore that which lies as unrealized desire and give it form, and his own artistic vision, Blake writes of "the Living Creatures" who cry

> Let the Indefinite be explored. and let every Man be Judged
> By his Works, Let all Indefinites be thrown into Demonstrations
> To be pounded to dust and melted in the Furnaces of Affliction:
> . . . .
> For Art and Science cannot exist but in minutely organized Particulars
> And not in generalizing Demonstrations of the Rational Power.
> The Infinite alone resides in Definite and Determinate Identity.
> (*Jer* 205, pl. 55, ll. 55–64)

Without "this Birth or Substance there could be nothing" (*TP* 2.12).

The love-play that brings about this birth and that sustains the movements to unity and multiplicity is in the state of divine temperature, the harmonious balance and interaction of "minutely organized Particulars." Blake's apprehension of the "lineaments of Gratified Desire" gives shape to this state of creative equilibrium. When Los and Enitharmon set to work at the end of the seventh Night of *The Four Zoas* they recognize the necessity of the "enjoyment and labour" (*SR* 16.14) of the temperature, and in their recognition create it. Enitharmon speaks of the temperature when she says to Los "in thy fires my soul delights / If mild they burn in just proportion" and if he "Wilt in sweet moderated fury, fabricate forms sublime." Los begins to "modulate his fires," "Dividing into just proportions" the "lovely form inspird" (370–71, Night 7, ll. 448–69). When the Seven Eyes of God are elected in *Jerusalem*, Blake portrays the temperature as necessary to the fulfillment of "sensual enjoyment":

Let the Human Organs be kept in their perfect Integrity
At will Contracting into Worms, or Expanding into Gods
. . . .
we
Contract or Expand Space at will: or if we raise ourselves
Upon the chariots of the morning. Contracting or Expanding Time!
Every one knows, we are One Family! One Man blessed for ever.
(205, pl. 55, ll. 36–46)

The temperature is alive in the "Divine Humanity." It is the condition "To which all Lineaments tend and seek with love and sympathy." The allaying of the No by the Yes is the attainment of the temperature, the realization of the "lineaments of Gratified Desire."

In the state of temperature the sound that is merely a painful "noise from the hardness" in the second property is purified through the fire and given harmonious expression in the sixth. Passively it is the sound of the properties' activities and actively the expression of them. They become the "Voices" of God's "eternal pregnant Harmony," "God's Instrument, in which the spirit of God *melodizes* in his Kingdom of Joy" (*MM[L]* 8.2). The sound in the sixth property heralds the birth in the light of the "Child" which is "the divine Word" (*TP* 4.52; *MM* 6.19). Where the Word "is only a Spirit" in the second property, it is "the substantial Power and Virtue" in the sixth (*Clavis* 128). It is spoken in Wisdom and is realized through her: "the manifested Word . . . puts forth itself in forms, for its expression. For the formed word hath the like might in it as to reproduce its likeness, viz. such a being as the birth of the spirit is" (*MM* 5.18). Again, the similitude is an affirmation of multiplicity. With the arising of the Word in the sixth property the Creation is conceived and springs forth. In other words, the sound expresses what the senses arising out of the fifth "discover." This is the "moment" spoken of earlier, in which the acts of perception and creation become one. In "a Pulsation of the Artery," between contraction and expansion, the senses perceive and the Word creates.

As the sound arising out of the sixth property expresses the other properties, and as "all forms belong unto the sound" (*MM* 5.17), in the renovation of the senses at the end of *Jerusalem* Blake speaks of the "Tongue" as "the Parent Sense" (257, pl. 98, l. 17). Boehme's Father is the speaker of the Word, his Son. In the same passage, Blake portrays language as actively creative. The love-play of the "Four Living Creatures" is a visionary activity in which the perceptual force of the senses and the creative drive of the language are interdependent and mutually formative:

they conversed together in Visionary forms dramatic which bright
Redounded from their Tongues in thunderous majesty, in Visions

> In new Expanses, creating exemplars of Memory and Intellect
> Creating Space, Creating Time according to the wonders Divine
> Of Human Imagination . . .
> . . .and the all tremendous unfathomable Non Ens
> Of Death was seen in regenerations terrific or complacent varying
> According to the subject of discourse and every Word and Every Character
> Was Human according to the Expansion or Contraction, the Translucence or
> Opakeness of Nervous fibres such was the variation of Time and Space
> Which vary according as the Organs of Perception vary.
> (*Jer* 257–58, pl. 98, ll. 28–38)

Creating similitudes in the mirror of Wisdom, the Word both articulates separate identities and expresses their unity in itself. Blake continues, evoking the state of temperature:

> they walked
> To and fro in Eternity as One Man reflecting each in each and clearly seen
> And seeing: according to fitness and order. And I heard Jehovah speak
> Terrific from his Holy Place and saw the Words of the Mutual Covenant Divine
> On Chariots of gold and jewels.
> (528, pl. 98, ll. 38–42)

The sound arising out of the sixth engages all the properties in "converse," in an articulate and "mutual intercourse" (*MM* 5.12) that speaks that which is to be created into being. Suggesting the relationship between the unitive fifth property, "wherein the sprouting forth of Paradise consists," as does the "sweet Water" of life and satiation, and the distinguishing sixth, the enactment of creative "converse," Blake describes "The Temple" which

> stands on the Mount of God from it flows on each side the River of Life on whose banks Grows the tree of Life among whose branches temples and Pinnacles tents and pavilions Gardens and Groves Display Paradise with its Inhabitants walking up and down in Conversations concerning Mental Delights. (*VLJ* 562)

The "tree of Life" is Boehme's "*Growing Tree,*" which "appeareth in the Center like a Cross, out of which the Essences of the desiring spring forth" (*TLM* 4.16). Blake continues: "Here they are . . . Conversing with Eternal Realities as they Exist in the Human Imagination" (*VLJ* 562). Through the fifth and sixth the properties are conceived and conceive in "the Human Imagination." As discussed in chapter 5, the mirror of Sophia and Jerusalem is a receptacle or medium for the creative and is necessary to expression and manifestation. Through it human creativity may work as a similitude of the divine love-play. As the Word continually seeks new forms for its manifestation, the sixth property opens up the possibility of expression to the creative individual. Blake's and Boehme's language is actively creative, creating what their senses discover in the *meonic*, the realm of potentiality. Creation being an act of discovery, the "Glass" is the receptacle in which this discovery takes place, that is, of that which is silent until language articulates it. As seen, the correspondence between divine and human "converse," and expression is given form in Blake's identification of himself with Los and of Los with Jesus, the Logos (*Milton* 117, pl. 22, l. 12; *Jer* 255, pl. 96, l. 7). He points up this love-play of identities: "let it be remembered that creation is. God descending according to the weakness of man for our Lord is the word of God and every thing on earth is the word of God and in its essence is God" (*Ann. Lav.* 599).

Blake underlines the importance of this correspondence:

> Lo the Eternal Great Humanity
> To whom be Glory and Dominion Evermore Amen
> Walks among his awful Family seen in every face
> As the breath of the Almighty. such are the words of man to man
> In the great Wars of Eternity, in fury of Poetic Inspiration,
> To build the Universe stupendous: Mental forms Creating.
> (*Milton* 129, pl. 30, ll. 15–20)

This again suggests the potency of Blake and Boehme's "converse in the spirit," "man to man," that the expressive quality of the properties was at work between them. The properties may be seen as alive in both visionaries' writings, working as "a continual making word in God's voice," may be seen as enacting a "converse" that brings "Visionary forms Dramatic" into being. As the Word is the "Child" that is born and declared in the fifth and sixth properties; as Los is associated with the Logos and Blake with both, as the "converse" of the "Four Living Creatures" makes "Every Word and Every Character . . . Human," and as the "Tongue" is the "Parent Sense," the Sons of Los may be understood as that which is expressed, as the words that create, the fruit of Los's—and by association Blake's—creative endeavors. They speak of the fecund interplay of the language of the properties:

> *These* are the Sons of Los, and *these* the Labourers of the Vintage
> Thou seest the gorgeous clothed Flies that dance and sport in summer
> Upon the sunny brooks and meadows: every one the dance
> Knows in its intricate mazes of delight artful to weave:
> Each one to sound his instrument of music in the dance,
> To touch each other and recede; to cross and change and return
> *These* are the Children . . .

> . . . loud they thunder thro' the darksom sky
> Uttering prophecies and speaking instructive words to the sons
> Of men: *These* are the Sons of Los! *These* the Visions of Eternity
> But we see only as it were the hem of their garments
> When with our vegetable eyes we view these wond'rous Visions.
> (*Milton* 123, pl. 26, ll. 1–12; emphasis added)

The last two lines underline the necessity of perceiving the spiritual sense of expression, the sense distinguished by Boehme: "{it is} as if the mind did play and melodise in a kingdom of joy within itself, and did hear in a most entire inward manner such a sweet pleasing melody and tune; and yet outwardly did neither hear nor understand it" (*MM* 5.19). This distinction is given form by Sophia:

> we Men can, in Eternity, see no more of the Spirit of God, but only the *Glance* of the Majesty: and his glorious *power* we feel in us, for it is our life, and conducteth us.
>
> But we know the Virgin in all her heavenly Similitudes or Images; whereas she giveth a *body* to all fruits, she is not the Corporeity of the fruit, but the Ornament and Luster. (*TLM* 5.51–52)

It is with such a vision in mind that Blake writes at the end of *Jerusalem:*

> I heard Jehovah speak
> Terrific from his Holy Place and saw the Words of the Mutual Covenant Divine
> On Chariots of gold and jewels.
> (*Jer* 258, pl. 98, ll. 40–42)

In part the "gold and jewels" are the "Ornament and Luster" of Sophia and Jerusalem, and the "Words," notably seen as in the mirror of Wisdom, are the Sons or fruit of Los-Blake. Together they are the fulfillment of the "gorgeous clothed Flies that dance and sport in summer." As the expression of the "Covenant Divine," Los's Sons give form to the merciful and "stubborn structure of the Language," the "embodied semblances" discovered in the mirror of Wisdom:

> The Spectres of the Dead howl round the porches of Los
> . . . .
> To devour the Body of Albion, hungring and thirsting and ravning
> The Sons of Los clothe them and feed, and provide houses and gardens.
> (*Jer* 229, pl. 73, ll. 46–49)

In their movement from Nothing to Something, Boehme's properties create the "stubborn structure of the Language."

MERCURY

The identification of Los with the Logos has particular resonance in the sixth property. As the second and sixth properties are paired and as the second is "the true original of the Mercurial life," in the sixth Mercury is at work in a purified form. He continues to act as "the separator of the powers and virtues," is the "Separator, Divider, and Former of every substance" (*Clavis* 162, 115). Mercury "cuts asunder the attracted desire" of the fifth property, "and brings it into multiplicity and variety." Purified through the fire, Mercury may now be associated with the Holy Ghost. With the realization of the "minute particulars" of creative language in the sound in the sixth property, he is "the sound in the spirit, understand, the separator of the sound, viz. of the tone; also of all pronunciations of speeches, and all the several cries and notes; all whatsoever sounds is distinguished by his might . . . he is the lutanist" (*SR* 9.20). Mercury is the "distinguisher (or articulator)" of the Word and the "master-workman" of the "Child" that is born and declared in the fifth and sixth properties (*SR* 4.27). At the same time he is the Word of God and with this "the worker, framer, and maker of the formings in the expressed wisdom" (*SR* 4.35). He

> is an heavenly and an earthly labourer, and labours in each form according to the property of the form. . . . In the holy angels the heavenly Mercury is holy and divine, and in the devils he is the poison and wrath of eternal nature according to the dark impression's property, and so on through all things, as the property of each thing is, so is its Mercury. (*SR* 9.22)

Mercury is therefore engaged with the correspondence between divine and human creativity, the movements to unity and multiplicity in the Word. His movements are

> to be understood in men and all creatures, in all whatever lives and moves; for the outward Mercury is the outward word in the outward world . . . and in the inward kingdom of the divine power he is the eternal word of the Father, whereby he has made all things in the outward [principle], understand, with the instrument of the outward Mercury.
>
> The outward Mercury is the temporal word, the expressed word; and the inward [Mercury] is the eternal word, the speaking word; the inward word dwells in the outward, and makes through the outward all outward things; and with the inward, inward things. (*SR* 9.23–24)

Present in discrete realms, Mercury acts as an intermediary: he works just as imagination does, building bridges—linguistic and otherwise—between the heavenly, the earthly, and the hellish.

Los's association with the creative activities of the Word similarly give form to the "stubborn structure" of "the temporal word, the expressed word." Through imagination and creative endeavor he keeps alive "the eternal word, the speaking word," maintaining the spiritual sense of the Word—that which is sounding in the sixth property—in the "outward." At the end of *Jerusalem* the Sons of Eden "praise" Los "in song / Because he kept the Divine Vision in time of trouble" (255, pl. 95, ll. 19–20). Los too is a "lutanist," "melodizing" with the "dance and sport" of his Sons. His separative activities have been seen at work in the "poison and wrath" of the second property and in the "holy and divine" sound of the sixth property. It is the Mercurial spirit, the artist in Los that knows that

> There is a Moment in each Day that Satan cannot find
> Nor can his Watch Fiends find it, but the Industrious find
> This Moment and it multiply, and when it once is found
> It renovates every Moment of the Day if rightly placed.
> (*Milton* 136, pl. 35, ll. 42–45)

Suggesting the "organization" of the temperature, Blake points out in his introduction to *Jerusalem*, "I . . . have produced a variety in every line, both of cadences and number of syllables. Every word and every letter is studied and put into its fit place" (146, pl. 3, "To the Public"). The "Moment that Satan cannot find" is the creative Word "that Satan cannot find," the "Mystery" guarded by the limit, the "strong lock and bar" of the spirit. Keeping the "Divine Vision in time of trouble," Los acts as the "Separator, Divider," and "distinguisher," drawing the "strong lock and bar," the "dividing Mark or bound," between the outward and inward Word.

As Mercury both "builds and breaks down," "distinguishes and dissipates" (*SR* 4. 35, 36), Los smashes the Spectre and his works for the sake of "Mystic Union." Taking up his hammer, "the active force of the Logos,"[4]

> he swung it round and at one blow,
> In unpitying ruin driving down the pyramids of pride
> Smiting the Spectre on his Anvil . . .
> . . . .
>
> Then he sent forth the Spectre all his pyramids were grains
> Of sand and his pillars: dust on the flys wing: and his starry
> Heavens: a moth of gold and silver mocking his anxious grasp
> Thus Los altered his Spectre . . .
> . . . .
> Till he had completely divided him into a separate space.
> (*Jer* 252, pl. 91, ll. 42–52)

The "grains of sand" are the "moments" that await "renovation," and the fly is the embodiment of the words, as seen with the Sons of Los, that carry the possibility of this renovation on their "wings." The "winged life" is expressed in the sixth property, is breathed forth as the Holy Spirit. Aubrey draws parallels between the Mercurial movements to unity and multiplicity and Los's construction of Golgonooza "In immense labours and sorrows, ever building, ever falling" (*Milton* 99, pl. 6, ll. 1–2).[5] Mercury "distinguishes and dissipates the hardness" first established in the first property, "breaks down" the "enclosed, and opens it to life: He opens the colours and makes forms and shapes" (*SR* 4.36). Working as Mercury does as "the opener of *hidden* Mysteries" (*TLM* 4.78), Los's task is

> To open the Eternal Worlds, to open the immortal Eyes
> Of Man inwards into the Worlds of Thought: into Eternity
> Ever expanding in the Bosom of God. the Human Imagination.
> (*Jer* 147, pl. 5, ll. 18–20)

This task is brought to fruition in the sixth property. The "Eternal Worlds" that are "Ever expanding in the Bosom of God" point to the "flowing and springing Spirit" that "is a Growing and Multiplying in one Will" in the sixth (*TP* 4.53). The "*hidden* Mysteries" that are opened are those contained within the Word. They are mysteries of creation, as unfolded or expressed in the sixth property. Guarding the "Divine Vision," enclosing it with the "strong lock or bar" against the outward and the hellish, Los opens it to creative imagination. In Boehme's terms, "the outward Essence reacheth not the inward in the soul, but only by the imagination. . . . For it {the soul} originally proceeded from the Imagination, and remains in it eternally" (*FQ* 11.9–10).

Laboring in the outward and inward word, and working as an agent of the divine imagination, Los acts like Mercury, as an intermediary between the heavenly, earthly, and hellish. In the major epics he brings the soul wailing to be created into a "Body" and life and delivers it into eternity, escorting the soul through Hell, Earth and into Heaven (*Milton* 123, pl. 26, ll. 13–17; 128, pl. 29, ll. 47–48; *FZ* 372, Night 8, ll. 15–43). In the same spirit Los compels his "harsh Spectre"

> Into the Furnaces and into the valleys of the Anvils of Death
> And into the mountains of the Anvils and of the heavy Hammers
> Till he should bring the Sons and Daughters of Jerusalem to be
> The Sons and Daughters of Los that he might protect them from
> Albions dread Spectres.
> (*Jer* 152, pl. 10, ll. 1–5)

The transformation of the Children of Jerusalem into the Children of Los is in part the opening up of the possibilities revealed in the mirror of Wisdom—Jerusalem—into merciful expression, "For without a Created body" of expression in which the inward Word might live, the Children of Jerusalem would become the Spectres of "Eternal Death." Los, the Mercurial "instrument" of divine imagination, brings about the marriage of Heaven and Hell, the allaying of the No by the expression of the Yes.

As the "converse" articulated in the sixth property creates "Mental Forms," the "Eternal Realities as they Exist in the Human Imagination," thought, and understanding are realized in the sixth. Mirroring Los's endeavors "to open the immortal Eyes / Of Man inwards into the Worlds of Thought," Mercury "makes the understanding . . . for he separates the thoughts, and makes them act and move." These movements are those of Blake's "Inhabitants" of Paradise, who walk "up and down in Conversations concerning Mental Delights." This is the "true intellective life," the love-play in which each of the properties remains distinct yet embraces and enters into all the others. In the spirit of the desire and energy of the love-play, Blake asserted that

> Men are admitted into Heaven not because they have <curbed and> governd their Passions or have No Passions but because they have Cultivated their Understandings. The Treasures of Heaven are not Negations of Passion but Realities of Intellect from which All the Passions Emanate <Uncurbed> in their Eternal Glory. . . . Those who are cast out Are All Those who having no Passions of their own because No Intellect. Have spent their lives in Curbing and Governing other Peoples. (*VLJ* 564)

Knowledge and desire are interdependent, as revealed in the mirror of Wisdom.

The "true intellective life" is the "manifestation of the understanding of the abyss, or God" (*MM* 5.12). Man being "a continual making word in God's voice," participating in His creation and manifestation, both visionaries intend that the individual participate in the love-play of "Mental Forms," for "there is no other / God, than that God who is the intellectual fountain of Humanity" (*Jer* 251, pl. 91, ll. 9–10). As the "heavenly" "flowing and springing Spirit" "forms and models the Divine understanding in the Wisdom" (*Clavis* 41), so too must the individual, because

> The inward Mercury is the life of the Deity, and all divine creatures; and the outward Mercury is the life of the outward world, and all external corporality in men and beasts, in vegetables and animals, and makes a peculiar principle, viz. a likeness of the divine world; and this is the manifestation of the divine wisdom. (*SR* 9.24)

As God comes to knowledge and understanding of Himself through the love-play of the "intellective life," the individual may, by engaging with the love-play of Boehme's properties, also come to know and understand the divine, and thus, by the correspondence of similitude, himself. This points again to the suggestion that in his reading of Boehme Blake was engaged with the similitude of the movements envisioned between God and the mirror of Wisdom. When Blake assimilates with Los in *Milton*, his identification is realized through a movement that speaks of the passage through the "lineaments" of Boehme's eternal and merciful properties to the articulate and creative intelligence of the sixth:

> I am that Shadowy Prophet who Six Thousand Years ago
> Fell from my station in the Eternal bosom. Six thousand Years
> Are finishd. I return! Both Time and Space obey my will.
> I in Six Thousand Years walk up and down: for not one Moment
> Of Time is lost, nor on Event of Space unpermanent
> But all remain: every fabric of Six Thousand Years
> Remains permanent: tho' on the Earth where Satan
> Fell, and was cut off all things vanish and are seen no more
> They vanish not from me and mine, we guard them first and last
> The generations of men run on in the tide of Time
> But leave their destind lineaments permanent for ever and ever.
>
> So spoke Los as he went along to his supreme abode.
>
> (*Milton* 117, pl. 22, ll. 15–26)

The "supreme abode" is found in the seventh property of Eternal Nature.

9

The Seventh Property and the Cycles of the Seven

THE SEVENTH PROPERTY

In themselves the first six properties are not externalized, but only the "spiritual essence of the manifested God" (*MM* 6.2). The "external essence" (*MM* 6.3) is realized in the seventh property. As "the First and Seventh property are accounted for one," the "first is the Desire which belongs to God the Father, yet is only a Spirit, but in the seventh Property, the Desire is substantial" (*Clavis* 126–27). The seventh is the "Substance" (*Clavis* 122) that arises from all the other properties, and is the "body," a "corporeal being" (*SR* 9.25) which incarnates the divine. That is, the seventh is that which is expressed into form, the spoken Word, and as such the "centre to which the desire of the six . . . tend" (*SR* 9.2). Maintaining the cycles of feeding and consuming, it feeds the other six with that for which they hunger, the externalized similitude. It is "a food of the fire, whence the fire draweth essence for its sustenance, wherein it burneth" (*MM* 6.20). Sustaining all the properties in the darkness and the light, it is the "house of the other six" and that "in which they are all substantially as the soul in the body" (*Clavis* 122). Without it the "Spirit is void . . . there is no understanding . . . the Spirit itself does not subsist without a body" (*TLM* 4.5). The first six properties live in the seventh. The seventh provides a place, a "mansion"

> wherein they should work; denoting that all whatsoever that they should work, manifest and produce out of the wonders of the eternal wisdom should re-enter into the one . . . which is the seventh property, viz. a house of the working life, wherein it should stand as a figure to the contemplation of the great glory of God. (*MM* 15.1)

In brief, the seventh is that "wherein every life should work as in one body" (*MM* 16.16).

The seventh property thus corresponds with Blake's "Divine Humanity," the "Only General and Universal Form / To which all Lineaments tend and seek with love and sympathy" (*Jer* 185, pl. 38, ll. 19–21). Where the seventh sustains the multiplicity of movements of the first six properties, the "Divine Humanity" "protects minute particulars, every one in their own identity" (*Jer* 185, pl. 38, l. 23). As the "body" of the seventh is the "house" of all that the first six give birth to, Blake evokes in Albion the Kabbalistic "tradition, that Man anciently containd in his mighty limbs all things in Heaven and Earth" (*Jer* 171, pl. 27, "To the Jews"). As the six forms are made substantial in the "divine corporality," the incarnation of the seventh, Blake wrote that "All Things are comprehended in their Eternal Forms in the Divine body of the Saviour the True Vine of Eternity The Human Imagination" (*VLJ* 555). The "Eternal Body of Man is The IMAGINATION. that is God himself The Divine Body Jesus we are his Members" (*Laocoön* 273). The seventh property is the "body" and "house" of imagination. It is that in which, as Blake perceived, "All Human Forms" are "identified" (*Jer* 258, pl. 99, ll. 1–2). With the understanding that the seventh is the "habitation" "wherein every life should work as in one body," working through multiplicity to reveal the unity and "great glory of God," this points back to Blake's "Universal Family": "We live as One Man; for contracting our infinite senses / We behold multitude; or expanding; we behold as one" (*Jer* 180, pl. 34, ll. 17–18). As Boehme's first six properties live in the seventh, Blake's "Divine Family" and "Council of God" (*FZ* 310–11, Night 1, ll. 469–75; 371, Night 8, ll. 1–2) give life to the seventh. They move and act in Blake's epics through the "divine corporality" envisioned there. For example, as the seventh property is the Word expressed through the activities of the other six, the "Divine Family" speaks in the epics "as One Man" (*Jer* 180, pl. 34, ll. 27–28; *Milton* 116, pl. 21, l. 58).

Incarnating the Word as "One Man," the seventh is also associated with the divine Wisdom, for "where the Word is, there is also the Virgin or Wisdom of God, for the Word is in the Wisdom, and the one is not without the other, or else the Eternity would be divided" (*TLM* 4.78). As seen, "There is no such thing in Eternity as a Female Will" (*VLJ* 562). The incarnation of Jesus in the seventh property is the "holy conjunction" of male and female: in him the sexes are "one image, viz. a manly virgin" (*MM* 19.17). It is with such a "body" in mind that Blake speaks of "the Mystic Union of the Emanation in the Lord" (*Jer* 203, pl. 53, l. 24). In the seventh "the eternal wisdom of God is manifest" (*MM* 16.27). She has moved from ideal or potential to actual existence and is realized as "the holy pure element" (*MM* 15.22). Where the first six properties are active, Wisdom is passive, "as a wife of all the other forms" (*SR* 9.25). Where the sun is active, imaginatively, in the fourth property as Sol, the passivity of Wisdom is associated with the moon: the "seventh form is called Luna" (*SR* 9.25). The first six properties

> do all cast their desire through Sol into Luna; for in Sol they are spiritual, and in Luna corporeal: Therefore the moon assumes to it the sunshine, and shines from the sun; whatever the sun is, and makes in the spirit-life in itself, the same Luna is, and makes corporeal in itself. (*SR* 9.25)

Working through the imaginative center of Sol, Mercury is Luna's "husband, which impregnates it" with imagination (*SR* 9.26). The seventh is "the seed" of the first six properties "which the desire impresses into a comprehensive body or essence wherein all lies" (*SR* 14.14). While Sol is associated with gold, Luna "receives only the white colour from the sun . . . in its property lies silver" (*SR* 9.26).

As noted in chapter 6, when the seven properties are in harmony they form Eternal Nature. To regard this another way, that which attains "corporality" and existence in the seventh property *is* Eternal Nature. All the properties lie in the seventh as one. As Martensen notes, if all seven properties were to be seen at once only the seventh would be seen, the others being hidden within it.[1] Blake perceived this unity and the necessity of the individual identities which make its manifestation possible in his "Divine Family":

> He who would see the Divinity must see him in his Children
> One first, in friendship and love; then a Divine Family, and in the midst
> Jesus will appear; so he who wishes to see a Vision; a perfect Whole
> Must see it in its Minute Particulars; Organized.
>
> (*Jer* 251, pl. 91, ll. 18–21)

The "body" of Eternal Nature, as "seen" in the seventh, sustains the properties in the state of temperature. The harmonious "place" of the seventh property is not only man's "house" but also his spiritual home. Accordingly, and as the properties are associated with the days of Creation, the seventh property is the Sabbath, "the perfection wherein . . . the six forms of the working power rest" (*SR* 9.2). As the six properties lie in the seventh as one, the Sabbath contains the six active days of Creation: "in the seventh property lieth the eternal day" (*MM* 16.23).

The sustaining, merciful, and overseeing structure of the seventh, in which the six may live and work, is reflected in Blake's Seven Eyes of God": they "continually / Guard round" man to sustain the eternal (*Milton* 119, pl. 24, ll. 7–8). When Blake has become "One Man" with Los in *Milton,* the "Eternal Prophet" declares that although "things vanish" "on the Earth," "They vanish not from me and mine, we guard them first and last." Los's "return" here at the end of "Six Thousand Years" to his "supreme abode" speaks of "the centre to which the desire of the six days tend . . . the Sabbath or resting-day" (*SR* 9.2). The "destined lineaments" which he and his "guard" and sustain are therefore those of the "supreme abode," the "body" of the Sabbath, man's spiritual home. Every "fabric of Six Thousand Years / Remains permanent" because each is contained, nourished, and upheld within this "body." In short, "not one Moment / Of Time is lost, nor one Event of Space unpermanent" in the "eternal day" of the seventh property. When Blake's Milton has departed from the "body" of this day in *Milton*, and as the seven properties make it possible to "see" this "body," the Seven Angels of the Presence afford Milton a sustaining vision of his own "resting" and "divine corporalty":

> As when a man dreams, he reflects not that his body sleeps,
> Else he would wake; so seem'd he entering his Shadow: but
> With him the Spirits of the Seven Angels of the Presence
> Entering; they gave him still perceptions of his Sleeping Body;
> . . . .
> . . . And the Seven comforted and supported him.
> (109, pl. 15, ll. 1–7)

Understanding with Boehme that Jesus is the "holy conjunction" of male and female in the seventh property, Blake writes a little later in *Milton*:

> Lo! I am with you alway
> . . . .
>
> So spake the Family Divine as One Man even Jesus
> Uniting in One with Ololon and the appearance of One Man
> Jesus the Saviour appeard coming in the Clouds of Ololon!
> (116, pl. 21, ll. 56–60)

Echoing the seventh as the place in which Jesus is incarnated, when the Seven Eyes of God are elected in *The Four Zoas* they are "one within the other the Seventh is named Jesus / The Lamb of God" (312–13, Night 1, ll. 551–56).

As Boehme's properties labor to prepare a place in which they may rest and, paradoxically, as they labor within that place, Eno is "occupied in labours / Of sublime mercy" in *Jerusalem* to realize this "kingdom." Notably,

> Los . . . saw her in his seventh Furnace, he also terrified
> Saw the finger of God go forth upon his seventh Furnace:
> . . to prepare Jerusalem a place.
> (197, pl. 48, ll. 44–46)

The seventh is the "place" where the female aspect of the properties gives birth to the "seed" sown by the first six. The association of the seventh property with Luna is re-expressed in "the Moony spaces of Eno" (*FZ* 305, Night 1, l. 232). It is significant that Eno is *seen* by Los and in *his* "seventh Furnace." His seeing here is active. Through the same activity as that in which the first six properties "do all cast their desire through Sol into Luna" and "the moon assumes to it the sunshine, and shines from the sun; whatever the sun is . . . that Luna is," Los, the counterpart of Sol, creates what he sees here. Perception is creation. The "seventh Furnace" is "his" because he has created it and the "Moony spaces of Eno" appear within what he has created. That which is "spiritual" in him becomes "corporeal" in these "Moony Spaces." His perception of the "finger of God" is one that participates in its creative activity. The "finger of God" is life- and form-giving: it creates "a place." In this it is like the first six properties, which give life to and actively form the "place" of the seventh property. The properties "cast their desire . . . into Luna." The going "forth" of the "finger of God" "upon" the "seventh Furnace" is a comparable activity, an act of spiritual impregnation. Bearing in mind that this impregnation is enacted "through" Sol, that Mercury is Luna's "husband, which impregnates it," and that Los works in the spirit of Mercury, it may be seen that he impregnates the "Moony spaces" with the "finger of God." It is the active expression of the divine "desire" which "impresses itself into a comprehensive body or essence wherein all lies." This "body or essence" is Jerusalem, "the holy pure element." The "finger of God" is that through which Wisdom is brought from ideal to actual existence. In this movement Jerusalem becomes the "place" that is being prepared for her.

The "finger of God" is also at work in the Sons of Los:

> Some Sons of Los surround the Passions with porches of iron and silver
> Creating form and beauty around the dark regions of sorrow,
> Giving to airy nothing a name and a habitation
> Delightful! with bounds to the Infinite putting off the Indefinite
> Into most holy forms of Thought: (such is the power of inspiration)
> They labour incessant; with many tears and afflictions;
> Creating the beautiful House for the piteous sufferer.
>
> (*Milton* 125, pl. 28, ll. 1–7)

The "power of inspiration" is that of the "finger of God." Working as the desire of Boehme's first six properties does, giving shape to the "Substance" of the seventh, the expressed Word, that which is "inspired" in the labors of the Sons of Los, is *expressed* in the "place" they are "Creating." Expression lives and works within the "body" or "Mansion" of the seventh property. Laboring with "many tears and afflictions," the Sons themselves are comprehended in the "piteous sufferer" for whom the "beautiful House" is being prepared. Their labor, as with that of the first six properties, is "incessant" until the "rest" of the Sabbath, the "beautiful House" into which they are to return as "One Man."

While these Sons create a spatial "habitation" and as the "eternal day" is within both space and time, in the same plate of *Milton* "others of the Sons of Los build Moments and Minutes and Hours / And Days and Months and Years and Ages and Periods." These too are "wondrous buildings" (126, pl. 28, ll. 44–45) within which life works and lives. Given that "Every Time less than a pulsation of the artery / Is equal in its period and value to Six Thousand Years" (127, pl. 28, ll. 62–63), that the first six properties may be understood in these "Years" and that "A Moment equals a pulsation of the artery" (126, pl. 28, l. 47), each "Moment" is realized in—and as—the "wondrous building" of the seventh property. The "pulsation of the artery" occurs in, and at the same time is the "body" and "place" of the seventh property. The Sabbath of the seventh is the eternal day of rest, the culmination of the "Period" in which "the Poet's Work is Done." Every "Moment" built by the Sons of Los "has a Couch of gold for soft repose" (127, pl. 29, l. 1; 126, pl. 28, l. 46). Understanding that the seventh property is the "food" of the other six, that it sustains the love-play of the active and passive aspects of the properties, Blake adds that "between every two Moments stands a Daughter of Beulah / To feed the Sleepers on their Couches with maternal care" (126, pl. 28, ll. 48–49). The satiation of desire or hunger gives form and substance to the similitude of that which is desired, in this case to the externalized similitude of the eternal "Moment."

To look more closely at the female aspect of the seventh property, as Jerusalem finds a "place" in the seventh and accordingly finds herself, and as the seventh sustains a state of harmony, it being the "eternal day . . . wherein God's love doth appease and atone the anger" (*MM* 16.23), the place in which the No is finally allayed by the Yes, she may be seen as the expression of the state of the temperature in the seventh: she is "A Tent and Tabernacle of Mutual Forgiveness" (*Jer* 203, pl. 54, l. 4). Within her "habitation" the merciful "body" of the seventh property resides. Like Sophia, she is the "Garment" of the "Divine Vision" (*Jer* 203, pl. 54, ll. 1–3). The necessity of the "body" of the seventh to the life of the spirit and the generation of this "body" in Luna through the first six properties is also re-expressed in Jerusalem, for she "is made receptive of Generation thro' mercy" (*Jer* 203, pl. 53, l. 27). Boehme's perception that "where the Word is, there is also the Virgin or Wisdom of God, for the Word is in the Wisdom," and that "the eternal Wisdom of God is manifest" in the seventh property is reflected in *The Four Zoas*:

> In Golgonoozas Furnaces among the Anvils of time and space
> . . . .
> appeard a Universal female form created
>
> And Enitharmon namd the Female Jerusa[le]m the holy
> Wondring she saw the Lamb of God within Jerusalems Veil
> The divine Vision seen within the inmost deep recess
> Of fair Jerusalems bosom in a gently beaming fire.
> (376, Night 8, ll. 186–93)

The "gently beaming fire" is that "fed" by the incarnation of the Yes in the seventh property. Equally, the fire gives birth to Jesus in the seventh: "the flames roll on / And after the flames appears the Cloud of the Son of Man / Descending from Jerusalem with power and great Glory" (*FZ* 393, Night 9, ll. 271–73).

Given that "the Word is in the Wisdom," that "the one is not without the other, or else the Eternity would be divided," Blake perceived that while "the Cloud of the Son of Man" descends, the Lamb of God "remains / Eternal" in the "bosom" of Jerusalem (*FZ* 391, Night 9, ll. 205–7). This is the "holy conjunction" of male and female in the seventh property. The Lamb of God and Jerusalem are ultimately one. The seventh being a place of sustenance, this conjunction is an act of mercy. To elaborate, because the six active properties are dependent upon the seventh and vice versa, the male can only be born through the female and the female through the male. Christ is the incarnation of this understanding. As Blake's "Eternal Man" perceives, the "manly virgin," the divine androgyne given form in the seventh makes life possible: "I thro him awake to life from deaths dark vale" (*FZ* 391, Night 9, l. 207). The seventh is not only the place of birth but rebirth. The active and passive aspects of the properties must be joined in a love-play that manifests the ultimate unity of the seventh property:

> Thus shall the male and female live the life of Eternity
> Because the Lamb of God Creates himself a bride and wife
> That we his Children evermore may live in Jerusalem.
> (*FZ* E391, Night 9, ll. 219–21)

The Mercurial creation of form in Luna, the "wife" of the active properties, is figured here in the Lamb's creation of Jerusalem, a creation which is the manifestation of himself. As the seventh property is both a "building" and the "place" in which the "seed" sown by the first six is "conceived," it is apt that the "Eternal Man" adds that Jerusalem is "a City yet a Woman / Mother of myriads redeemd and born in her spiritual palaces" (391, Night 9, ll.

222–23). The "myriads" may be understood as the possibilities first seen in the mirror of Wisdom, and given birth in the "spiritual palaces" of the seventh property. The seventh is the place of redemption.

Dependent on each other, male and female feed each other with the "food" of the seventh property. Evoking the "rest" of the Sabbath, man's true spiritual home and "body," Blake writes that when Milton

> enterd into his Shadow: Himself:
> His real and immortal Self: was as appeard to those
> Who dwell in immortality, as One sleeping on a couch
> Of gold; and those in immortality gave forth their Emanations
> Like Females of sweet beauty. to guard round him and to feed
> His lips with food of Eden in his cold and dim repose!
> (*Milton* 109, pl. 15, ll. 10–15)

Milton sleeps, as does Albion, in the "place" of the seventh property. In the seventh resides the true life that sustains their wandering "Shadows." Milton's "real and immortal Self: was as appeard to those / who dwell in immortality" because it is the reflection, in the mirror of the seventh property, of themselves, of their unity in the "One Man." The giving "forth" of their Emanations here speaks again of the "finger of God" which creates a place for Jerusalem and in the same moment creates her. The reciprocity of this "feeding" is conveyed in *Jerusalem*:

> The Female searches sea and land for gratification to the
> Male Genius: who in return clothes her in gems and gold
> And feeds her with the food of Eden. hence all her beauty beams.
> (223, pl. 69, ll. 16–18)

The "Male Genius" that desires gratification lies in the active properties. This desire is gratified in the "lineaments" of the seventh property. The "gems and gold" with which the male "clothes" the female point back to the "Garment" of Jerusalem, and, in many respects, they are the "food" with which he "feeds her": "casting" his desire "through Sol into Luna," the male gives form to the female and "hence her beauty beams," reflecting and thus fed with the light of Sol. This correspondence with the property of Luna is enforced in the next lines:

> She Creates at her will a little moony night and silence
> With Spaces of sweet gardens and a tent of elegant beauty:
> . . . .
> And a little tender moon.
> (223, pl. 69, ll. 19–22)

This "little moony night" is Beulah, a place that suggests notable parallels with the female aspect of Boehme's seventh property. It is "A Tent and Tabernacle of Mutual Forgiveness":

> There is a place where Contraries are equally True
> This place is called Beulah, It is a pleasant lovely Shadow
> Where no dispute can come. Because of those who Sleep.
> (*Milton* 129, pl. 30, ll. 1–3)

"Beulahs moony shades and hills" (*Milton* 129, pl. 30, l. 5) are the "Shadow" "cast" by Sol. As the seventh property is a "House" and also, like Jerusalem, "a City yet a Woman,"

> Beulah is evermore Created around Eternity; appearing
> To the Inhabitants of Eden, around them on all sides.
> But Beulah to its Inhabitants appears within each district
> As the beloved infant in its mothers bosom round incircled
> With arms of love and pity and sweet compassion.
> (*Milton* 129, pl. 30, ll. 8–12)

The Word is born in Wisdom. Blake's vision of Beulah suggests the merciful Sabbath of the seventh property:

> There is from Great Eternity a mild and pleasant rest
> Namd Beulah a Soft and Moony Universe feminine lovely
> Pure mild and Gentle given in Mercy to those who sleep
> Eternally. Created by the Lamb of God around
> On all sides within and without the Universal Man
> The Daughters of Beulah follow sleepers in all their Dreams
> Creating Spaces lest they fall into Eternal Death.
> (*FZ* 303, Night 1, ll. 93–100)

Mirroring the movements of the six active properties, which cast the "seed" of their desire into the "place" or "womb" of the seventh, Blake writes that "in Beulah the Feminine / Emanations Create Space. the Masculine Create Time, and plant / The Seeds of beauty in the Space" (*Jer* 243, pl. 85, ll. 7–9). The "holy conjunction" of male and female gives form to the "seed" sown in the seventh property. The "sweet gardens" of Beulah are those in which the "Seeds of beauty" are sown. Kathleen Raine has noted in respect of Vala's "Garden of Delight" that these "gardens" have distinct parallels with Boehme's seventh property, which is also "a Garden of Delight, into which the Master of it sows all manner of Seeds, according to his Pleasure, and then enjoys the Fruit of it" (*Aur* 16.21–22).[2] It is from these "Seeds" that the "corporality" of Eternal Nature, manifest in the seventh property, springs.

The seventh is the place in which Blake's Spectres are redeemed from their torment:

> The Spectres of the Dead howl round the porches of Los
> . . . .
> To devour the Body of Albion, hungring and thirsting and ravning
> The Sons of Los clothe them and feed, and provide houses and gardens
> And every Human Vegetated Form in its inward recesses
> Is a house of ple[as]antness and a garden of Delight Built by the
> Sons and Daughters of Los.
>
> (*Jer* 229, pl. 73, ll. 46–52)

This cooperation or "holy conjunction" of male and female is given further expression in *Milton.* Reiterating Boehme's understanding that desire needs the "body" of the seventh property, Blake depicts the "Souls" who

> incessant wail, being piteous Passions and Desires
> With neither lineament nor form but like to watry clouds
> The Passions and Desires descend upon the hungry winds
> For such alone Sleepers remain meer passion and appetite;
> The Sons of Los clothe them and feed and provide houses and fields
>
> And every Generated Body in its inward form,
> Is a garden of delight and a building of magnificence,
> Built by the Sons of Los in Bowlahoola and Allamanda
> And the herbs and flowers and furniture and beds and chambers
> Continually woven in the Looms of Enitharmons Daughters.
>
> (*Milton* 123, pl. 26, ll. 26–35)

Los and Enitharmon also bring about the "holy conjunction" realized in the seventh property. The "stern desire" they feel to "fabricate embodied semblance in which the dead / May live" in the seventh Night of *The Four Zoas* attains "corporality" in the eighth. Mirroring the penetration of the female property, the "dead" "descend thro the Gate of Pity," the "Gate of Enitharmon." She weaves "the Spectres / Bodies of Vegetation" and in the spirit of the temperature sings "lulling Cadences to drive away / Despair." The "finger of God" and the divine similitude are at work here:

> Los loved them
> With a parental love for the Divine Hand was upon him
> And upon Enitharmon and the Divine Countenance shone
> In Golgonooza. Looking down the Daughters of Beulah saw
> With joy the bright Light and in it a Human form
> And knew he was the Saviour Even Jesus.
>
> (372, Night 8, ll. 25–43)

The seventh property is "nothing else but Paradise regenerate anew" (*MM* 17.8), the "kingdom of the divine glory" (*MM* 6.20), the "inward spiritual holy heaven, which is the mansion of the power of God" (*MM* 15.9).

THE CYCLES OF THE SEVEN

The movement of the properties is cyclic. Working in the body of the seventh property, the first six proceed out of it and work through a cycle that returns them to it. It is through this that "the First and Seventh property are accounted for one." The seventh is the "seed" of the other six, "which the desire impresses into a comprehensive body or essence wherein all lies" (*SR* 14.14). This is the impression that takes place in the first property. With it the cycle of the properties moves from the seventh to the first. That which is impressed in the first property is the objectified Eternal Nature as realized in the seventh property, and which now "proceeds forth {as} an essence" (*SR* 14.17) through all the properties. The first and the seventh property are associated with the female because each is impregnated with desire. The first property is the "first mother" or *prima materia* that, laboring through the cycle of all the properties, attains fruition in the "body" of the seventh, forming a wheel of birth (*SR* 14.15). That which attains essence in the seventh enters again into the impression of the dark desire of the first. The movement between the two properties is one that plays out the eternal cycles of spiritual death and rebirth.

This is the wheel of God "wherein many wheels are made *one in another*." As the seventh property is bound to enter into the first it forms the "unbeginning and indissoluble Band." The seven properties can never be free of the cycles of rest and activity. As the Yes must enter into a relationship with the No, that which is incarnated in the seventh property must enter the dark impression of the first and all that follows therefrom. To put this another way, through this wheel the "divine corporality" realized in the seventh "feeds" the other six with its "gentle beneficence" (*ToI* 2.5.6) and thus makes possible their return to it. The Word that is expressed in the seventh property speaks through the other six. The wheel sounds in both the mind of God and man: it is the unitive "wheel of the mind . . . and . . . is so proportioned [or composed] as a mind of a man" (*SR* 14.16). Through its cycles man may move to God and God to man. Working as an "eternal Band" the beginning gives shape to the end and the end to the beginning. The seven properties form cycles of ascent and descent, progressive and regressive.

Suggesting Boehme's "mother of all beings," who labors through the wheel of birth to bring the impression of the *prima materia* into the pure essence of the "eternal day" of the seventh, Eno, in *The Four Zoas*, takes the "seed" sown in the "Garden of Delight" of the seventh and brings it "into the first day of the beginning of all essences" and all that follows therefrom. She

> took a Moment of Time
> And drew it out to Seven thousand years with much care and affliction
> And many tears and in Every year made windows into Eden
> She also took an atom of space and opend its center
> Into Infinitude.
>
> (304–5, Night 1, ll. 222–26)

The "Seven thousand years" form the eternal cycle of days that proceed out of and return to the "eternal day" of the seventh. The "Infinitude" into which the "atom of space" is "opend" is that which is impressed in the first property and which, unfolding through the activities of all the properties, finds a place or "habitation" in the seventh. "Infinitude" is understood in the "eternal band" of the properties. The "windows into Eden" which Eno makes "in Every year" point to how Boehme's seven properties are "each within the other," each leading into—and ultimately contained within—the "Garden" of the seventh.

Expanding the "unbeginning and indissoluble Band" of the seven properties to the "Twenty-seven Heavens and their Churches" "formd by Los" in *Jerusalem*, Blake states that

> where Luther ends Adam begins again in Eternal Circle
> To awake the Prisoners of Death; to bring Albion again
> With Luvah into light eternal, in his eternal day.
>
> (231, pl. 75, ll. 24–26)

The cycles of spiritual death and rebirth are cycles of sleep and awakening. As seen in the previous section, the "real and immortal Self" of both Milton and Albion may be understood as sleeping in the place of the seventh property. Their wandering "Shadows" may be seen as moving through the cycles that depart from the seventh. As the "eternal Band" returns to the seventh, its entrance into the "eternal day" is an awakening in the seventh. Both Milton and Albion awake to their "true and immortal" selves in the seventh. When Albion begins to awaken in the eighth Night of *The Four Zoas*, for instance, he awakens to and in the sustaining and "divine corporality" of the seventh property, "In the saviours arms, in the arms of tender mercy and loving kindness" (372, Night 8, l. 14). Similarly, because Jerusalem finds a place and thus herself in the seventh, at the climax of *Jerusalem* she is exhorted to awaken in the seventh property—as the "Tent and Tabernacle" of the seventh—and thus to herself:

> Awake! Awake Jerusalem! O lovely Emanation of Albion
> Awake and overspread all Nations as in Ancient Time
> For lo! The Night of Death is past and the Eternal Day
> Appears upon our Hills.
>
> (256, pl. 97, ll. 1–4)

Toward the end of *Milton* Blake's "Starry Seven" exhort the awakening in the seventh, suggesting the Word that speaks and "proceeds forth" through the wheel of the properties:

> there went forth from the Starry limbs of the Seven: Forms
> Human; with Trumpets innumerable, sounding articulate
> As the Seven spake . . .
> . . . .
>
> Awake Albion awake! Reclaim thy Reasoning Spectre. Subdue
> Him to the Divine Mercy . . .
> . . . .
> Let the Four Zoas awake from Slumbers of Six Thousand Years
> Then loud the Furnaces of Los were heard! And seen as Seven Heavens.
>
> (140, pl. 39, ll. 3–14)

Boehme likewise envisioned each of the seven properties as a "Heaven" (*MM* 16.21).

As the Word incarnated in the seventh property enters the "seed" impressed in the *prima materia* of the first, and as man's "true and immortal self" rests in the "Garden of Delight" of the seventh, Blake writes:

> when Man sleeps in Beulah, the Saviour in mercy takes
> Contractions Limit, and of the Limit he forms Woman: That
> Himself may in the process of time be born Man to redeem.
>
> (*Jer* 189, pl. 42, ll. 32–34)

Blake's Christ participates in the eternal wheel of birth. He appears "within the Furnaces" as "the Divine Vision," gathering "Jerusalems Children in his arms" and bearing them "like / A Shepherd" toward the place of the seventh (*Jer* 210, pl. 60, ll. 5–9). As suggested, the wheel of the properties draws cycles of ascent and descent between man and the divine. It is because of the necessity that compels the seventh to enter again into the first that the "Divine voice" declares "Albion goes to Eternal Death: In Me all Eternity. / Must pass thro' condemnation , and awake beyond the Grave!" (*Jer* 177, pl. 31, ll. 3, 9–10). Through this movement Albion is able to say to Jesus at the end of *Jerusalem*, "I behold the Visions of my deadly Sleep of Six Thousand Years." Jesus replies, "Fear not Albion unless I die thou canst not live / But if I die I shall arise again and thou with me" (*Jer* 255, pl. 96, ll. 11–15). As the entrance into the first property is a "darkening" of desire, an "overshadowing," Blake adds here:

> So Jesus spoke! the Covering Cherub coming on in darkness
> Overshadowd them and Jesus said Thus do Men in Eternity
> One for another to put off . . . every sin.
>
> (255, pl. 96, ll. 16–19)

It is at this point that Albion casts himself into the cycles of death and rebirth, throwing himself into the "Furnaces of affliction." The furnaces become "Fountains of Living Waters flowing from the Humanity Divine," and "all the Cities of Albion . . . and All / The Sons and Daughters of Albion" arise from sleep (256, pl. 96, ll. 35–39).

Forming cycles of ascent and descent between God and man, the wheel of the properties is not only at work in the divine and harmonious loveplay, but in everything in Heaven, Hell, and on Earth. Whatever the first six properties desire and hunger for is realized in the "body" of the seventh. Accordingly, as the wheel of the properties is at work in man as the "wheel of the mind," and as Sophia is realized in the seventh property, Blake understood that "Every Mans Wisdom is peculiar to his own Individ[u]ality" (*Milton* 98, pl. 4, l. 8). "As a man is So he Sees" (*Letters* 702). In the cycle of the properties, that which is seen also determines the individual. Los's perception of the "finger of God" is creative, participating in what it gives form to in "his seventh Furnace." In *The Four Zoas* he sees "The Finger of God touch the Seventh furnace in terror." "Pale terror seiz'd the Eyes of Los," and he becomes "terrifid at the shapes / Enslavd humanity put on he became what he beheld / He became what he was doing he was himself transformd" (338, Night 4, ll. 276–87). Similarly, Blake writes in *Milton* that "as the Spectres choose their affinities / So they are born on Earth." This is affected "not by Natural but by Spiritual power alone," for "every Natural Effect has a Spiritual Cause" (*Milton* 124, pl. 26, ll. 38–46). Boehme's properties are the "Spiritual Cause" of the "Natural Effect" of the external world. In the seventh property the earthly is "coagulated" and takes on "essence" (*MM* 10.38), and in the same moment eternity enters into time (*SR* 14.28; *TLM* 3.41). As the wheel of the mind moves between the spiritual and the earthly, man is "created into the externall world, that he might bring the external Figures into the internall" (*Ep* 5.22). The wheel of the properties describes how they "introduce themselves into good and evil, and again bring themselves out of good and evil" (*SR* 14.16).

At the same time the Wheel of the properties has a fallen aspect that can be wrathful and destructive and as such produces a place in the seventh in which the devil may hold sway, as "a Prince of this World" (*TLM* 8.43). This destructive aspect has been seen at work in Blake in the discussion of the contrariety between darkness and light. As the desire of the properties is given form through Mercury and as Mercury can be a "poison-source," the "outward Mercury" transforms the wheel of the properties into the divisive "poisonful mercurial wheel" (*SR* 13.29–30). Blake speaks of this in *Jerusalem*, of

> Wheels rising up poisonous against Albion
> Urizen, cold and scientific: Luvah, pitying and weeping
> Tharmas, indolent and sullen: Urthona, doubting and despairing
> Victims to one another and dreadfully plotting against each other
> To prevent Albion walking about in the Four Complexions.
>
> (184, pl. 38, ll. 1–5)

This destructive wheel of the mind is figured in Hand, Hyle, and Coban, who desire in plate 18 of *Jerusalem* to "destroy the Divine Saviour" and Albion: "forth from his bosom they went and return'd. / Like Wheels from a great Wheel reflected in the Deep. / Hoarse Turn'd the Starry Wheels, rending a way in Albions Loins" (163, ll. 37–44). In *The Four Zoas* Luvah and Vala depart from the "Garden of Delight" and, entering Boehme's dark world, descend and, enter into "the shadows of Valas Garden / Where the impressions of Despair and Hope for ever vegetate" (395, Night 9, ll. 375–77).

The hellish and earthly cycles shut off possibility, separating the "heavenly, diabolic," and "terrestrial" (*TQ* 3.2) into discrete enclosed realms. Blake envisions the imagination embodied in the seventh property as being forsaken by the wheel of the mind for the "Reasoning Power":

> The Spectre is the Reasoning Power in Man; and when separated
> From Imagination, and closing itself as in steel, in a Ratio
> Of the Things of Memory. It thence frames Laws and Moralities
> To destroy Imagination! The Divine Body.
>
> (*Jer* 229, pl. 74, ll. 10–14)

As perception is creative that which is perceived diminishes: "If Perceptive Organs vary: Objects of Perception seem to vary: / If the Perceptive Organs close: their Objects seems to close also" (*Jer* 177, pl. 30, ll. 55–56). The "diabolic" and "terrestrial" cycles of the properties illustrate how "man has closed himself up, till he sees all things thro' narrow chinks of his cavern" (*MHH* 39, pl. 14). The divine place of the seventh property becomes this "cavern," the shrunken "habitation" of the wheel of the mind. Where in harmony Boehme's properties actively explore the possibilities of the senses, their enclosure is a diminishment of possibility. After the seven "Ages" of the regressive creation of Urizen in *The Book of Urizen* (74–76, pls. 10–13), Blake describes the fate of the "Inhabitants" of his "Cities":

> weaken'd
> The Senses inward rush'd shrinking,
> Beneath the dark net of infection
> Till the shrunken eyes clouded over
> . . . .
>
> Six days they shrunk up from existence
> And on the seventh day they rested
> . . . .
>
> No more could they rise at will
> In the infinite void, but bound down
> To earth by their narrowing perceptions.
> (82–83, pl. 25, ll. 28–47; pl. 28, ll. 1–3)

As the cycles are at work in all things and Blake's furnaces correspond to the properties, it is not only Los who has furnaces. Hand, Bowen, Molech and Urizen also possess them. Tirzah declares in *Jerusalem*:

> These fibres of thine eyes that used to beam in distant heavens
> Away from me: I have bound down with a hot iron.
> These nostrils that expanded with delight in morning skies
> I have bent downward with lead melted in my roaring furnaces
> Of affliction . . .
> My soul is seven furnaces.
> (221, pl. 67, ll. 47–52)

Blake perceived the "diabolic" aspect of the seven, that "the Seven Eyes of God . . . walk even to Satans Seat" (*Milton* 136, pl. 35, l. 64). Satan, the "Prince of this World," speaks from the heart of the Nay-saying will:

> to my eternal Will and to my dictate bow
> I hold the balances of Right and Just and mine the Sword
> Seven Angels bear my name and in those Seven I appear
> But I alone am God and I alone in Heavn and Earth.
> (*Milton* 139–40, pl. 38, ll. 53–56)

Where the properties in harmony create the holy place of the seventh, the "Tabernacle" that houses in its "bosom" the Lamb of God, "Satans Seat" or place is one of corruption and destruction. Where Jerusalem and Sophia's

"Tent" is ultimately the place of awakening and revelation, Satan's is one of enclosure and secrecy, an expression of the "poisonful mercurial wheel":

> I . . . stood in Satans bosom and beheld its desolations!
> A ruind Man: a ruind building of God . . .
> . . . .
> Its furnaces of affliction in which his Angels and Emanations
> Labour . . .
> . . . .
> In which dwells Mystery Babylon, here in her secret place
> . . . .
> Here is her Cup filld with its poisons, in these horrid vales
> And here her scarlet Veil woven in pestilence and war:
> Here is Jerusalem bound in chains, in the Dens of Babylon.
> (*Milton* 139, pl. 38, ll. 15–27)

By contrast with the purity of the seventh property, which reveals the "holy conjunction" of male and female, the "manly virgin" or divine androgyne, Urizen beholds in *The Four Zoas*

> a form
> Which he intended not a Shadowy hermaphrodite black and opake
> The Soldiers namd it Satan but he was yet unformd and vast
> Hermaphroditic it at length became hiding the Male
> Within as in a Tabernacle Abominable and Deadly.
> (374, Night 8, ll. 102–6)

In this "Abominable" "tabernacle," the seven become poisonous Sins. Inverting the movements in which the seventh property "feeds" and sustains all the properties, Blake writes in *The French Revolution*, "In the den nam'd Religion, a loathsome sick woman, bound down / To a bed of straw; the seven diseases of earth, like birds of prey, stood on the couch, / And fed on her body" (E287, ll. 35–37). In *The Four Zoas* the "Prester Serpent" declares, "Take thou the seven Diseases of Man store them for times to come / In store houses in secret places" (363, Night 7b, ll. 119–20).

Without the "indissoluble" contrariety and entrance of the Yes into the No there would be no movement and thus no life. The movements and interactions of the properties are inexhaustible, continually proposing and revealing new possibilities. Their cycles give life to the understanding that the movements of the mind and spirit can reach no fixed and irrevocably final form. The association of Jerusalem's and Sophia's "Tent and Tabernacle" with the seventh property is apt because the "Tent and Tabernacle" are moveable, are "places" that can have no fixed location and form; they are continually determined anew by the desire and imagination of the properties. If they were to become fixed and final, they would become, as Frosch has argued, the "enduring idol Vala."[3] The life that lives through the properties is in perpetual motion, the cycles of activity and rest being part of this movement. Man in his natural or "Vegetable" existence can attain no final, temporally enduring state of harmony and revelation. The "moment" of illumination revealed in the seventh property passes, and life moves on. As long as life persists, the cycles continue. This lies behind Blake's assertion that "Many Persons . . . say we will not Converse concerning Good and Evil we will live in Paradise and Liberty You may do so in Spirit but not in the <Mortal> Body" (*VLJ* 564). For the best part the cycles do not open into the full satiation of the higher properties. This is conveyed in "The Crystal Cabinet," where the narrator suggests the desire that is cast into the seventh property, and which in turn is impressed in the first:

> I strove to seize the inmost Form
> With ardor fierce and hands of flame
> But burst the Crystal Cabinet
> And like a Weeping Babe became
>
> A weeping Babe upon the wild
> And Weeping Woman pale reclind
> And in the outward air again
> I filld with woes the passing Wind.
>
> (*SB* 488–89, ll. 121–28)

Likewise, the ongoing and intricate cycles of "The Mental Traveller" convey those of Boehme's that fall short of the light, the protean movements there between youth and age, male and female, suggesting Boehme's "wheels within wheels" of progression and regression, the constant determination of the end by the beginning, the beginning by the end (*SB* 483–86).

Ultimately, however, as the "finger of God" is creative in the seventh the seven properties and Blake's seven Furnaces and Eyes lead back to the source of creation. They present an imaginative structure through which man may move beyond the enclosing cycles of the "diabolic" and "terrestrial," both of which are not fixed and final forms. With a view to this Blake calls upon the Lamb of God in *Jerusalem* to "Descend" and "take away the imputation of Sin / By the Creation of States and the deliverance of Individuals Evermore" (170, pl. 25, ll. 12–13). There are correspondences between the ongoing movement of Boehme's properties and Blake's perception of man's movement through "States." Indeed in *Milton* the Seven Angels of the Presence "converse," declaring "We are not Individuals but

States" (131, pl. 32, l. 10). As the "Mortal Body" can find no final and all-embracing place in the seventh property, because life is a process of becoming, the movement through successive forms of life, and as "time coucheth in eternity" and the temporal activities of the properties are the outward forms or reflections of eternal, "Spiritual Causes," Blake writes in *A Vision of the Last Judgment*:

> Man Passes on but States remain for Ever he passes thro them like a traveller who may As well suppose that the places he has passed thro exist no more as a Man may suppose that the States he has passd thro exist no more Every Thing is Eternal. (556)

Blake "passd thro" certain States already visited by Boehme.

The very fact that the movement through the properties and States is ongoing is itself redemptive: while properties and States are eternal, man is able to pass beyond any given form they create. As seen, the wheel of the properties describes how they "introduce themselves into good and evil, and bring themselves out of good and evil." This movement may be compared to that of the *Songs of Innocence and of Experience*, which passes from the State of Innocence, through Experience to a higher Innocence or Wisdom. Similarly, the "Divine voice" declares in *Jerusalem*:

> Albion hath enterd the State Satan! Be permanent O State!
> And be thou for ever accursed! that Albion may arise again;
> And be thou created into a State! I go forth to Create
> States: to deliver Individuals evermore! Amen.
> So spoke the voice from the Furnaces.
> (177–78. pl. 31, ll. 13–17)

The darkness of Boehme's lower ternary is an eternal darkness, one side of the "indissoluble" contrariety between Yes and No:

> There is a State namd Satan learn distrinct to know . . .
> The Difference between States and Individuals of those States
> The State namd Satan never can be redeemd in all Eternity.
> (*FZ* 380, Night 8, ll. 379–81)

In *Milton* the Seven Angels speak of "the Human Imagination: which is the Divine Vision and Fruition / In which Man liveth Eternally" and of the "Qualities" (as seen, Boehme also referred to the properties as qualities), "which are Servants of Humanity, not Gods or Lords" (132, pl. 32, ll. 18–21). Blake states in *Jerusalem*:

> Learn therefore O Sisters to distinguish the Eternal Human
> That walks about among the stones of fire in bliss and woe
>
> Alternate! From those States or Worlds in which the Spirit travels.
> (199, pl. 49, ll. 72–74)

In other words, the movement of Boehme's properties is an imaginative movement, the imagination being the life of the properties. The properties move through the necessary cycles of death and rebirth, destruction and creation, and with such an understanding in view Blake perceived that "The Imagination is not a State: it is the Human Existence itself / Affection or Love becomes States, when divided from Imagination" (*Milton* 132, pl. 32, ll. 32–33). The imagination is kept alive in Boehme's three principles.

10
The First and Second Principles

THE FIRST PRINCIPLE

The first principle is Boehme's dark world and the second is the light world. They are "mutually in one another as one Being" (*Ep* 6.18). However, their separation is necessary to understand all that proceeds from the manifestation of the Deity: "Indeed there is no difference in God, only when it is enquired from whence Evil and Good proceed, it is to be known, what is the first and original fountain of Anger, and also of Love" (*TP* 1.4). As the "one only Will" introduces itself into the first of the seven properties and all that follows therefrom, the dark world of the first principle is "the first Ground to the Eternal Nature" and to life (*MM* 5.9). A "Principle is nothing else but a new Birth" (*TP* 5.6). The first principle is comprehended in the first four properties as they stand in themselves before the opening of the light world. In itself it is the dark, unconscious, insubstantial, and insatiable "anguish-source," "the Anger and the Wrath," the fire that is "biting, wrathful, devouring and consuming" (*Ep* 6.28; *TLM* 2.44, 7.63). It is associated with the first person of the Trinity. In the first principle the Father is "a consuming fire" (*MM* 7.13), "attracting all things to himself, and devouring them" (*TLM* 7.66). God "is not called God according to the first Principle; but according to that, he is called Wrathfulness, Anger, the earnest [severe or tart] Source, from which Evil, and also the woful tormenting Trembling, and Burning, have their Original" (*TP* 1.8). Hell is in the first principle.

The first principle is a formless and unconscious world, a state of "Eternal Death." It is into this world that Thel enters in *The Book of Thel.* Suggesting the wheel of anguish that turns ceaselessly in every mind, and the "root" of each individual as first impressed or compacted in the first property, she sees

> the secrets of the land unknown;
> She saw the couches of the dead, and where the fibrous roots
> Of every heart on earth infixes deep its restless twists:
> A land of sorrows and of tears where never smile was seen.
>
> (6, pl. 6, ll. 2–5)

Aubrey has suggested that the unconscious and insubstantial aspect of Boehme's first principle may also be compared to the first two worlds of Blake's "fourfold vision" (*Letters* 722), Ulro and Generation.[1] Dark Ulro is a place of "dread sleep" and "deepest night"; it is the place of the "Grave" "where Tirzah and her Sisters / Weave the black Woof of Death" (*Milton* 110, pl. 17, l. 5; *FZ* 376, Night 8, l. 216; *Jer* 189, pl. 42, l. 17; *FZ* 377, Night 8, l. 222; *Milton* 128, pl. 29, ll. 55–56). The formless spectral existence of the first principle is expressed here in "the unreal forms of Ulro's night"; it is a place "where the Dead wail Night and Day" in doubt and despair (*FZ* 318, Night 2, l. 112; 317, Night 2, l. 71; *Jer* 171, pl. 25, ll. 15–16). The "forms" that "burst forth" from "Enitharmons shadow" in the seventh Night of *The Four Zoas* are "Cruel and ravening with Enmity and Hatred and War / In the dreams of Ulro dark delusive" (360, Night 7, ll. 328–31). Where the first principle is the "first Ground" of birth and life, "Such is the nature of Ulro: that whatever enters: / Becomes Sexual, and is Created, and Vegetated, and Born" (*Jer* 186, pl. 39, ll. 21–22). This points again to the "first mother" who appears in the dark properties. Insofar as Boehme's dark properties may be seen as the "eternal beginning" of the birth of Christ, the first principle may be compared to the world of Generation, which Blake envisions as the "Birthplace of the Lamb of God incomprehensible" (*Jer* 150, pl. 7, ll. 64–67). The "seed" which is sown in the seventh property is impressed in the first. In its more adverse aspect Generation is suggestive of the self-will of the first principle, for it is a world in which "Life lives upon Death and by devouring appetite / All things subsist on one another" (*FZ* 369, Night 7, ll. 389–90). Blake speaks in *A Vision of the Last Judgment* of the "Eternal Fire which is the fire of Generation or Vegetation it is an Eternal Consummation" (558).

Certain parallels may also be drawn with Blake's associated realms of Udan-Adan and Entuthon Benython. The formless mystery of Boehme's first principle is reflected in the "deeps of indefinite Udan Adan" (*Jer* 149, pl. 7, l. 22), which are "Perturbd black" with "death and despair" (*FZ* 377, Night 8, ll. 226, 231). As the first principle is one of unsatiated hunger, it is "around / The Lake of Udan-Adan, in the Forests of Entuthon Benython" that the "Souls incessant wail, being piteous Passions and Desires / With neither lineament nor form" (*Milton* 123, pl. 26, ll. 24–29). Where Boehme's first principle is a "dark valley" (*TP* 4.56) of "woful tormenting," Entuthon Benython is a place of "Gloom" and "dismal vales," of "terrors" and "shadows of torment and woe" (*FZ* 342, Night 5, ll. 149–51; *Jer* 147, pl. 5, l. 24; *FZ* 378, Night 8, l. 269). As with the "Eternal Death" of Boehme's dark world, Entuthon Benython is "A dark and unknown night, indefinite, unmeasurable, without end" (*Jer* 148, pl. 5, l. 57); a "world of deep darkness where all things in horrors are rooted" (*FZ* 330, Night 3, l. 181) in the eternal beginning of the dark properties. Mirroring the labor of the "first mother" in the first principle, Jerusalem is seen "bending / Her revolutions . . . in maternal anguish . . ./ In Entuthon Benythons deep Vales" (*Jer* 158, pl. 14, ll. 31–34).

Each of the Four Zoas descends into a condition that brings to mind the first principle. Percival argues that Blake might well have drawn on Boehme's dark world in his portrayal of Urthona, "who is heard relentlessly hammering in the darkness of the subconscious at the substance of thought."[2] "Dark Urthona" remains largely shadowy and mysterious, at work "In the deep caves" and "dens" "beneath" (*FZ* 406, Night 9, ll. 806, 841; 343, Night 5, ll. 189–90). When he falls in *The Four Zoas* he falls into Boehme's raging wheel of anguish, becoming "a raging serpent rolling round" (*FZ* 312, Night 1, ll. 531–32). When divided from the other Zoas his is a world of "solid Darkness / Unfathomable without end" (*Jer* 209, pl. 59, ll. 19–20), "Shut up in stifling obstruction rooted in dumb despair" (*FZ* 351, Night 6, ll. 268–69).

Franklin proposes that the process of indrawing, "overshadowing," and darkening in the first principle may be seen in Tharmas's movements in the first Night of *The Four Zoas*.[3] When Tharmas is first mentioned he is "darkning in the West" (301, Night 1, l. 23). Following this his world is seen as one of secrecy and labyrinthine darkness, as a world of "Terror" and "dreadful dolor and pain" in which he declares, "I am like an atom / A Nothing left in the darkness yet I am an identity / I wish and feel and weep and groan" (302, Night 1, ll. 62–63). The Spectral existence of Boehme's dark world then emerges "in flames of fire / In gnawing pain": "this Spectre of Tharmas / Is Eternal Death" (*FZ* 302, Night 1, ll. 77–80; 303, ll. 108–9). Tharmas's emanation, Enion, then perceives "the Shadow of the dead," the "darkness and solitude" and "Doubt" of the "Created Phantasm" of the first principle (303, Night 1, ll. 115–20). With that the Spectre of Tharmas acts in the spirit of the self-will, becoming self-righteous, "Glorying in his own eyes Exalted in terrific Pride" (303, Night 1, ll. 128–29, 147–49). Asserting this will and evoking Boehme's "bitter poisonful" "Sting," he declares to Enion:

> That dark and dismal infinite where Thought roams up and down
> Is Mine and there thou goest when with one Sting of my tongue
> Envenomd thou rollst inwards to the place whence I emergd.
> (303–4, Night 1, ll. 151–53)

As Boehme's dark desire draws itself into itself and "makes essence" (*SR* 2.10), the "Song" at the "Feast of Los and Enitharmon" recalls how with Tharmas's descent "a barren waste sunk down / Conglobing in the dark confusion" (309, Night 1, ll. 419–20).

Luvah is associated with love and Christ. In both *Jerusalem* and *The Four Zoas* he enters the "Furnaces of affliction," following the movement between the seventh and first property. As the first principle is shut up in darkness, Los's Spectre says in *Jerusalem,*

> O! thou seest not what I see! what is done in the Furnaces.
> Listen, I will tell thee what is done in moments to thee unknown:
> Luvah was cast into the Furnaces of affliction and sealed,
> And Vala fed in cruel delight, the Furnaces with fire:
> . . . .
> With joy she heard his howlings, and forgot he was her Luvah,
> With whom she liv'd in bliss in times of innocence and youth!
>
> (149–50, pl. 7, ll. 28–37)

The casting of Luvah into this condition is that of Boehme's vision of the casting or impression of desire in the dark world. With his descent love has become a dark desire. The "sealed" "Furnaces" suggest the hermetically sealed "place" in which the alchemical fire works, and the will that "frames or compacts itself" and which "has . . . inclosed the {free} Will" (*EOG* 9.38; *TP* 14.62). Luvah's condition is that in which "nature opposes the free-will, and a thing is at enmity in itself" (*SR* 2.14–15). The "times of innocence and youth" point to the freedom of the love-will as it stands outside or distinct from the first principle. At this point, however, Luvah is trapped in Boehme's wheel of anguish. Vala's "feeding" of the "fire" and of his "howlings" expresses the hunger that cannot be satiated. Luvah is cast into despair, and "Love turns into anguish" (*SR* 4.10). He has entered into "Eternal Death / . . . our Primeval Chaos . . .of incoherent / Discordant principles of Love and Hate." He speaks of this from "the unreal forms of Ulros night" (318, Night 2, ll. 101–3, 111–12). There being nothing substantial to "feed" and sustain Luvah and his emanation here, Blake adds that

> when Luvah age after age was quite melted with woe
> The fire of Vala faded like a shadow cold and pale
> An evanescent shadow. last she fell a heap of Ashes
> Beneath the furnaces a woful heap in living death.
>
> (*FZ* 318, Night 2, ll. 113–16)

When Luvah is cast into the "Furnaces of affliction" "Stern Urizen" is "urgd by necessity to keep / The evil day afar, and . . . with iron power / . . . avert his own despair" (*Jer* 150, pl. 7, ll. 30–34). Where Luvah suggests the will that is "inclosed" in the first principle and that would be free of it, Urizen suggests the necessity worked by the constrictive Nay-saying will that "desires only . . . to find itself in itself" (*SR* 2.33–34; *MM* 3.26). It was shown earlier that Urizen acts as Boehme's constrictive Father who would "hold and shut in the disobedient son." He is the Father who in the first principle is a "consuming fire," "attracting all things to himself, and devouring them." His wrath and anger is that of Boehme's dark world. He is engulfed in

> Rage, fury, intense indignation
> In cataracts of fire blood and gall
> In whirlwinds of sulpherous smoke:
> And enormous forms of energy;
> All the seven deadly sins of the soul
> In living creations appear'd
> In the flames of eternal fury
> . . . .
>
> But no light from the fires, all was darkness
> In the flames of Eternal fury.
> (*BU* 72–73, pl. 4, ll. 45–49; pl. 5, ll. 1–2, 17–18)

Boehme's first principle seems a very probable source of Blake's "Father of Jealousy" (*VDA* 50, pl. 7, l. 12), as particularly manifested in the character of Urizen. By comparison with most Christians both visionaries could appear heretical in their placing of God the Father in this dark principle. Urizen is, as Oothoon laments, the "Creator of men! mistaken Demon of heaven" (*VDA* 48, pl. 5, ll. 3–4). Fuzon asks in *The Book of Ahania*, "Shall we worship this Demon of smoke, / . . . this abstract non-entity / This cloudy God" (84, pl. 2, ll. 10–12). In *Jerusalem* Los's Spectre also speaks of Boehme's "aspiring wrathfulness" (*SR* 2.34), of a God who is "Righteous" rather than "a Being of Pity and Compassion." He "feeds on Sacrifice and Offering" (*Jer* 153, pl. 10, ll. 46–50). Urizen himself announces in "awful pride," "I am a God from Eternity to Eternity . . . / . . . I am God the terrible destroyer and not the Saviour" (*FZ* 307, Night 1, ll. 334–47). The first principle is that which gives shape to "the Great Selfhood / Satan: Worshipd as God by the Mighty Ones of the Earth" (*Jer* 175, pl. 29, ll. 17–18).

The poem "The Tyger" (*SoE* 24–25) is a potent expression of the wrath and terror of the dark world, and the creature itself one of Blake's foremost manifestations of the first principle. The voice that addresses the Tyger makes felt the sense of "woful tormenting Trembling" that arises with Boehme's apprehension of the source of wrath. The same spirit accompanies Blake's depiction of Orc, in whom the fierce energy of the first principle burns. His flames

roll heavy
Around the limbs of Albions Guardian, his flesh consuming.
Howlings and hissings, shrieks and groans, and voices of despair
Arise around him.

(*Eur* 65, pl. 12, ll. 32–35)

Bound, his is a "Human fire fierce glowing, as the wedge / Of iron heated in the furnace," in which there is "heat but not light" (*Am* 53, pl. 4, ll. 8–11). Orc's anguish can only be quenched by the "swallowing" of the "substance" of the light, through which it "burneth like *kindled* Oil" (*TLM* 8.31–33; *SR* 14.12). In the dark world in itself, in the "Caves of Orc," this "oil" serves only to fuel the wrath. Orc's is "A Cavernd Universe of flaming fire" in which "justice" is "Consuming in the raging lamps of mercy." The "holy oil rages thro all the cavernd rock" (*FZ* 352–53, Night 7, ll. 5–12). The first principle is a potent unconscious force that lies behind man's activities:

Men understand not the distress and the labour and sorrow
That in the Interior Worlds is carried on in fear and trembling.

(*Jer* 209, pl. 59, ll. 50–51)

THE SECOND PRINCIPLE, SEPARATION, AND INTERDEPENDENCE

God is manifest in the second principle "as a great fiery flame of light and love" (*MM* 7.13). As He is wrathful in the first, the "Father is called a holy God" only according to the Light, "in the Son" (*MM* 7.14). The correspondences between Ulro and Generation and the first principle are rounded out in the second two worlds of Blake's "fourfold vision." The similarities between Beulah and the mercy of the "pleasant," "sweet yielding," and "heavenly Essence" of the second principle have already been drawn. Eden is like Boehme's light world in that it too is a "land" of "Perfect Unity," of "Giving, receiving, and forgiving" (*FZ* 300, Night 1, ll. 4–5; *Jer* 180, pl. 34, l. 22). The second principle is the "place . . . in which the spirit of Christ takes on human being" (*WC* "On the New Birth," 1.19) and "wherein we understand the Divine body" (*FQ* 1.305). Blake envisioned the "garment of immortal texture / Woven in looms of Eden," and that Jesus "is all in all / In Eden: in the garden of God." As "One Man all the Universal Family . . . / Live in perfect harmony in Eden the land of life" (*Jer* 180, pl. 38, ll. 52–53, 24–25, 17–21). Where Boehme's "Light is the eternal Liberty" (*TLM* 7.65), Blake describes the "wheels" "in Eden which / Wheel within Wheel in freedom revolve in harmony and peace" (*Jer* 159, pl. 15, ll. 19–20). The "heavenly Essence" of this "free lubet" is embodied in Jerusalem, who "is called Liberty among the Children of Albion" (*Jer* 203, pl. 54, l. 5). Wisdom is "the *Expressed Essence of the Divine Power*" (*Ep* 6.21) in the second principle. She appears to Los in a vision of the "great fiery flame of light and love." She "Reflects Eternity" and reveals "the flames of holiness" which "like a Veil of Seraphim / In flaming fire unceasing burns from Eternity to Eternity" (*Jer* 244–45, pl. 86, ll. 1–25). Through her Blake's vision of Innocence gives form to Boehme's light world: "<I have seen when at a distance Multitudes of Men in Harmony appear like a single Infant sometimes in the Arms of a Female <this> represented the Church>" (*VLJ* 557), or Jerusalem. As the second is the "Principle of the holy divine Birth" and understanding, Blake portrays Jesus as "surrounded by Beams of Glory in which are seen all around him Infants emanating from him these represent the Eternal Births of Intellect from the divine Humanity" (*VLJ* 562). Jerusalem evokes

> the sweet regions of youth and virgin innocence:
> Where we live . . .
> . . . .
> Where we delight in innocence before the face of the Lamb:
> Going in and out before him in his love and sweet affection.
> (*Jer* 165, pl. 20, ll. 6–10)

Given that the Lamb of God and Jerusalem are ultimately one, where the Tyger is a creature of the wrath of the first principle, Blake's Lamb embodies the "great meekness" and love of the second.

Much of Blake's work, not least in the epics, is concerned with the passage through the darker and more adverse aspects of existence toward the light, rather than with the light as it stands in itself. This tallies with Boehme's focus on the relationship of the light world to the dark world. Whatever "is a desiring love in the light . . . that, in the darkness, is an enmity" (*MM* 5.6). This relationship is drawn in "The Clod and the Pebble." The Clod of Clay speaks of the second principle:

> Love seeketh not Itself to please,
> Nor for itself hath any care;
> But for another gives its ease,
> And builds a Heaven in Hells despair.

The Pebble speaks from the first principle:

> Love seeketh only Self to please,
> To bind another to Its delight:
> Joys in anothers loss of ease,
> And builds a Hell in Heavens despite.
> (*SoE* 19, ll. 1–4, 9–12)

In Boehme's words, where God's "Love is *hid* in any Thing there his Anger is *manifest*" (*MM[L]* 8.24). The separation or closing off of the dark principle from the light is marked by a phrase that appears with some frequency in Blake's work: "no light from the fires. all was darkness" (*BU* 73, pl. 5, ll. 17–18). In itself the first principle is not painful to itself: "No creature . . . created out of the darkness, has pain from the darkness, even as a poisonous snake has no pain from his poison" (*WC* "On True Resignation," 2.6). The "sorrow triumpheth in itself, that it is a might and strength . . . Hence arise pride and self–will" (*MM* 5.8). However, in relation to the second principle the first is "as a great fear before the light" (*MM* 3.26), for if "a good thing is brought within it . . . this will become its pain and death" (*WC* "On True Resignation," 2.6). Blake understood this:

> No one Envies or Hates one of his Own Party even the devils love one another in their Way they torment one another for other reasons than Hate or Envy these are only employd against the Just. . . . In Hell all is Self Righteousness. (*VLJ* 564–65)

When Satan attempts to approach Albion in *Milton* he stands

> trembling round his Body, he incircled it
> He trembled with exceeding great trembling and astonishment
> Howling in his Spectre round his Body hungring to devour
> But fearing for the pain for if he touches a Vital,
> His torment is unendurable: therefore he cannot devour.
> (140, pl. 39, ll. 16–20)

The pain of the first principle arises out of that which it is not.

If there were no separation there could be no aspiration and desire for the light. The opposition and interdependence of the first and second principles are essential to life, for the first in or of itself is as Blake's Negation: "Negations are not Contraries: Contraries mutually Exist: / But Negations Exist Not . . . / . . . nor shall they ever be Organized for ever and ever" (*Jer* 162, pl. 17, ll. 33–35). The relationship between the dark and light worlds is both potent and paradoxical, for while "they are mutually bound to each other; and the one were a Nothing without the *other*" (*MM[L]* 8.26), "the Light has shone from Eternity in the Darkness, and the Darkness has not comprehended it" (*Clavis* 52). The "one holds the other hidden or closed up in it" (*SR* 2.29), and yet each stands "in its order, in its own principle" (*ToI* 1.1.34). The movement that comprehends the relationship between the two is imaginative. While Orc is bound he is nonetheless open to the benevolent and nourishing life that is hidden from the darkness, to a sphere of vision and experience that his "chains" cannot "hold" or "comprehend":

His limbs bound down mock at his chains for over them a flame
Of circling fire unceasing plays to feed them with life and bring
The virtues of the Eternal worlds ten thousand thousand spirits
Of life lament around the Demon going forth and returning
At his enormous call they flee into the heavens of heavens
And back return with wine and food. Or dive into the deeps
To bring the thrilling joys of sense to quell his ceaseless rage
His eyes the lights of his large soul contract or else expand.
(*FZ* 341, Night 5, ll. 114–21)

A little later Urizen views this embodiment of Boehme's principles, seeing only Orc's "woful place" of "fierce fires" and "bitter anguish." Lacking imagination, Urizen is amazed at Orc:

Yet thou dost laugh at all these tortures and this horrible place
Yet throw thy limbs these fires abroad that back return upon thee
While thou reposest throwing rage on rage feeding thyself
With visions of sweet bliss far other than this burning clime
Sure thou art bathd in rivers of delight on verdant fields
Walking in joy in bright Expanses sleeping on bright clouds
With visions of delight so lovely that they urge thy rage.
(353–54, Night 7, ll. 44–45, 59–65)

Orc gives form to the will in the darkness that is nourished by the desire of release and which breaks through the fourth property into the light. That which is "bitter" in the darkness is purified through the fire and transformed into a "sweet delight." When Orc arises in *America* he declares:

The fiery joy, that Urizen perverted to ten commands,
. . . .
That stony law I stamp to dust . . .
. . . .
. . . to renew the fiery joy . . .
. . . .
For every thing that lives is holy, life delights in life;
Because the soul of sweet delight can never be defil'd.
Fires inwrap the earthly globe, yet man is not consum'd;
Amidst the lustful fires he walks.
(54, pl. 8, ll. 3–16)

The life that lives in the second principle "can never be defil'd," Though largely hidden it is eternally present, guarded by the separative limit of the fourth property. Blake's works persistently reach toward this life and light. Aspiring to the passage through the fire and the condition of Sophia,

Oothoon says "I call with holy voice! . . . / Rend away this defiled bosom that I may reflect. / The image of Theotormon on my pure transparent breast" (*VDA* 46, pl. 2, ll. 14–16). Stressing the paradoxical necessity of the passage through the darkness to the light she adds:

> If Theotormon once would turn his loved eyes upon me;
> How can I be defild when I reflect thy image pure?
> Sweetest the fruit that the worm feeds on. And the soul prey'd on by woe.
> (47, pl. 3, ll. 15–17)

Urizen is depicted in "the dark deep,"

> seeking for delight . . .
> Seeking the Eternal which is always present to the wise
> Seeking for pleasure which unsought falls round the infants path.
> (*FZ* 390, Night 9, ll. 170–72)

As Oothoon declares, "the soul of sweet delight / Can never pass away" (*VDA* 46, pl. 1, ll. 9–10). The second principle is the world in which Los realizes "all that has existed in the space of six thousand years: / Permanent" (*Jer* 157, pl. 13, ll. 59–60). With this in view Enitharmon sings "Oer Los reviving him to Life" (*FZ* 323, Night 2, l. 342) in *The Four Zoas*: "I wake sweet joy in dens of sorrow and I plant a smile / In forests of affliction / And wake the bubbling springs of life in regions of dark death" (324, Night 2, ll. 371–73). Blake's view that "Without Contraries is no progression" is thoroughly Behmenist:

> Roses are planted where thorns grow.
> And on the barren heath
> Sing the honey bees.
> (*MHH* 33, pl. 2, ll. 6–8)

Similarly, he perceived that "the Grave is Heaven's golden Gate," and wrote of his "Visions": " 'The Grave produc'd these Blossoms sweet / In mild repose from Earthly strife; / The Blosoms of Eternal Life!' " (*SB* 480 "To the Queen," ll. 7, 18–20). As long as the light is allaying and governing the darkness, maintaining the state of temperature, the first principle can "make the desarts blossom" (*Am* 54, pl. 8, l. 8) and "renew the fiery joy."

This is the marriage of Heaven and Hell. It is not surprising that Blake acknowledges Boehme in *The Marriage.* Boehme understood that "the Will which is in Hell, and the Will which is manifested in Heaven, both of them, in the inward Ground, without and beyond the Manifestation, are *one* Thing" (*EOG* 8.285). Blake's "Heaven and Hell are born together" (*Ann.*

DLDW 609) as are Boehme's, which are "verily in one another, as Day and Night: and Hell is a Ground for Heaven" (*EOG* 8.286): "for the Flame of Anger is the Manifestation of the great Love, and in the Darkness the Light is made known" (*MM[L]* 8.27). Following this, Blake saw that "under every *Good* is a hell. i.e. hell is the outward or external of heaven. and is of the body of the lord. for nothing is destroyd" (*Ann. HH* 602). Urizen addresses Luvah, recalling the state of temperature: "thou didst keep with Strong Urthona the living gates of heaven / But now thou art bound down with him even to the gates of hell . . . / When Thought is closd in Caves. Then love shall shew its root in deepest Hell" (*FZ* 344, Night 5, ll. 232–33, 241). As seen in "The Clod and the Pebble," "*Heaven is in Hell,* and the *Hell is in Heaven,* and yet the one is not manifest to the other" (*MM[L]* 8.28). However, with the advent of Christ, who breaks "thro' the Central Zones of Death and Hell," the "gates of hell" are transformed and "Hell is opend to Heaven . . . / The dungeons burst and the Prisoners set free" (*Jer* 231, pl. 75, l. 21; 233, pl. 77, ll. 34–35). As Boehme's love-play sustains the temperature or "fearful symmetry" of the first and second principles and creates through it, Blake describes the "Plow of ages" as "ornamented / With beautiful art the study of angels the workmanship of Demons / When Heaven and Hell in Emulation strove in sports of Glory" (*FZ* E293, Night 9, ll. 297–98). In an inscription to *The Marriage,* he wrote, "Death and Hell / Team with Life" (673). A peculiar characteristic of both Blake's and Boehme's vision is the understanding that "Energy is Eternal Delight" (*MHH* 34, pl. 4). Blake's "God is within, and without! he is even in the depths of Hell!" (*Jer* 155, pl. 12, l. 15). As Boehme saw that "that which in the dark is a fear, terror and trembling, is in the light a shout of joy, a ringing forth and singing" (*SP* "Six Theosophic Points," 2.3), Blake's God

> speaks in thunder and fire!
> Thunder of Thought, and flames of fierce desire:
> Even from the depths of Hell his voice I hear,
> Within the unfathomd caverns of my Ear.
> Therefore I print; nor vain my types shall be:
> Heaven, Earth and Hell, henceforth shall live in harmony.
> (*Jer* 145, pl. 3, ll. 5–10)

Boehme's first principle is a world of wrath and judgment, the fire that drives prophetic vision; the second is of loving mercy and compassion and the fulfillment of the prophetic spirit. Through them Blake's "Universal Family" live "Mutual in one anothers love and wrath all renewing" (*Jer* 180, pl. 34, l. 16). The separation of the "one only Will" casts desire through the darkness and into the light:

a World of Mercy, and
A World of Justice: the World of Mercy for Salvation
To cast Luvah into the Wrath, and Albion into the Pity
In the Two Contraries of Humanity.

(*Jer* 216, pl. 65, ll. 1–4)

This finds further resonance in the "impression" of Los's hammer: "The blow of his Hammer is Justice. the swing of his Hammer: Mercy. / The force of Los's Hammer is eternal Forgiveness" (*Jer* 247, pl. 88, ll. 49–50). For Boehme "the God of the holy World, and the God of the dark World, are *not two* Gods; there is but *one* only God. He himself is the whole Being" (*MM[L]* 8.24). Blake's Jesus "is the God [*of Fire*] and Lord [*of Love*] to whom the Ancients look'd and saw his day afar off, with trembling and amazement" (*Jer* 145, pl. 3, "To the Public"). In an inscription to his "Epitome of Hervey's Meditations among the Tombs" Blake wrote that "God out of Christ is a Consuming Fire." This is notably framed by the words "MERCY" and "WRATH" (*Inscrip.* 691). He states in *A Vision of the Last Judgment* that

> Thinking as I do that the Creator of this World is a very Cruel Being and being a Worshipper of Christ I cannot help saying the Son O how unlike the Father <First God Almighty comes with a Thump on the Head Then Jesus Christ comes with a balm to heal it>. (*VLJ* 565)

Like Boehme, Blake turns to the "sweet Water" of the second principle: "O Saviour pour upon me thy Spirit of meekness and love: / Annihilate the Selfhood in me, be thou all my life!" (*Jer* 147, pl.5, ll. 21–22).

When the Four Zoas have fallen from the state of temperature, this loving "symmetry" of the first and second principles becomes truly "fearful": "If we are wrathful Albion will destroy Jerusalem with rooty Groves / If we are merciful, ourselves must suffer destruction on his Oaks!" (*Jer* 38.8–9 p.184). However, as Los understands,

They have divided themselves by Wrath. they must be united by
Pity: let us therefore take example and warning O my Spectre,
O that I could abstain from wrath! O that the Lamb
Of God would look upon me and pity me in my fury.

(*Jer* 150, pl. 7, ll. 57–60)

While "we live not by wrath. by mercy alone we live" (*Milton* 119, pl. 23, l. 34), Los cannot "abstain from wrath" insofar as it is an "indissoluble" aspect of "pity." In the ninth Night of *The Four Zoas* the "Eternal Man" approaches the necessity that works through the second principle, addressing the "dragon of the Deeps":

> O how couldst thou deform those beautiful proportions
> Of life and person . . .
> Let Luvah rage in the dark deep even to Consummation
> For if thou feedest not his rage it will subside in peace.
>
> (389, Night 9, ll. 138–43)

This prophecy finds fulfillment a little later when the "Eternal Man" has arisen into the second principle and thus cannot

> put off his new risen body
> In mental flames the flames refusd they drove him back to Beulah
> His body was redeemd to be permanent thro Mercy Divine.
>
> (395, Night 9, ll. 355–57)

The "Immortal" adds,

> Luvah and Vala henceforth you are Servants obey and live
> You shall forget your former state return O Love in peace
> Into your place the place of seed.
>
> (395, Night 9, ll. 363–65)

Thus Los declares "I will quell my fury and teach / Peace to the Soul of dark revenge and repentance to Cruelty" (368, Night 7, ll. 368–69). For Blake and Boehme it was vital that everything remain in the "beautiful proportions" of the temperature.

THE FALL OF LUCIFER

Boehme's angels were created "that they might increase the paradisical Joy, and abide [therein] eternally" as " a holy Sport in Paradise" (*TP* 4.65, 66). They were able through imagination to move or look through the fourth property into "the first or second Principle, and to manifest themselves" (*EOG[E]* 4.25). As a similitude of the divine free will, "what the angels will and desire is by their imagination brought into shape and forms" (*TQ* 6.10). It is through this movement that Lucifer fell. Rather than casting their imagination into the light the "great potent princely Angels . . . cast their Imaginations back into themselves, and formed [or created] a Will [or Purpose] in the {dark} Matrix" (*TP* 5.25). Lucifer saw here "that he was a Prince" and "despised the Meekness of the Heart of God. He would not set his Imagination therein" (*TP* 4.68) and "would not continue in renunciation, but willed to rule over the thrones, and broke himself off from the Unity" (*TQ* 7.5). Lucifer "*awakened* the Matrix of the Fire" (*TLM* 8.44) and "entered with his will into self" (*MM* 9.7). His fall is one of "pride and self-will" (*MM* 5.8). Lucifer is therefore responsible for his own fall and "lost the light of the Heart of God" (*TLM* 2.48; *SR* 7.16). That is, when he turned away from the light "the properties of enmity instantly arose in him, for in the light they could not be manifest; but when the light extinguished they were manifest, and he became a devil" (*MM* 17.28). The "holy power in the light of God" has "concealed itself" from him, and he is "as wood that is burnt to a coal, which only glows, and has no more any true light in it" (*EOG[E]* 4.46; *SR* 7.10). The "apostate will . . . died to the kingdom of heaven or the good will" (*EOG[E]* 4.46).

Shut up in the darkness of the first principle, he "lost his beautiful, [fair, bright,] and glorious Image" (*TP* 4.67) and "forfeited the Divine image or the idea" (*TQ* 8.10), becoming a "Loathsomeness" to Paradise and an "eternal Enemy to the Heart of God" (*TP* 4.68, 72). His fall first brings the seven properties of Eternal Nature out of the state of temperature. Lucifer and his followers can no longer raise their imagination up into God "for there is in them all no longer any longing or desire towards humility or repentance" (*TQ* 8.5). The devil's imagination can only give form to the "Will striving against itself, an eternal Despair of all Good" (*TP* 4.70). While his is a "Will continually aspiring to . . . destroy the Heart of God . . . {it or he} could never at all be able to reach it,"

> For he is always shut up in the first Principle (as in the eternal Death,) and yet he raises himself up continually, thinking to reach the Heart of God, and to domineer over it . . . but he attains nothing . . . his Refreshing is ... the eternal Hunger in the Bitterness, an eternal Thirst in the Source of the Fire; his climbing up is his Fall, the more he climbs up in his Will, the greater is his Fall. (*TP* 4.70–71)

Hell is a "State" of eternal damnation. Although "the Devil should go many Millions of Miles, desiring to enter into Heaven, and to see it, yet he would still be in Hell, and not see it" (*MM[L]* 8.28). This blindness arises from the fact that Lucifer has broken himself off from the one true will. Hell is thus "the Kingdom of *Phantasy*" (*EOG* 6.50), and the devils "can now do no otherwise than what the property of phantasy implies, namely, practise foolery, transform themselves, and break down the existing being" (*EOG[E]* 4.30).

In *The Book of Urizen* Blake suggests the condition of Boehme's angels before their fall, their ability to turn themselves with the free will to the first or second principle:

Earth was not: nor globes of attraction
The will of the Immortal expanded
Or contracted his all flexible senses.
Death was not, but eternal life sprung.
(71, pl. 3, ll. 36–39)

As the movement of the will into self brings with it the loss of the light of "the Heart of God," of "the Divine image or idea," the second Night of *The Four Zoas* opens with Albion "Rising upon his Couch of Death . . . / Turning his Eyes outward to Self. losing the Divine Vision" (313, Night 2, ll. 1–2). Lucifer "wished with the No to rule over the Yes" (*TQ* 7.6), meaning "to be a very potent terrible Lord" (*TP* 4.68). Blake's Satan appears in *Milton* as the "God" of the "Consuming Fire," disrupting the temperature of the seven properties:

Satan flaming with Rintrahs fury . . .
. . . .
. . . created Seven deadly Sins drawing out his infernall scroll,
Of Moral laws and cruel punishments upon the clouds of Jehovah
To pervert the Divine voice in its entrance to the earth
. . . .
. . . Saying I am God alone
There is no other . . .
. . . .
. . . I rend this accursed Family from my covering.
(103, pl. 9, ll. 19–29)

This movement into the enclosure of self and the first principle is then identified as the fall into the "Kingdom of *Phantasy*" of the dark Matrix:

Albions
Dread Tomb immortal on his Rock, overshadowd the whole Earth:
Where Satan making to himself Laws from his own identity.
Compell'd others to serve him in moral gratitude and submission
Being Call'd God: setting himself above all that is called God.
. . . .
In a feminine delusion of false pride self-deciev'd.
(104–5, pl. 11, ll. 8–12, 26)

A product of his own delusions and despising the "Meekness of the Heart of God," Satan later anticipates the time when "All Things become One Great Satan, in Holiness / Oppos'd to Mercy, and the Divine Delusion Jesus be no more" (140, pl. 39, ll. 1–2). As Boehme's devil "willed to rule over the thrones" and to "destroy the Heart of God," and accordingly awakened and took possession of the dark "Matrix of the Fire," "Albions Twelve Sons" are seen in *Jerusalem*

> raging against the Lamb and against Jerusalem,
> Surrounding them with armies to destroy the Lamb of God.
> They took their Mother Vala, and they crown'd her with gold:
> They nam'd her Rahab, and gave her power over the Earth
> . . . .
> Even to the stars exalting her Throne, to build beyond the Throne
> Of God and the Lamb, to destroy the Lamb and usurp the Throne of God
> Drawing their Ulro Voidness round the Four-fold Humanity.
>
> (234, pl. 78, ll. 13–20)

The fall of Lucifer actualizes the process of "overshadowing" or "darkening." The light that was "extinguished from his fire-life," leaving him "as wood that is burnt to coal, which only glows, and has no more any true light in it" appears when Satan asserts his self-will:

> his bosom grew
> Opake against the Divine Vision; the paved terraces of
> His bosom inwards shone with fires, but the stones becoming opake!
> Hid him from sight, in an extreme blackness and darkness.
>
> (*Milton* 103, pl. 9, ll. 30–33)

Similarly, when Urizen declares "I am God . . . eldest of things!" in *The Book of Ahania* Blake suggests the loss of Lucifer's "beautiful [fair, bright,] and glorious Image":

> Sudden sings the rock, swift and invisible
> On Fuzon flew, enter'd his bosom;
> His beautiful visage, his tresses,
> That gave light to the mornings of heaven
> Were smitten with darkness, deform'd.
>
> (86, pl. 3, ll. 38–43)

Revealed as a "Loathsomeness" to Paradise, Satan appears as a "form dishumanizd monstrous," "Fo[r]lorn of Eden and repugnant to the forms of life," "Being multitudes of tyrant Men in union blasphemous / Against the divine image" (*FZ* 377–78, Night 8, ll. 252–58).

The fall of Albion's Angel in *Europe* is that of self-will. He flees from "the heavens . . . / . . . smitten with his own plagues" (63, pl. 9, ll. 6–16). While Boehme places far more emphasis on the destructive and illusory aspects of imagination than Blake, both perceived its ability through desire to corrupt. Blake repeatedly writes of his characters, "they became what they beheld"

(*Jer* 177, pl. 30, ll. 50, 54; 178, pl. 32, ll. 9, 15, 19; 217–18, pl. 65, ll. 75–79; 218, pl. 66, l. 36). Under the influence of the dark Matrix the "tree of Mystery" takes root and Urizen is ensnared by his own self-will:

> Misplacing every Center hungry desire and lust began
> Gathering the fruit of that Mysterious tree till Urizen
> Sitting within his temple furious felt the num[m]ing stupor
> Himself tangled in his own net.
>
> (*FZ* 375–76, Night 8, ll. 171–81)

Leutha recalls how Satan drove the Harrow which "cast thick flames and orb'd us round in concave fires / A Hell of our own making . . . / . . . Satan in pride of heart / Drove the fierce Harrow" (*Milton* 106, pl. 12, ll. 22–25). As Lucifer "despised the Birth of the Heart of God, and . . . would not set his Imagination therein," and there is "in the devils . . . no longer any longing or desire towards humility and repentance," Leutha adds that Satan's "former life became like a dream / . . . in selfish holiness demanding purity / Being most impure, self-condemn'd to eternal tears" (106, pl. 12, ll. 45–47). By contrast with him she says "I humbly bow in all my Sin before the Throne Divine. / Not so the Sick-one" who "despises the Saviour. / Glorying to involve Albions Body in fires of eternal War" (106, pl. 13, ll. 3–6). Los declares here "Satan! Ah me! is gone to his own place" (*Milton* 104, pl. 10, l. 12).

Satan's fall is an irrevocable closing off of possibility. He stands "opake immeasurable / Covering the east with solid blackness, round his hidden heart" and rends apart pity and wrath: "and wrath was left to wrath, and pity to pity. / He sunk down a dreadful Death . . . / The Separation was terrible" (*Milton* 103–4, pl. 9, ll. 39–49). Satan is "fall'n from his station and never can be redeem'd" (*Milton* 105, pl. 11, l. 19) and is "Abhorrd accursed ever dying an Eternal death" (*FZ* 377, Night 8, l. 256). Unable to be "fed from the Word of the Lord" (*TP* 4.68), standing captive in the "sharp, hard, piercing, bitter, stinging, poisonous, anxious, painful fire-root" (*TQ* 8.4), the devil is the "Objecting and cruel Spite / And Malice and Envy" of Blake's Negation which can "never! never! . . . be Organized / But as a distorted and reversed Reflexion in the Darkness," "an Unquenchable Fire," "a Hell and Despair for ever and ever" (*Jer* 162, pl. 17, ll. 37–47). Enclosed in "the deep dens of Urthona," Urizen enters this State and finds that the "mountains . . . of silver where the sons of wisdom dwelt" and the "gardens of wisdom are become a field of horrid graves" (*FZ* 343, Night 5, ll. 189–97). Los speaks of this State in *Jerusalem*, addressing the seventh property:

> Birthplace of the Lamb of God incomprehensible!
> The Dead despise and scorn thee, and cast thee out as accursed:

Seeing the Lamb of God in thy gardens and thy palaces:
Where they desire to place the Abomination of Desolation.
(150, pl. 7, ll. 67–70)

A harsh necessity is attendant upon the will that breaks itself "off from the Unity" as the "Eternal Man" warns Urizen:

if thou darest obstinate refuse my stern behest
Thy crown and scepter I will sieze and regulate all my members
In stern severity and cast thee out into the indefinite
Where nothing lives, there to wander. and if thou returnst weary
Weeping at the threshold of Existence I will steel my heart
Against thee to Eternity and never recieve thee more.
(*FZ* 390, Night 9, ll. 144–49)

If Urizen did not repent he would become as one of Boehme's devils who, having lost "any longing or desire towards humility and repentance" are "cast out" and unable to "reach the Heart of God." Blake depicts the consequences of this "endless curse" in *Jerusalem:*

had the Body of Albion fall'n down, and from its dreadful ruins
Let loose the enormous Spectre on the darkness of the deep,
At enmity with the Merciful and fill'd with devouring fire,
A nether-world must have recievd the foul enormous spirit,
. . . .
There to eternity chain'd down, and issuing in red flames
And curses, with his mighty arms brandish'd against the heavens
Breathing cruelty blood and vengeance, gnashing his teeth with pain
Torn with black storms, and ceaseless torrents of his own consuming fire.
(182, pl. 36, ll. 29–39)

While "the State Satan" cannot escape Hell, it or he can be "Organized / . . . as a distorted and reversed Reflexion in the Darkness," "Eternal Death" being indissolubly bound to the "Eternal life" of the "divine image":

Loud Satan thunderd, loud and dark . . .
Coming in a Cloud with Trumpets and with Fiery Flame
An awful Form . . .
so permitted
(Lest he should fall apart in his Eternal Death) to imitate
The Eternal Great Humanity Divine.
(*Milton* 140, pl. 39, ll. 22–27)

"Each creature" is in Boehme's view "to remain in that in which God created it or it will walk into the opposition and enmity of the will of God" (*WC*

"On True Resignation," 2.6). Blake explores this in *Milton*:

> Enitharmon brought forth Satan Refusing Form, in vain
> The Miller of Eternity made subservient to the Great Harvest
> That he may go to his own Place Prince of the Starry Wheels.
> (97, pl. 3, ll. 41–43)

Los continues,

> Every Mans Wisdom is peculiar to his own Individ[u]ality
> O Satan my youngest born, art thou not Prince of the Starry Hosts
> And of the Wheels of Heaven, to turn the Mills day and night?
> . . . .
>
> Anger me not! Thou canst not drive the Harrow in pitys paths.
> Thy Work is Eternal Death, with Mills and Ovens and Cauldrons.
> Trouble me no more. thou canst not have Eternal Life.
> (98, pl. 4, ll. 8–18)

Satan has "died to the kingdom of heaven or the good will." However, just as the devil "raises himself up continually, thinking to reach the Heart of God" and "climbing up is his Fall," Satan endeavors to assume the "station" of the Harrow and thus disrupts the state of temperature. Palamabron states that

> he hath assum'd my place
> For one whole day, under pretence of pity and love to me:
> My horses hath he maddend! and my fellow servants injur'd:
> How should he[,] he[,] know the duties of another?
> (101, pl. 7, ll. 25–28)

Satan brings "the eternal will out of the temperature into division, namely, into the dissimilarity of imagination or phantasy" (*EOG[E]* 4.29). He "can do no otherwise than what the property of phantasy implies, namely, practise foolery, transform" himself, "and break down existing being." Like Boehme's devil, who in his "phantasy" is blind to the fact that he cannot move beyond his own principle, Palamabron speaks here of "Satans mildness and his self-imposition, / Seeming a brother, being a tyrant, even thinking himself a brother / While he is murdering the just" (100, pl. 7, ll. 21–23). Satan weeps "And mildly cursing Palamabron him accus'd of crimes / Himself had wrought": "Satans self, believ'd / That he had not oppres'd the horses of the Harrow, nor the servants" (101, pl. 7, ll. 33–35, 39–40). When Satan returns to his Mills, as tended by Palamabron, he also "found all confusion / And back return'd to Los." Los "beheld"

> The servants of the Mills drunken with wine and dancing wild
> With shouts and Palambrons songs, rending the forests green
> With ecchoing confusion.
>
> (101, pl. 8, ll. 4–10)

Los declares here "let each his own station / Keep" (101, pl. 7, ll. 41–42).

11

The Third Principle

HARD MATTER, CREATION, AND ADAM

When Lucifer fell and disrupted the temperature he "entered with his will into self; and in self is the centre of nature" (*MM* 9.7). With this there first arose "hard Matter, (*viz.* Stones and Earth,) whereupon followed the gathering together of the Earth . . . and the creating of the third Principle" (*TP* 5.7). The third principle is that of this world. Beginning with the first movements out of the *Ungrund,* Boehme envisioned the Creation as taking place in stages. The beginning of Genesis was not for him the beginning of the Creation. As the seven properties are equated with the days of Creation, Lucifer's fall brings their cycles into the first day, and the Creation begins anew. The fall of the devils "shut up existence into a compaction and brought it into a mass" (*EOG[E]* 4.32). Lucifer is "a cause of the Third Principle" and "therefore Christ called him . . . a Prince of this World" (*TLM* 8.43). He aspires to be "an omniscient artist: he would domineer in and above the whole creation, and be a co-former in all properties" (*MM* 7.27). He therefore has something of the character of the Gnostic demiurge.

Creation and Fall are eternal events. Blake shared Boehme's view of Genesis:

> Many suppose that before [*Adam*] <the Creation> All was Solitude and Chaos This is the most pernicious Idea that can enter the Mind as it takes away all sublimity from the Bible and Limits All Existence to Creation and to Chaos To the Time and Space fixed by the Corporeal Vegetative Eye and leaves the Man who entertains such an Idea the habitation of Unbelieving Demons. (*VLJ* 563).

Blake mirrors the fall of Boehme's "Unbelieving Demons" "into the centre of Nature" in *Milton,* evoking "the Earth, where Satan / Fell, and was cut off" (117, pl. 22, ll. 21–22). In an annotation to *Divine Love and Divine Wisdom* he speaks of "meer Nature or Hell" (605). As seen there are notable correspondences between Boehme's devil and Urizen. Each has been a "Prince of Light" (*FZ* 307, Night 1, l. 341). As Paley notes, Orc tells Urizen "I stole thy light and it became fire / Consuming" (*FZ* 356, Night 7, ll. 147–48).[1] With his fall Urizen also enters the wrathful "centre of Nature": "Satan is Urizen / Drawn down by Orc and the Shadowy Female into Generation" (*Milton* 104, pl. 10, ll. 1–2). He too may be seen as "a cause of the Third Principle": "Then burst the center from its orb, and found a place beneath; / And Earth conglob'd, in narrow room, roll'd round its sulphur Sun" (*Am* 58, pl. b, ll. 4–7). It is through this movement that he arises in *The Book of Urizen* as "A wide world of solid obstruction" (72, pl. 4, l. 23). The seven ages of the creation of his body are seven stages of his fall into "hard Matter." As has often been noted, Urizen may also be compared to the demiurge. He is the "God of This World. A God Worshipd in this World as God and Set above all that is calld God" (*Ann. Wat.* 618). This God is at work in *Jerusalem*, aspiring to be a "co-former in all properties":

> Such is the Ancient World of Urizen in the Satanic Void
> . . . .
> Furious in pride of Selfhood the terrible Spectres of Albion
> Rear their dark Rocks among the Stars of God: stupendous
> Works! A World of Generation continually Creating; out of
> The Hermaphroditic Satanic World of rocky destiny.
> (208, pl. 58, ll. 44–51)

Where Lucifer would be "an omniscient artist," Urizen appears in the second Night of *The Four Zoas* as "the great Work master": "Build we a Bower for heavens darling in the grizly deep / Build we the Mundane Shell around the Rock of Albion" (314, Night 2, ll. 22–25). "Petrifying all the Human Imagination into rock" (314, Night 2, l. 38) he creates the worlds of Newton and the Druids (314–19).

However "there is a separation made in the creation of this world" (*SR* 4.16). The third principle "was created out of both inward properties" (*SR* 3.31), out of Love and Wrath, Light and Darkness. While the devil "would domineer in and above the whole creation," as he is shut up and captive in the first principle he can only reach part of the third. He is "in the world, and also not in the world" (*SR* 3.31). The "separation made in the creation" is an act of mercy. While the four dark properties are in themselves in a state of enmity, the third principle does not "stand . . . in such a wrathful source [or property;] . . . the *Light* out of the second Principle . . . doth enlighten" and "*tempereth*" it (*TLM* 2.47). The light is the "allaying, or mitigating" of the darkness, and the "third Principle is the second's proper own, not separate, but one Essence in it" (*TP* 5.15). Arising from both "inward properties" the third "has a Beginning, and proceeds from the Eternal; it is a manifestation of the Eternal, an awakening, image and similitude of the

Eternal" (*SP* "Six Theosophic Points" 2.15). The "Light springs up still" through it (*TP* 8.4).

This springing forth of the similitude points again to the "outbreathing" of divine activity from the movements out of the *Ungrund* onward. As the Creation takes place in stages, the appearance of the third principle is a continuation or image of the movements to divine consciousness: "One emanation has advanced out of another down to the coarsest matter or compaction of earth and stones" (*TQ* 6.13). The "whole creation, both of the eternal and also of the temporal creatures and beings lies in the Word of divine power" (*EOG[E]* 4.3). The "inner, holy, spiritual world is the speaking Word of God" (*EOG[E]* 4.17) and the outward world "the *Verbum Fiat* (*viz.* the Naturall word of God)" (*Ep* 6.25), the expressed Word which has "immassed" or compacted itself "into a palpable tangible being" (*EOG[E]* 4.13–14). This compaction is the Creation of Genesis (*EOG* 4.13). Through the third principle the "word has been spoken into a time and brought into a being with a beginning and end" (*EOG[E]* 4.18). The "Earth was coagulated in the seventh form of nature" (*MM* 10.38). "In the beginning" Paradise "was nothing else but the seventh day's property" (*MM* 17.4) and "grows and buds . . . in the temperament of the one element" (*EOG* [*E*] 4.16). That is, it is "the pure Element" (*EOG[E]* 4.10) that holds all three principles in the state of temperature. Paradise is hidden to the "earthly nature," residing as it does in "another Principle" (*EOG*[*E*]4.16). Boehme thus distinguishes between Paradise and the Garden of Eden: "The Garden of Eden was a place upon the earth, where man was tempted; and the Paradise was in heaven; and yet was in the Garden of Eden" (*MM* 17.3).

As the divine will is merciful and created "another Principle" in the place of the Paradise lost by the fall of the devils, God "would give to the Place of this World an angelical Host again, which should continue to stand for ever" (*TP* 10.8). Created "in the stead and place of extruded Lucifer" (*MM* 17.31), man's is "a creaturely image . . . a figure of the invisible being" of God (*EOG[E]* 5.30), a similitude made possible by the mirror of Wisdom. Adam was the "one only Man that God created" (*ToI* 1.7.56), and "God created him perfect" (*MM* 19.23). The creation of Eve is not part of Adam's pristine state. In "heaven there is neither male nor female" (*MM* 19.23). Adam "was a man and also a woman, and yet none of them [distinct], but a virgin," the divine androgyne who maintains the masculine and feminine within him in a state of temperature (*MM* 18.2). He "loved himself" within the "fair Paradisical rose-garden of delight," "without further propagation, in an eternal confirmation" (*MM* 18.2, 19.23). Everything stood within him. The similitude of God, he stands as the precursor of the ultimate unity of Blake's Lamb and Jerusalem: "the true woman from the being of the heavenly world, when she was still in Adam . . . was virgin Sophia," his true bride (*EOG[E]* 7.33; *TP* 12.39).

God created a "twofold" body for Adam, "a spiritual body and a corporeal" (*MM* 15.10). The corporeal is "out of the [one] Element, or Root of the four Elements," air, water, fire, and earth, and the "[one Element] is the fifth essence, [or Quintessence]" of alchemy (*TP* 4.19). Through the Word the outward is an "image of the inward, viz. an instrument of the inward" (*MM* 16.14). Adam had "only one" body, but with "a twofold essence, viz. one inward, heavenly, holy; and one from the essence of time; which were espoused and betrothed to each other to an eternal [being]" (*MM* 18.8). As the inward world is itself twofold Boehme draws correspondences between the body, soul, and spirit and the three principles, the body corresponding to the third principle, the soul to the first, and the spirit to the second (*MM* 15.15). Adam was "created out of all the three Principles," wherein he stood as "only one soul" (*MM* 17.17, 15.15). He existed in the state of temperature, in "an agreeing harmony" and "the divine light temperised all the properties, so that there was a mutual melody and play of unanimous love between them" (*MM* 17.17). Paradise "was the temperature in Man" (*Ep* 8.27). The outward world was thus originally hidden in the "inward man" "as the darkness dwelleth in the light" (*MM* 16.6–7). The "inward man" is the "true human body" (*MM* 16.4). Adam "had no such Hard Bones in his Flesh [as we now have]" (*TP* 10.21), and there was "nothing without the body that could either destroy or annoy" his temperature (*MM* 16.12).

Placed in the "mutual melody" of the properties, he participated in the divine love-play: "The outward spirit and body was unto the inward as a wonder of divine manifestation . . . a mirror of the great omnipotence and omniscience of God: and the inward was given unto it for a ruler and a guide" (*MM* 16.9). Everything was subject to Adam; "he ruled in heaven and earth and over all the elements" (*MM* 16.11), possessing the full creative capacities of will, desire, and imagination. He "saw with pure eyes . . . The inward man, viz. the inward eye, saw through the outward" (*MM* 18.13). As the Creation is the speaking forth of the Word, Adam "knew the property of all creatures, and gave names to all creatures . . . He understood the Language of Nature, viz. the manifested and formed Word in every one's essence" (*MM* 19.22). This view of the Word highlights again the immense creative possibilities of language. The "inward divine man should play with the outward . . . and open the divine wisdom" (*MM* 16.10). A "Particular or *Parcel* of the highest Omnipotence of the Substance of all Substances is understood to be *in the Soul*" (*EOG* 6.43) of the individual. There is nothing "that can destroy or shatter it" (*EOG* 6.44). All three principles "lie in the Soul: All that God has, and can do, and that God is in his Ternary, that the

Soul is in its Essence" (*FQ* 2.1). It is in the spirit of Adam that Boehme states that he has written out of his "own Book which was opened in me, being the Noble similitude of God":

> My Booke hath only three leaves, the same are the three Principles of Eternity, wherein I can finde all whatsoever *Moses*, and the Prophets; Christ and the Apostles have taught, and spoken; I can find therein the foundation of the World, and all Mysteries; yet not I, but the Spirit of God doth it according to the measure, as he pleaseth. (*Ep* 2.14–15)

The "Spirit that is in us, which one Man inheriteth from the other, that was breathed out of the Eternity into *Adam*, that same Spirit has seen it all, and in the Light of God it sees it still" (*TP* 7.6). "I saw, that I, in the essence of my soul and body, when I was not yet I, but when I was in Adam's essence, was there" in Paradise (*MM* 18.1).

As the creation of man in his pristine state is an image of the inward movements to divine revelation, Blake's vision of that state has already been dealt with extensively in the discussion of the light and dark worlds of the seven properties and first and second principles. For instance, as the third principle "was created out of both inward properties" he perceived "the Two Contrary States of the Human Soul" (*SoIE* 7) and the distinction between "Natural Effect" and "Spiritual Cause" (*Milton* 124, pl. 26, ll. 43–46), that "We who dwell on Earth can do nothing of ourselves, {for} every thing is conducted by spirits" (*Jer* 145, pl. 3, "To the Public"). Alongside the understanding that Satan is "hungring to devour" the "Body" and yet cannot, "for if he touches a Vital, / His torment is unendurable" (*Milton* 140, pl. 39, ll. 16–21), he asserted that "every one remains in his own energy" (*Milton* 122, pl. 25, l. 43) and that the angry "God in the dreary Void / Dwells from Eternity, wide separated from the Human Soul" (*Jer* 168, pl. 23, ll. 29–30). Accordingly, "no mortal man can find the Mill / Of Satan in his mortal pilgrimage of seventy years / For Human beauty knows it not: nor can Mercy find it" (*Jer* 181, pl. 35, ll. 4–6). Blake's Satan is "in the world, and also not in the world" and cannot distinguish between the outward and inward man:

> Truly My Satan thou art but a Dunce
> And does not know the Garment from the Man
> Every Harlot was a Virgin once
> Nor canst thou ever change Kate into Nan.
>
> (*GP* 269, "Epilogue," ll. 1–8)

Blake also saw that the "separation made in the creation of this world" "was an act of Mercy" (*VLJ* 563). Distinguishing between the third principle and

Satan's confinement in the first, he believed that although the devil "made himself a God" man can partake of the free love-play of Paradise:

> the Divine Humanity and Mercy gave us a Human Form
> Because we were combind in Freedom and holy Brotherhood
> While those combind by Satans Tyranny first in the blood of War
> And Sacrifice and, next, in Chains of imprisonment: are Shapeless Rocks.
> (*Milton* 131–32, pl. 32. ll. 14–17)

The light that "springs up still" lies behind the lines in "The Little Black Boy" that "we are put on earth a little space, / That we may learn to bear the beams of love" (*SoI* 9, ll. 13–14). The "beams of love" appear in *A Vision of the Last Judgment*: "Around the Throne Heaven is opend and the Nature of Eternal Things Displayd All Springing from the Divine Humanity All beams from him" (561). Jerusalem reflects this light. Aubrey compares that which "*tempereth*" the third principle to Blake's vision of her as she "overspread all Nations . . . in Ancient Time" (*Jer* 256, pl. 97, l. 2).[2] Through Jerusalem the third principle is realized as "the second's proper own."

The light that "beams" from the "Divine Humanity" is the same as the "outbreathing" or expression of Boehme's creative Word. In *The Design of the Last Judgment* Blake speaks of "the Eternal Creation flowing from the Divine Humanity" (554). The "Lord is the word of God and every thing on earth is the word of God and in its essence is God" (*Ann. Lav.* 599), right "down to the coarsest matter or compaction of earth and stones." As "every thing that lives is Holy," the created "beams" with—or reflects back—the life of the divine. In *Europe* the "Fairy" evokes the living interplay of the principles. The narrator asks "what is the material world, and is it dead?" Having sung of "the eternal world that ever groweth"—as Boehme's Paradise "grows and buds" through the "essence of time"—the "Fairy" promises "I'll . . . shew you all alive / The world, when every particle of dust breathes forth its joy" (60, pl. iii, ll.13, 4, 17–18). The descent or imaginative penetration that the second makes in the third makes it possible for Blake to write:

> To see a World in a Grain of Sand
> And a Heaven in a Wild Flower
> Hold Infinity in the palm of your hand
> And Eternity in an hour.
> (*AoI* 490, ll. 1–4)

Following Boehme's apprehension of the Word, which is spoken into "a beginning and end," time "is the work of Fairy hands" (*Milton* 127, pl. 28, l. 60) and "Eternity is in love with the productions of time" (*MHH* 36, pl. 7, l. 10).

While Paradise and the Garden of Eden may be distinguished, the latter manifests the former. As God "would give to the Place of this World an angelical Host" Blake works from "The Eternal Great Humanity Divine" who "planted his Paradise" in "the Portals of my Brain" (*Milton* 96, pl. 2, ll. 7–8).

This points once more to Blake's insight into the similitude, that "human nature is the image of God" (*Ann. Lav.* 597), a nature rooted in Adam's original perfection. Boehme's view that Adam "was the one only Man that God created" is given new form in Blake's that in Adam all is "united into One Man" (*Jer* 210, pl. 60, l. 16). His perfection has been seen in the poet's projection of the divine androgyne. Blake's argument that "There is no such thing in Eternity as a Female Will" (*VLJ* 562) agrees with Boehme's that the creation of Eve is not part of the true temperature of Paradise. The divine "Humanity is far above / Sexual organization" (*Jer* 236, pl. 79, ll. 73–74). Suggesting the "mutual melody" of Adam's love-play within himself, his union with Sophia in the "fair Paradisical rose-garden of delight," the "Spectre of Urthona" speaks to the "Shadow of Enitharmon" of

> those mild fields of happy Eternity
> Where thou and I in undivided Essence walkd about
> Imbodied, thou my garden of delight and I the spirit in the garden
> Mutual there we dwelt in one anothers joy revolving
> Days of Eternity with Tharmas mild and Luvah sweet melodious.
> (*FZ* 358, Night 7, l. 217; 359, Night 7, 270–74)

The distinction contained within Adam's "twofold" body is expressed in the early work *All Religions are One*: "the Poetic Genius is the true Man. and . . . the body or outward form of Man is derived from the Poetic Genius . . . As all men are alike in outward form, So, (and with the same infinite variety) all are alike in the Poetic Genius" (1). The all-embracing fecundity of the "inward spiritual man" is the source of "infinite variety" in the outward. The relationship makes possible "converse in the spirit." Boehme's belief that Adam had "one only" body which marries the "twofold" essence in "an eternal [being]" is reiterated in *The Marriage*: "Man has no Body distinct from his Soul for that calld Body is a portion of Soul discernd by the five Senses" (*MHH* 34, pl. 4). The "Energy" that is thus "Eternal Delight" springs from the play of Boehme's fiery love-desire, as first manifested by Adam.

Because the outward is an image or "instrument of the inward,"

> man cannot know
> What passes in his members till periods of Space and Time
> Reveal the secrets of Eternity: for more extensive
> Than any other earthly things, are Man's earthly lineaments.
> (*Milton* 115, pl. 21, ll. 8–11)

The "one only" body of Adam speaks again of the "tradition, that Man anciently containd in his mighty limbs all things in Heaven and Earth" (*Jer* 171, pl. 27, "To the Jews"). For Blake "every thing is Human" (*Jer* 180, pl. 34, l. 48). The body, soul, and spirit of his "One Man" unite the discrete spheres embodied in Boehme's three principles. As Albion unites within him the Four Zoas, who are associated with the "Four Elements" (*Jer* 178, pl. 32, ll. 25–27, 31–32), he may be seen in terms of the "Quintessence." He stands originally in the "agreeing harmony" of "the divine light":

> Four Mighty Ones are in every Man; a Perfect Unity
> Cannot Exist, but from the Universal Brotherhood of Eden
> The Universal Man. To Whom be Glory Evermore Amen.
>
> (*FZ* 300, Night 1, ll. 4–6)

"Paradise was the temperature in Man." As Paradise is hidden to the "earthly nature," residing as it does in "another Principle," Blake adds:

> [*What*] are the Natures of those Living Creatures the Heavenly Father only [*Knoweth*] no Individual [*Knoweth nor*] Can know in all Eternity.
>
> (301, Night 1, ll. 7–8)

Equally, as the outward is hidden in the unfallen Adam, as darkness in light, Blake understood that "Eternity Exists and All things in Eternity Independent of Creation" (*VLJ* 563). He also perceived that those "in Paradise . . . have no Corporeal <and Mortal> Body" (*VLJ* 564). The "Hard Bones" of existence "Appear only in the Outward Spheres of Visionary Space and Time" (*Jer* 252, pl. 92, l. 17) or third principle. Following Boehme's view that there was "nothing without the body that could either destroy or annoy" Adam, Blake wrote "You cannot go to Eternal Death in that which can never Die" (*Milton* 132, pl. 32, l. 24).

"The Human Imagination" is the "true Man." The correspondences with the creative capacities of Boehme's Adam are evident. Blake re-expresses Boehme's view that "the inward was given unto" the "outward spirit" "for a ruler and guide" and that the Word manifests itself in the compaction of the third principle:

> the Voice Divine went forth upon the rocks of Albion
>
> I elected Albion for my glory; I gave to him the Nations,
> Of the whole Earth. He was the Angel of my Presence: and all
> The Sons of God were Albions Sons: and Jerusalem was my joy.
>
> (*Jer* 191, pl. 43, ll. 5–8)

Once more, God "would give to the Place of this World an angelical Host again." Adam's sovereignty over creation lies behind Los's assertion as the agent of imagination that "both Time and Space obey my will" (*Milton* 117, pl. 22, l. 17). The play of Adam is also reflected in *The Four Zoas*:

> Los and Enitharmon walkd forth on the dewy Earth
> Contracting or expanding their all flexible senses
> At will to murmur in the flowers small as the honey bee
> At will to stretch across the heavens and step from star to star
> . . . .
> While round their heads the Elemental Gods kept harmony.
> (322, Night 2, ll. 295–301)

The outward world is "a mirror of the great omnipotence and omniscience of God." To "the Eyes of the Man of Imagination Nature is Imagination itself" (*Letters* 702). The pure and "inward eye" of Adam that sees "through the outward" looks out at the end of *A Vision of the Last Judgment*: "I question not my Corporeal or Vegetative Eye any more than I would Question a Window concerning a Sight I look thro it and not with it" (566). Similarly, as Blake appreciated the "all-powerful" possibility of "Human Words" (*Jer* 169, pl. 24, l. 1) his world of Innocence reverberates with the "Language of Nature," echoing or reflecting the Word compacted in and creating through Adam:

> A Rock a Cloud a Mountain
> Were . . . Vocal . . . in Climes of happy Eternity
> Where the lamb replies to the infant voice and the lion to the man of years
> Giving them sweet instructions Where the Cloud the River and the Field
> Talk with the husbandman and shepherd.
> (*FZ* 348, Night 6, ll. 134–38)

As in this expression of the Word, Blake's "breath of the Almighty" is therefore equated in *Milton* with "Poetic Inspiration" (129, pl. 30, ll. 18–19). That which is breathed out of the *Ungrund* is breathed into the body, soul, and spirit of man, "To build the Universe stupendous: Mental forms Creating" (*Milton* 129, pl. 30, l. 20). Boehme's vision resonates through the Word in the poet's art: "The Primeval State of Man, was Wisdom, Art and Science" (*Jer* 146, pl. 3, "To the Public"). The "Divine Body" of imagination "manifests itself in . . . works of Art" (*Laocoön* 273). "Poetry, Painting, and Music" are "the three Powers <in Man> of conversing with Paradise which the flood did not Sweep away" (*VLJ* 559).

Nothing "can destroy or shatter" the "Particular or *Parcel* of the highest Omnipotence" that makes possible Man's creative "Powers": "There is a Throne in every Man, it is the Throne of God" (*Jer* 176, pl. 30, l. 27). As there is the "Spirit . . . which one Man inheriteth from the other" and "the three Principles lie in the Soul," Blake also wrote out of the "Book which was opened" within him and spoke prophetically from "the foundation of the World," the compaction of the Word:

> I am Inspired! I know it is Truth! for I Sing
> According to the inspiration of the Poetic Genius
> Who is the eternal all-protecting Divine Humanity
> To whom be Glory and Power and Dominion Evermore Amen.
> (*Milton* 107–8, pl. 13, l. 51; pl. 14, ll. 1–3)

As illuminated by Boehme, all

> equal share
> Divine Benevolence and joy, for the Eternal Man
> Walketh among us, calling us his Brothers and his Friends.
> (*Jer* 204, pl. 55, ll. 8–10)

Likewise,

> All these things are written in Eden. The artist is an inhabitant of that happy country; if every thing goes on as it has begun, the world of vegetation and generation may expect to be opened again to Heaven, through Eden, as it was in the beginning. (*DC* 543)

The movement out of the *Ungrund* is from the *meonic* to the actual. Everything "possible to be believ'd is an image of the truth" (*MHH* 37, pl. 8, l. 38). It is through this movement that God "planted his Paradise" in "the Portals" of the poet's "Brain," "when I was not yet I."

THE FALL OF MAN

The Fall of Adam mirrors the Creation in that it also takes place in stages. Following Lucifer he too disrupted the temperature through self-will. Although Adam stood in the temperature of Paradise, "the properties were in themselves an awakened hunger, each in itself" (*MM* 17.36). Each of "the three Principles . . . would accomplish [or work forth] its wonders in him" (*MM* 18.27). For his part the devil in the first principle "introduced continually his imagination into the soul, and into the outward flesh" (*MM* 18.28). The "first Principle in the soul" was therefore "moved to speculate itself in the devil's imagination . . . to contemplate in the magical birth how and what evil and good were . . . in the unlikeness of the essence" (*MM* 18.28). With this "Adam's free-will in the fiery attraction became infected . . . by which a first will to individual desire arose" (*EOG[E]* 6.14). The "earthly lust to eat of the manifold properties did arise in the outward part of the soul;

and in the inward fiery part of the soul the lust of pride did arise" (*MM* 18.29). While "yet in Paradise," Adam "brought his imagination into the earth" (*MM* 17.39), and "his will departed out of the equal concord into the multiplicity of the properties" (*MM* 17.37). His "hunger . . . drew forth the Tree of Temptation" (*MM* 18.31): "For the essence in the Tree of the Knowledge of Good and Evil, and the hunger of the desire in Adam, were alike; what he desired was represented unto him by the Fiat; Adam's imagination was the cause of it" (*MM* 17.40).

At this point in the movement out of the temperature Adam "did not eat thereof in the mouth, only with the imagination or desire did he eat thereof" (*MM* 18.32). However, "the outward man did awake in him, and obtained the dominion" (*MM* 18.33), and Adam "discovered himself in the great Deep of the Kingdom of this World." He "fell into Lust" (*TP* 17.54), "the Form of this World" (*TP* 12.54) "took hold of him, as a Mother makes a Mark upon a Child in the Mother's Womb" (*TP* 17.54), and he "lost his clear pure steady eyes and sight, which was from the divine essence" (*MM* 18.33). In other words, Adam "broke himself off from God" and became "blind as to God, and saw neither God nor the Virgin any more in his Mind" (*TP* 17.54). The "heavenly image of the angelical world's essence did disappear" (*MM* 19.3): Sophia or the "Virgin departed" (*TP* 13.2). He then "became feeble as to the Kingdom of God, and so fell down and slept" (*TP* 17.54). His sleep is a movement "into an unability, which signifieth the death: for the image of God, which is immutable, doth not sleep" (*MM* 19.4), and "his heavenly Body became Flesh and Blood" (*TP* 13.2). His decline is further marked by the decision to "make . . . an help meet for him,"[3] the "Woman of this World" who is "built [or formed] out of him" (*TP* 17.55). Eve replaces Sophia: "*Adam* has lost the Virgin by his Lust, and has received the Woman in his Lust" (*TP* 12.60). The original union of male and female in the divine androgyne thus divided into two separate beings: "Eve was half the Adam, viz. the part wherein Adam should have loved and impregnated himself" (*MM* 18.11).

Adam "slept in the angelical world, and awaked to the outward world" (*MM* 19.4). He "saw his wife Eve standing before him . . . and [he] cast the property of his desire upon her, as he had done before when he loved himself" (*MM* 20.1). While Adam and Eve "were made into creatures of the outer world" (*EOG[E]* 6.46), the "Body had not then such hard Grisles and Bones" as it has now (*TP* 13.13). They "both stood yet in Paradise, in the garden of Eden, and knew neither evil nor good" (*MM* 20.2). They were "yet in innocence" (*TP* 17.31) and "the heavenly image . . . did yet live both in Adam and Eve, but in a very obscure and impotent manner" (*MM* 19.24). Nonetheless, as "Eve was half the Adam" her "essence was . . . already somewhat poisoned and infected by Adam's imagination" (*MM* 20.23). When the serpent "saw Eve, he then knew his insinuated desire in her," knew that she "did . . . long after the fruit of the Tree of the Knowledge of Good and Evil" and tempted her (*MM* 20.5, 22). Here "Eve's desire and the devil's desire were espoused" (*MM* 20.24), and she "laid hold on the Tree, and broke off [an Apple,] and did eat of the Fruit of the four Elements and Stars, and gave to *Adam;* and when *Adam* saw that *Eve* died not, then he eat also" (*TP* 17.57). With the eating of the apple "the heavenly part of man" (*MM* 20.26) fully disappeared and the "divine light . . . was extinct" (*SR* 7.19). However, Boehme adds that "we are {not} to understand that man's heavenly ens {divine spark, essence} became nothing; it remained in man, but it was as 'twere a nothing to man in its life; for it stood hidden in God" (*MM* 20.28). God's "cursing is a withdrawing . . . into its own principle" (*SR* 7.19). By it Adam and Eve "saw the Paradise no more, but the Garden in Eden" and they "could set no Will [or Desire] into it" (*TP* 17.59).

With the complete closure of the divine light man's eyes opened fully "to the kingdom of Nature" (*EOG[E]* 7.6), and Adam and Eve "knew that they had Flesh and Blood, and were quite naked" (*TP* 17.58). The "Spirit of this World" overwhelmed them (*TP* 17.60), and the "flesh became gross, hard, thick and corruptible" (*MM* 21.3). Adam "saw that he had a bestial Form" and "was ashamed of his monstrous Form [or Shape] and hid himself behind the Trees in the Garden" (*TP* 10.6). While "the Spirit of this World held the Body," "the Abyss of Hell held the Soul" (*TP* 17.61): "the wrath of God's anger did awake in the monstrous image, viz. the properties of the dark world" (*MM* 20.31). The "awakening of the anger" in Adam and Eve (*MM* 20.38) revealed the contrariety that lies at the core of Boehme's vision, a contention that was also manifested in the world outside Adam. That is, "the one element did manifest and put forth itself into four properties," and "each property desired . . . an essence out of and according to itself" (*MM* 11.17). The fallen world of the third principle both arises through Adam and reflects his Fall.

Blake's view of the movements behind man's Fall have been seen in the falls, divisions, and contentions of the Zoas, emanations, and Albion. Similarly, the source of the earthly and the "Tree of Temptation" appears in Blake's repeated use of "he became what he beheld / He became what he was doing He was himself transformd" (*FZ* 338, pl. 4, ll. 286–87). "The Bible says that God formed Nature perfect but that Man perverted the order of Nature" (*Ann. Wat.* 614). The self-willing movement into the "unlikeness of the essence," into "the multiplicity of the properties" that brings with it the appearance of good and evil may be seen at the beginning of *Jerusalem.* While "the Saviour" appears "spreading his beams of love,"

> the perturbed Man away turns down the valleys dark;
> [*Saying. We are not One: we are Many, thou most simulative*]
> Phantom of the over heated brain! Shadow of immortality!
> Seeking to keep my soul a victim to thy Love.
>
> (*Jer* 146, pl. 4, ll. 4–5, 22–24)

As this movement of the "lust of pride" is accompanied in Adam by an "earthly lust," in which the female "Form of this World" captivated and overwhelmed him, Blake's Vala emerges as the "form / That drew the body of Man from heaven into this dark Abyss" (*FZ* 340, Night 5, ll. 46–47). Blake shared Boehme's view that the outward spirit of the third principle "took hold" of Adam "as a Mother makes a Mark upon a Child in the . . . Womb" and that "the soul was moved to speculate itself in the devil's imagination . . . in the magical birth":

> The nature of a Female Space is this: it shrinks the Organs
> Of Life till they become Finite and Itself seems Infinite.
>
> And Satan vibrated in the immensity of the Space! Limited
> To those without but Infinite to those within.
>
> (*Milton* 104, pl. 10, ll. 6–9)

The "heavenly image" of Sophia thus leaves "the perturbed Man" through his own selfhood and vanity. He announces "Jerusalem is not!," "My mountains are my own, and I will keep them to myself!": "So spoke Albion in jealous fears, hiding his Emanation / . . . dissembling / His jealousy before the throne divine, darkening, cold!" (*Jer* 147, pl. 4, ll. 27–35). Following Boehme, this "overshadowing" of Man is arrived at in stages. Although Jerusalem had originally been "assimilating in one with Vala" (*Jer* 164, pl. 19, ll. 40–51) Albion cast his desire into the latter. As Jerusalem says to Vala:

> Albion lov'd thee! He rent thy Veil! he embrac'd thee! he lov'd thee!
> . . . .
> I redounded from Albions bosom in my virgin loveliness.
> The Lamb of God reciev'd me in his arms he smiled upon us:
> He made me his Bride and Wife; he gave thee to Albion.
>
> (*Jer* 165–66, pl. 20, ll. 36–40)

This was "as yet" "a time of love" (166, pl. 20, l. 41). The opening of *Jerusalem* suggests how far Albion has declined since that "time." Jesus speaks of this to him:

> the Divine Vision is darkened:
> Thy Emanation that was wont to play before thy face,

Beaming forth with her daughters into the Divine bosom
Where hast thou hidden thy Emanation lovely Jerusalem
From the vision and fruition of the Holy-one?
(146, pl. 4, ll. 13–17)

Jerusalem is hidden through the "darkening" of Albion's "clear pure steady eyes," as the "Grain of Sand . . . that Satan cannot find."

Albion has therefore become "feeble as to the Kingdom of God" and subject to necessity: "Refusing to behold the Divine image which all behold / And live thereby. he is sunk down into deadly sleep" (Cancelled lines from *FZ* 825, Night 1). He has moved into the sleep of Adam, the "unability, which signifieth death": "Behold these sickning Spheres," "I am weary, and must sleep in the dark sleep of Death" (*FZ* 313, Night 2, ll. 3, 6). As the outward world overcame Adam Albion is the "sleeper of the land of shadows" (*Jer* 146, pl. 4, l. 6), the "shadows" being the forms reflected "in the great Deep of the Kingdom of this World." He is "our Ancestor . . . whose History Preceded that of the Hebrews and in whose Sleep <or Chaos> Creation began" (*VLJ* 558); that is, the creation of Genesis. As "Flesh and Blood" first became apparent in Adam's sleep, Blake also wrote that the "Corporeal <and Mortal> Body . . . originated with the Fall" (*VLJ* 564). Milton enters into "his own Shadow; / A mournful form double; hermaphroditic: male and female / In one wonderful body" (*Milton* 108, pl. 14, ll. 36–38). His "real and immortal Self . . . appeard . . . / . . . as One sleeping" and his "heavenly Body" became earthly: "Like as a Polypus that vegetates beneath the deep! / . . .his Shadow vegetated underneath the Couch of death" (*Milton* 109, pl. 15, ll. 8–11). As Adam grows "blind as to God" and yet the "divine light" remains "in its own Principle" eternally, Milton is fed "with food of Eden in his cold and dim repose! / But to himself he seemd a wanderer lost in dreary night" (*Milton* 109, pl. 15, ll. 15–16).

The separation of the divine androgyne into the "Flesh and Blood" of male and female divides Los. With the creation of the body of Urizen in seven ages Los's "dark visions" are of "dark separation":

At length in tears and cries imbodied
A female form trembling and pale
Waves before his deathy face

All Eternity shudderd at sight
Of the first female now separate.
(*BU* 78, pl. 15, ll. 1–13; pl. 18, ll. 6–10)

The "Feminine separates from the Masculine and both from Man, / Ceasing to be His Emanations, Life to Themselves assuming!" (*Jer* 249, pl. 90, ll.

1–2). Lusting as the "inward man" does after the earthly, Los is "Lured by" Enitharmon's "beauty outside of himself" (*Jer* 245, pl. 86, l. 60). She is "the part wherein" Los "should have loved and impregnated himself," as she herself remarks: "In Eden our loves were the same here they are opposite" (*Jer* 246, pl. 87, l. 17). Adam "has lost the Virgin by his Lust, and has received the Woman in his Lust." When Albion desires Vala instead of Jerusalem,

> a double form Vala appeard. A Male
> And female shuddring pale the Fallen Man recoild
> From the Enormity and calld them Luvah and Vala. turning down
> The vales to find his way back into Heaven but found none
> For his frail eyes were faded and his ears heavy and dull.
> (*FZ* 358, Night 7, ll. 246–50)

In *Milton* Orc asks the "Shadowy Female," "When wilt thou put on the Female Form as in times of old," "like the Garment of God"; "Jerusalem is his Garment and not thy Covering Cherub O lovely / Shadow of my delight" (112, pl. 18, ll. 34–38). As Adam "slept in the angelical world, and awaked to the outward world" the third principle may be seen as that which is dreamed by the "inward Man." It is the "dreary night" of which the "immortal" Milton dreams: "As when a man dreams, he reflects not that his body sleeps, / Else he would wake; so seem'd he entering his Shadow" (*Milton* 109, pl. 15, ll. 1–2). This again marks the separation of the principles. Where Adam "awoke" and "saw his wife," Enitharmon is seen as "a vegetated mortal Wife of Los: / His Emanation, yet his Wife till the sleep of death is past" (*Jer* 158, pl. 14, ll. 12–13). Nonetheless, the bodies first created for Los and Enitharmon were not of "such hard Grisles and Bones" as now. Although "Shrunk into fixed space . . . / . . . mighty bulk and majesty and beauty remaind" (*FZ* 339, Night 5, ll. 11–13). The "heavenly image . . . did yet live . . . but in a very obscure and impotent manner." The desire that Adam cast upon Eve while "yet in Paradise," "in innocence," participates in the forming of the male and female bodies. Los and Enitharmon "wanderd hand in hand like two Infants . . . / . . . terrified at each others beauty / Envying each other yet desiring, in all devouring Love" (*Jer* 246, pl. 86, ll. 62–64). Enitharmon is seen by Los "Filling with Fibres from his loins" and his "wild fibres shoot in veins / Of blood thro all" his "nervous limbs" (245, pl. 86, l. 51; 246, pl. 87, ll. 5–6).

Enitharmon asserts her "individual desire" here: "I will seize thy Fibres and weave / Them: not as thou wilt but as I will"; "I have Loves of my own" (*Jer* 246, pl. 87, ll. 12–13, 18). This is an assertion of the self-will that first "poisoned and infected" the androgynous Adam, and that led to its separation into the "Two Wills," masculine and feminine. The "individual desire" of the "Female Will" precipitates the fall into "the four elements and stars." Vala's "joy and love" are "a shade of sweet repose: But animated and vegetated, she is a devouring worm" (*Jer* 155, pl. 12, ll. 2–3). The "devouring worm" speaks here of the "espousal" of "Eve's desire and the devil's desire" through the serpent. Blake picks up on this in *A Vision of the Last Judgment*, arguing that the eating of the knowledge of good and evil is "for Satan's Gratification" (565). As "the heavenly part of man" and the "divine light" fully disappeared with the eating of the apple, and as the fallen world of the third principle is as a dream to the "real and immortal Self," Los's "eternal life / Like a dream was obliterated" (*BU* 77, pl. 13, ll. 33–34). The Eternals announce in respect of Los and "the first female form":

> "Spread a Tent, with strong curtains around them
> "Let cords and stakes bind in the Void
> That Eternals may no more behold them"
>
> They began to weave curtains of darkness.
>
> (*BU* 78, pl. 19, ll. 2–5)

With the departure of the "divine power . . . into its own principle," "The Visions of Eternity, by reason of narrowd perceptions, / Are become weak Visions of Time and Space, fixd into furrows of death" (*Jer* 198, pl. 49, ll. 21–22).

Man's eyes closed to the divine and opened to the "kingdom of Nature" and "Flesh and Blood." Fallen, Blake's "Adam is only The Natural Man and not the Soul or Imagination" (*Laocoön* 273). Because Adam and Eve became conscious of and therefore captive to their earthliness, "He who sees the Infinite in all things sees God. He who sees the Ratio only sees himself only" (*NNR* 3). The correspondence between the shrinking of the senses and the world has been discussed. The relationship is described in *Europe*:

> when the five senses whelm'd
> In deluge o'er the earth-born man; then turn'd the fluxile eyes
> Into two stationary orbs, concentrating all things.
> The ever-varying spiral ascents to the heavens of heavens
> Were bended downward; and the nostrils golden gates shut
> Turn'd outward, barr'd and petrify'd against the infinite
>
> (63, pl. 10, ll. 10–15)

Blake underlines the source of the Fall in *The Four Zoas*, that Adam and Eve "could set no Will [or desire]" into the Deity:

> every one opend within into Eternity at will
> But they refusd because their outward forms were in the Abyss
> . . . .

the eyelids quiverd
Weak and Weaker their expansive orbs began shrinking.
(350–51, Night 6, ll. 252–57)

Overwhelmed by the "Spirit of this World" and "naked," Man thus appears to the "Selfhood" to be "Creeping in reptile flesh upon the bosom of the ground" and each of the senses "comprehending great, as very small" (*Jer* 198, pl. 49, ll. 33, 37).

The "bestial Form" of man thus became apparent and he hid himself in shame "behind the Trees in the Garden":

man fled from its face and hid
In forests of night; then all the eternal forests were divided
Into earths rolling in circles of space, that like an ocean rush'd
And overwhelmed all except this finite wall of flesh.
(*Eur* 63, pl. 10, ll. 17–20)

Shame itself, as consciousness of the earthly body, extinguishes the "divine light": "Shame siezd us, we could not look on one-another for abhorrence: the Blue / Of our immortal Veins and all their Hosts fled from our Limbs" (*Jer* 169, pl. 24, ll. 7–8). Likewise, "Albions Sons" build "A Strong / Fortification against the Divine Humanity and Mercy, / In Shame and Jealousy to annihilate Jerusalem" (*Jer* 174, pl. 28, ll. 25–27). With this Albion turns

his back to the Divine Vision, his Spectrous
Chaos before his face appeard: an Unformed Memory.

Then spoke the Spectrous Chaos to Albion darkning cold
....

I am your Rational Power O Albion and that Human Form
You call Divine, is but a Worm seventy inches long
That creeps forth in a night and is dried in the morning sun.
(*Jer* 175, pl. 29, ll. 1–7)

The separation of Boehme's Man from the principle of Light thus suggests Blake's Spectre. As the "heavenly ens," the divine essence that remains in the fallen man is hidden to the earthly, "the Reasoning Spectre / Stands between the Vegetative Man and his Immortal Imagination" (*Jer* 178, pl. 32, ll. 23–24). Milton realizes this, that the Spectre is "a false Body: an Incrustation over my Immortal / Spirit; a Selfhood" (*Milton* 142, pl. 40, ll. 34–36). As the third principle "held the Body," the first "held the Soul" as a "monstrous Form" or "image":

Thou knowest that the Spectre is in Every Man insane brutish
Deformd that I am . . . a ravening devouring lust continually
Craving and devouring but my Eyes are always upon thee O lovely
Delusion and I cannot crave for any thing but thee . . .
for I am as the Spectre of the Living
For till these terrors planted round the Gates of Eternal life
Are driven away and annihilated we never can repass the Gates.
(*FZ* 360, Night 7, ll. 297–303)

The "awakening of the anger" in Adam and Eve reveals the contention and wrath that arise through the first principle, and which bar "the Gates of Eternal Life" to man. Jerusalem distinguishes between the fallen and unfallen body and in so doing points to Boehme's bar or limit:

The Infant Joy is beautiful, but its anatomy
Horrible ghast and deadly! nought shalt thou find in it
But dark despair and everlasting brooding melancholy!
(*Jer* 167, pl. 22, ll. 22–24)

Man's "exteriors are become indefinite opend to pain / In a fierce hungring void" (*FZ* 312, Night 1, ll. 543–44). With this in view Albion addresses his "Children," suggesting the awakened enmity of the first and second principles: "are you born to feed the hungry ravenings of Destruction / To be the sport of Accident! to waste in Wrath and Love" (*Jer* 169, pl. 24, ll. 14–15). Adam's and Eve's Fall revealed the contrariety that lies at the heart of Boehme's vision. Los

Filled with doubts in self accusation beheld the fruit
Of Urizens Mysterious tree . . . Enitharmon thus spake

When in the Deeps beneath I gathered of this ruddy fruit
It was by that I knew that I had Sinnd and then I knew
. . . .
That Life lives upon Death and by devouring appetite
All things subsist on one another.
(*FZ* 369, Night 7, ll. 383–89)

The "hungry" contention between the properties gives shape to that between male and female. Through it Blake presents a perverse and divided "shadow" of the state in which the divine androgyne "loved and impregnated himself":

Los saw the Female and pitied
He embrac'd her, she wept, she refus'd

In perverse and cruel delight
She fled from his arms, yet he followd

Eternity shudder'd when they saw,
Man begetting his likeness,
On his own divided image.

(*BU* 79, pl. 19, ll. 10–16)

As the Fall manifests the contention of the properties in the world outside Adam, Ololon asks in *Milton*

How are the Wars of Man which in Great Eternity
Appear around, in the External Spheres of Visionary Life
Here renderd Deadly within the Life and Interior Vision
How are the Beasts and Birds and Fishes, and Plants and Minerals
Here fixd into a frozen bulk subject to decay and death[?]
Those visions of Human Life and Shadows of Wisdom and Knowledge

Are here frozen to unexpansive deadly destroying terrors.

(134–35, pl. 34, ll. 50–55; pl. 35, l. 1)

The responsibility lies with man. His Fall from the temperature of the inward world disrupts that which held the outward. With Adam's exile "outside himself" "the Starry Heavens are fled from the mighty limbs of Albion" (*Jer* 171, pl. 27, "To the Jews"). They are "drivn forth" by his "disease" (*Jer* 166, pl. 12, ll. 5–10). The awakened enmity of the properties "separated the stars from the mountains: the mountains from Man / And left Man, a little grovelling Root, outside of Himself" (*Jer* 162, pl. 17, ll. 31–32). This state of exile is seen among the "Peoples and Nations of the Earth": "Their eyes their ears their nostrils and tongues roll outward they behold / What is within now seen without they are raw to the hungry wind" (*FZ* 314, Night 2, ll. 54–55).

Paradoxically, the very exile of man "outside of Himself" confines him to himself. Blake writes of the fallen "children": "Beyond the bounds of their own self their senses cannot penetrate / As the tree knows not what is outside of its leaves and bark" (*FZ* 347, Night 6, ll. 94–95). This is the "curse" or "withdrawing" of the "divine power . . . into its own principle" through which the four elements are at enmity with each other:

the Four Zoas who are the Four Eternal Senses of Man
Became Four Elements separating from the Limbs of Albion

. . . .

And they divided into Four ravening deathlike Forms.

(*Jer* 178, pl. 32, ll. 31–32)

The one pure element contained within the body of the "Quintessence" separates and

> all the Living Creatures of the Four Elements, waild
> With bitter wailing . . .
> . . . .
> These are the God's of the Kingdoms of the Earth: in contrarious
> And cruel opposition: Element against Element, opposed in War
> Not Mental, as the Wars of Eternity, but a Corporeal Strife.
> (*Milton* 130, pl. 31, ll. 17–18, 23–25)

Each Zoa desires "an essence out of and according to itself," and their fall mirrors the collapse of Boehme's elements into "the centre of Nature":

> All fell towards the Center in dire ruin, sinking down.
> And in the South remains a burning fire; in the East a void.
> In the West, a world of raging waters; in the North a solid.
> (*Milton* 112–13, pl. 19, ll. 21–23)

Urizen's "children" similarly emerge out of the "monstrous image" as the four elements, Thiriel as air, Utha as water, Grodna as earth, and Fuzon as fire. Urizen "in darkness clos'd, view'd all his race / And his soul sicken'd! he curs'd / Both sons and daughters" (*BU* 81, pl. 23, ll. 8–18, 22–24). In Albion's "Chaotic State of Sleep, Satan and Adam and the whole World was Created" (*Jer* 171, pl. 27, "To the Jews"). "Satan and Adam" represent the "Limits" to the Fall.

12

Incarnation and Judgment

MERCY

While the falls of Adam and Lucifer are similar in that they both "entered into a self-fullness" the nature of the desire of each distinguishes the two: "the Devil made himself Hell, and that he has; and Adam made himself Earth, and that he is" (*ToI* 1.5.82). Lucifer was thrown into "the Kingdom of *Phantasy*, into the Darkness," whereas Adam was cast "into . . . the Creation, into the *bestial* Property" (*EOG* 6.50). In this the created world or third principle appears as an act of Mercy and as a limit to Man's Fall: "*Adam* might have been a Devil; but the outward Looking-Glass hindered that" (*FQ* 16.13). While the devil is "shut up" eternally in the first principle and can reach only part of the third, "God created man out of three Principles in one, that . . . he did not live wholly in the place of Lucifer, that so he might help him" (*MM* 17.33). As seen the "heavenly ens" was "shut up" in Adam. The "divine love-will would not forsake this disappeared angelical matrix" (*MM* 11.19) and would "generate the new Man in the Soul, which is hidden in the old" (*TP* 10.5):

> as the Devil's Word had spoken itself into the Soul, so the Word of the Love of God came and spake itself again into the faded *Ens.*
>
> Signifying thereby, that it is an Aim, Mark, or Limit, of an Eternal *gracious* Covenant, wherein God's Love, in the name JESU, would destroy the *Works* of the Devil. (*EOG* 7.39–40)

Eve is associated with the light of the second principle, "the Son's property" (*MM* 19.16–17) and as such the Covenant is realized or born through her. She is the "Mother of all Men" (*EOG* 7.48): in "*Eve* Sin began, and in *Eve* also *Grace* began" (*EOG* 7.61). Man is not predestined to share the devil's state of "Eternal Death." As the "new Man" lies "hidden in the old" the "outward life . . . is most profitable to us" (*FQ* 16.7): "the powers of eternity do work through the powers of time" (*MM* 12.29). The soul is therefore "still powerful . . . It can by magic alter all things whatsoever that are in the outward world's essence, and introduce them into another essence" (*MM*

17.43). As the "inward Ground of the Soul" arising out of the liberty of the *Ungrund* "is neither Evil nor Good" (*EOG* 8.275), "every Man is *free*, and is as a *god* to himself; in this life man may *change* and alter himself either into wrath or into light" (*Aur* 18.43). "*We* ourselves are God's Will to Evil and Good" (*EOG* 8.288). Equally, "God is *no* Creature, also *no* Maker, but a Spirit and an *Opener*" (*ToI* 1.5.83).

Blake also perceived the "Limit" that prevents man's fall into the condition of the devil. While "the torments of Eternal Death, waited on Man," he is saved from the "endless curse" by "the Merciful-One, for he is of tender mercies" (*Jer* 182, pl. 36, ll. 25–30, 43). Urizen beholds Heaven and the merciful movement from the *meonic* to the actual. He sees

> The wondrous work flow forth like visible out of the invisible
> For the Divine Lamb Even Jesus who is the Divine Vision
> Permitted all lest Man should fall into Eternal Death
>
> . . . .
>
> Thus were the stars of heaven created like a golden chain
> To bind the Body of Man to heaven from falling into the Abyss.
>
> (*FZ* 321–22, Night 2, ll. 260–67)

Whatever "is visible to the Generated Man, / Is a Creation of mercy and love, from the Satanic Void" (*Jer* 157, pl. 13, ll. 44–45). As the devil aspires above the separation of the principles and thus the division of the male and female, Los labors

> To Create a World of Generation from the World of Death:
> Dividing the Masculine and Feminine: for the comingling
> Of Albions and Luvahs Spectres was Hermaphroditic.
>
> (*Jer* 207, pl. 58, ll. 18–20)

Separate but in conjunction with Los, Enitharmon's "Looms vibrate with soft affections, weaving the Web of Life / Out from the ashes of the Dead" (*Milton* 100, pl. 6, ll. 28–29). "The Ruins of Time builds Mansions in Eternity" (*Letters* 705). In his labors Los speaks of the mercy of the created:

> O holy Generation! [*Image*] of regeneration!
> O point of mutual forgiveness between Enemies!
> Birthplace of the Lamb of God incomprehensible!
>
> (*Jer* 150, pl. 7, ll. 65–67)

Working through Boehme's vital distinction between Adam and Satan, Los participates in the creation of the "Limits":

> Luvahs World of Opakeness grew to a period: It
> Became a Limit, a Rocky hardness without form and void
> Accumulating without end: here Los, who is of the Elohim
> Opens the Furnaces of affliction in the Emanation
> Fixing The Sexual into an ever-prolific Generation
> Naming the Limit of Opakeness Satan and the Limit of Contraction
> Adam.
>
> (*Jer* 228, pl. 73, ll. 22–28)

The "World of Opakeness" speaks of the "*Phantasy*" and "Darkness" of the devil's condition, and that of "Contraction" of man's entrance into "hard Matter," from or through which the "powers of eternity" can expand in the cycles of contraction and expansion drawn by the seven properties. Notably, the "Two Limits" of Adam and Satan are established in *Milton* in the election of the Seven Eyes of God, and as a result

> the Elect shall say to the Redeemd. We behold it is of Divine
> Mercy alone! of Free Gift and Election that we live.
> Our Virtues and Cruel Goodnesses, have deserv'd Eternal Death.
>
> (107, pl. 13, ll. 32–34)

The "inward Ground of the Soul . . . is neither Evil nor Good." Thus Blake writes that "in every human bosom these limits stand" and that they were established "While yet those beings {Adam and Satan} were not born nor knew of good or Evil" (*FZ* 338, Night 4, ll. 272–75).

The "divine love-will would not forsake" Man:

> I see Albion sitting upon his Rock in the first Winter
> And thence I see the Chaos of Satan and the World of Adam
> When the Divine Hand went forth on Albion in the mid Winter
> And at the place of Death when Albion sat in Eternal Death
> Among the Furnaces of Los.
>
> (*Jer* 159, pl. 15, ll. 30–34)

The "new man" watches over the "faded *Ens*" of the "old":

> as the Will must not be bended but in the day of Divine
> Power: silent calm and motionless, in the mid-air sublime,
> The Family Divine hover around the darkend Albion.
>
> (*Jer* 186, pl. 39, ll. 18–20)

Blake gives expression to the Grace of the "living Eternal Word" (*EOG* 7.38) in "To the Jews." The "Human Form"

became a Mortal Worm:
But O! translucent all within.

The Divine Vision still was seen
Still was the Human Form, Divine
Weeping in weak and mortal clay
O Jesus still the Form was thine.

And thine the Human Face and thine
The Human Hands and Feet and Breath
Entering thro' the Gates of Birth
And passing thro' the Gates of Death.
(*Jer* 173, pl. 27, ll. 53–64)

The "Gates of Birth" and "Death" point to the Covenant established in Eve:

> There is a limit of Opakeness, and a limit of Contraction;
> In every Individual Man . . .
> . . . .
> the Saviour in mercy takes
> Contractions Limit, and of the Limit he forms Woman: That
> Himself may in the process of time be born Man to redeem
> But there is no Limit of Expansion! There is no Limit of Translucence.
> In the bosom of Man for ever from eternity to eternity.
> (*Jer* 189, pl. 42, ll. 29–36)

Blake's view that there is "no Limit of Expansion" echoes Boehme's that "every Man is free, and is as a God to himself." That which Man desires forms the object of his belief. Thus, though more antinomian than Boehme, Blake writes that "Satan thinks that Sin is displeasing to God he ought to know that Nothing is displeasing to God but Unbelief and Eating of the Tree of Knowledge of Good and Evil" (*VLJ* 564). Blake understood that the "inward Ground of the Soul . . . is neither Evil nor Good," that man should not be "talking of what is Good and Evil" but "Conversing with Eternal Realities as they Exist in the Human Imagination" (*VLJ* 562). The eating of the Tree of Knowledge made man "blind as to God": "Questions concerning Good and Evil . . . hinder the Vision of God" (*VLJ* 554). God is "a Spirit and an *Opener*": "O search and see: turn your eyes inward: open O thou World / Of Love and Harmony in Man: expand thy ever lovely Gates"(*Jer* 187, pl. 39, ll. 41–42).

However, as the contrariety between good and evil is necessary to life and "the one cannot be without the other" (*MM* 11.15), "good and evil . . . have each of them their usefulness, *the evil as well as the good*" (*TP* 9.13). Boehme saw the "stinging" pain and anguish of the dark world as necessary in that they drive man beyond them. As the second principle is man's "proper own," the first and third are to him sources of "Woe, Misery, Sorrow, and Distress; for he is not in his native Country . . . Therefore the poor Soul must thus be plagued and tormented, that it may attain its native Country again" (*TP* 17.73). The created is a goad to imaginative activity. This sense of revelation through contrariety proposes, from the point of fallen man, the necessity of the Fall. Given that man is fallen he must have a myth through which he can recognize it. Equally, the Fall prepares the way for the entrance of Grace in the Incarnation, and Redemption. This again stresses the mercy of Creation, that the eternal may redeem man in or through time. Sophia manifests "herselfe through the thornes of God's anger, as a faire Rose on a thorny Bush" (*Ep* 23.2).

Blake perceived in Chaucer's Pardoner and Summoner the embodiment of the understanding that without the "stinging" "poison . . . there is no Life":

> the pardoner . . . is sent in every age for a rod and scourge, and for a blight, for a trial of men . . . he is suffered by Providence for wise ends, and has also his great use, and his grand leading destiny.
>
> His companion the Sompnour, is also a Devil of the first magnitude . . . The uses to society are perhaps equal of the Devil and of the Angel, their sublimity who can dispute. (*DC* 535)

The "sublimity" of this view extends to that of the poet's art: "the grandest Poetry is Immoral . . . Poetry is to excuse Vice and shew its reason and necessary purgation" (*Ann. Boyd* 634). "Falshood" is given a body "that it may be cast off for ever" (*Jer* 155, pl. 12, l. 13). "All Life consists of these Two Throwing off Error . . . continually and recieving Truth . . . Continually . . . to be an Error and to be Cast out is a part of God's Design" (*VLJ* 562). This again extends to Blake's vision of his work: "No man can Embrace True Art till he has Explored and Cast out False Art" (*VLJ* 562). "The Combats of Truth and Error is Eating of the Tree of Life" (*VLJ* 563). With this in mind Milton announces "I will go down to self annihilation and eternal death," that "All that can be annihilated must be annihilated" (*Milton* 108, pl. 14, l. 22; 142, pl. 40, l. 30). The necessity of Milton's descent into "Eternal death" again proposes that of the Fall. Similarly, as Man attains revelation and Grace through contrariety, Mary declares in *Jerusalem:*

> if I were pure, never could I taste the sweets
> Of the Forgiven[ne]ess of Sins! if I were holy! I never could behold the tears
> Of love! of him who loves me in the midst of his anger in furnace of fire.
> . . . .

O Mercy O Divine Humanity!
O Forgiveness and Pity and Compassion! If I were Pure I should never
Have known Thee; If I were Unpolluted I should never have
Glorified thy Holiness, or rejoiced in thy great Salvation.
(211–12, pl. 61, ll. 11–13, 43–46)

None can "consummate bliss without being Generated / On Earth" (*Jer* 245, pl. 86, ll. 42–43). "Time is the mercy of Eternity; without Times swiftness / Which is the swiftest of all things: all were eternal torment" (*Milton* 121, pl. 24, ll. 72–73).

INCARNATION

As the "living Eternal Word . . . came of meer Grace, and spake itself again into the faded *Ens* of the heavenly World's Substance" (*EOG* 7.38) in man, the necessity of the Fall brings with it the necessity of the Incarnation. Viewed eternally, the Incarnation is finally inseparable from the Fall, both being part of the eternally cyclic "Band" of the seven properties. As the Word speaks through the cycles of the seven, the "Voice of Grace ... assumed" in man "a Soul." This "Voice of Grace in the Voice of Christ" calls to the soul that lies "shut up in Darkness" (*EOG* 10.63). In other words, "none can see God, unless God become first man in him, which is brought to pass in faith's desire" (*SR* 11.88). Boehme writes of Christ, "in respect of the Deity he is no Creature; but in respect of the Heavenly Essence . . . he is in the Humanity creaturall, and without the Humanity uncreaturall" (*Ep* 2.54). That "which he introduced out of the Deity into the humanity, that is neither nature nor creature, yet in our humanity formatively . . . immense, uncircumscribed" (*MM* 37.44). Christ "became a God-man . . . God and man one person undivided" (*MM* 37.32). He reveals the imaginative bridge between the divine and the human. The "divine love-will" would "by the *Fiat* generate the new Man in the Soul, which is hidden in the old" and Christ is the "Second Adam." "Paradise is *revealed to us again in Christ*" (*Ep* 8.27). That which "disappeared in *Adam* . . . must born again through Christ" (*MM[L]* 8.15), who wills "the true Ground of the first generated Soul . . . wherein the Voice of God lyes" (*EOG* 9.194). Beginning and end meet in Christ. As Adam "fell asleep to the divine world" (*EOG[E]* 6.42), "the new regenerate life in Christ's humanity must enter into Adam's sleep, and awaken it again to the eternal life, and bring it out of time into the eternal" (*MM* 19.5). Christ "became man in the woman's part, and brought the man's part again into the holy matrix, so that {the two} . . . were again one image, viz. a manly virgin" (*MM* 19.17). Through Christ "Adam receiveth again into his arms his most precious and endeared bride," Sophia (*MM* 25.14).

What "Adam had merited as a malefactor, Christ himself must take upon him in Adam's person, and bring again the life out of death" (*MM* 23.9). This is again the cross-birth. It is on the cross that Christ accomplishes the "redemption of our virgin-like image from the divided sex of male and female" (*MM* 19.7). He must on the cross "drink down" the "wrathful anger, which was awakened in Adam's essence, into his holy heavenly ens, and change it with great love into divine joy" (*MM* 23.5). As Adam "exalted his own will . . . the humanity of Christ upon the Cross must give this own self-will unto the anger for to devour it" (*MM* 23.7). Christ therefore "entered into the image of the first Adam" (*SR* 12.7). Boehme makes an important distinction in respect of the crucifixion: "we must not think, that the holy Man in Christ died, for that died not; but the mortal [Man] from the Kingdom of the World [is that which died]" (*TP* 22.46).

The importance of Christ's Incarnation lies in that it is primarily eternal rather than temporal. Man is therefore to act with or through Christ. The "new *birth* is not a grace imputed from without," and the soul "must be Regenerated upon the Cross of Christ" (*TLM* 11.49). Every "man hath Christ in him; but the own-will doth not apprehend Christ, but it crucifieth him, and will not die to its selfness" (*MM* 51.11). However, "the Son of the Virgin hath regenerated us again on the Cross to a Heavenly Image" (*TLM* 5.34). An essential part of the necessity of the Fall and Incarnation lies in man's dependence on Christ: "God's word became Man, that it might unite him into God again, that he might be *totally* born again in God" (*ToI* 1.4.24). This brings with it a potent view of man's "station": "Let none climb above the Cross, or if he does, he will fall into Hell to the Devil" (*FQ* 1.347). The human must and can only be human. The cross-birth "united the human time with eternity" (*SR* 11.70). It is the point at which the divine and the human meet: "the Soul is from the Eternal, and the external from Time" (*MM[L]* 8.15). All "men are but one man, Adam. God created only him, and the other creating he left to man" (*MM* 71.31). Similarly, "the most inward Ground *in* Man is CHRISTUS, *Christ*," not "according to the Nature of Man, but according to the *Divine* Property in the heavenly substance" (*EOG* 7.98). "Christ is born in the faith *in us*" (*MM* 52.9), and "Faith is nothing else but the uniting of one's will to God . . . that so both these, viz. God's will and man's will, become both one substance and essence" (*MM* 39.8).

The *Ungrund* is unfathomable. No "man hath ever seen God; the Sonne alone who is in the unmeasurable bosome of the Father, declareth unto us the Word and Will of God in our selves" (*Ep* 1.10). The "soul cannot see God, save only in its new-born image: only through and in virgin Sophia . . . in the name of Jesus" (*MM* 52.10). Again, "none can see God, unless God become first man in him." Such a view makes possible the statement that "the Son is many thousand times Greater than the Father" (*TLM* 6.98). From this Boehme argues that "If *Christ* be *not* in the Soul, there is no Grace nor Forgiveness of Sins in it," for "Christ himself is the Forgiveness of Sins" (*EOG* 13.37–38). To regard this another way, "when God fogiveth thee thy sins, when thou callest upon him, he taketh nothing away from thee, neither doth he fly down from Heaven into thee for *He is from Eternity in thy soul*, but in his own Principle; thy soul as to him is only gone out from his Principle" (*TLM* 11.54).

Christ's desire to awaken man from "Adam's sleep" is given form in Blake's "Divine Lamb," who must "drink down" the "wrathful anger" and of necessity takes on the fallen man's "Humanity":

> when Luvah sunk down himself put on the robes of blood
> Lest the state calld Luvah should cease. and the Divine Vision
> Walked in robes of blood till he who slept should awake.
> (*FZ* 321, Night 2, ll. 261–65)

As Milton's descent "to Eternal Death" suggests the necessity of the Fall, and as this necessity is finally inseparable from that of the Incarnation, he moves through the "passage" Christ "hath made . . . through the Death and Anger to the Majesty of God" (*TLM* 11.54), through the Incarnation (*Milton* 108–9, pl. 14, ll. 14–42; pl. 15, ll. 1–16). His search for his Emanation and "the daughters of inspiration" (108, pl. 14, ll. 28–29) similarly suggests the necessary reunion of the male and female. As the "Voice of Grace" calls to the soul "shut up in Darkness," that which lies hidden in the "old" man returns the call with a hunger for the restoration of man's pristine state:

> in the cries of birth and in the groans of death his voice
> Is heard throughout the Universe whereever a grass grows
> Or a leaf buds The Eternal Man is seen is heard is felt
> And all his Sorrows till he reassumes his ancient bliss.
> (*FZ* 385, Night 8, ll. 580–83)

This desire may be seen as the beginning of the Incarnation, the movement of Faith through or in man. The "Voice of Christ" is also heard in the "Introduction" of *Songs of Experience*, in an invocation of the "moment" in which beginning and end meet:

> Hear the voice of the Bard!
> Who Present, Past, and Future sees
> Whose ears have heard,

The Holy Word,
That walk'd among the ancient trees.

Calling the lapsed Soul

(18, ll. 1–6)

The conjunction of the "voice of the Bard" and the "Holy Word" here points to the union of the divine and the human in the "ancient tree" of the cross-birth.

Christ became a "God-man" and must take upon him "what Adam had merited as a malefactor": "Sin was begun in Eternity, and will not rest to Eternity / Till two Eternitys meet together" in one (*Milton* 107, pl. 13, ll. 10–11). End and beginning must meet in the second Adam. The "Divine Vision" thus recalls the "liberty and life" of Jerusalem that "were as Adam before me: united into One Man" (*Jer* 210, pl. 60, ll. 10, 16). In *The Four Zoas* the "Eternal Man" asks "When shall the Man of future times become as in days of old?" (389, Night 9, l. 115). The "new Man . . . hidden in the old" is seen in the "Shadowy Eighth" "Eye" or "Image Divine" that "hid in Albions Forests" (*Milton* 114, pl. 20, l. 47; 109, pl. 15, ll. 1–7; *Jer* 205, pl. 55, l. 33). The eighth opens with the fulfillment of the Incarnation and the awakening of Man "again to the eternal life" (*Milton* 143, pl. 42, ll. 7–15). As "Christ became man in the woman's part, and brought the man's part again into the holy matrix," and "the Son of the Virgin hath *regenerated* us again in the Cross to a Heavenly Image,"

Los said to Enitharmon Pitying I saw
Pitying the Lamb of God Descended thro Jerusalems gates
To put off Mystery time after time and as a Man
Is born on Earth so was he born of Fair Jerusalem
In mysterys woven mantle and in the Robes of Luvah

He stood in fair Jerusalem to awake up into Eden
The fallen Man but first to Give his vegetated body
To be cut off and separated that the Spiritual body may be Reveald.

(*FZ* 378, Night 8, ll. 260–67)

Man must enter into the union with Sophia that distinguished the "Nature of Man" from the "*Divine* Property of the Heavenly Substance," and thus through Christ cast off Adam's self-will:

Crave not for the mortal and perishing delights, but leave them
To the weak . . . Break not
Forth in your wrath lest you also are vegetated by Tirzah
. . . .

> . . . rush forward with me into the glorious spiritual
> Vegetation; the Supper of the Lamb and his Bride; and the
> Awaking of Albion our friend and ancient companion.
> (*Milton* 122, pl. 25, ll. 56–62)

The "Sexes must vanish and cease / To be, when Albion arises from his dread repose" (*Jer* 252, pl. 92, ll. 13–14).

Blake's man is "redeemd and born" in Jerusalem's "spiritual palaces / By a New Spiritual birth Regenerated from Death" (*FZ* 391, Night 9, ll. 223–34). Accordingly, as Christ would "bring again the life out of death" through the cross-birth, Blake writes in *Milton* that

> Jesus, the image of the Invisible God
> Became . . . a curse, an offering, and an atonement,
> For Death Eternal in the heavens of Albion, and before the Gates
> Of Jerusalem his Emanation.
> (96, pl. 2, ll. 12–15)

This mirrors Christ, who "took on Sin in the Virgins Womb, and put it off on the Cross" (*Milton* 98, pl. 5, l. 3). Boehme's distinction between the "mortal" and the "holy Man" is drawn in the "Universal Humanity." The

> Universal Humanity who is One Man blessed for Ever
> Recievest the Integuments woven Rahab beholds the Lamb of God
> She smites with her knife of flint She destroys her own work
> Times upon times thinking to destroy the Lamb blessed for Ever
> He puts off the clothing of blood he redeems the spectres from their bonds
> He awakes the sleepers in Ulro.
> (*FZ* 377, Night 8, ll. 232–37)

The love-will that is "the true Ground of the first generated Soul" is then evoked:

> we now behold
> Where Death Eternal is put off Eternally
> Assume the dark Satanic body in the Virgins womb
> O Lamb divin[e] it cannot thee annoy O pitying one
> Thy pity is from the foundation of the World and thy Redemption
> Begun Already in Eternity.
> (377, Night 8, ll. 339–44)

Christ

> in his Body tight does bind
> Satan and all his Hellish Crew
> And thus with wrath he did subdue

The Serpent Bulk of Natures dross
Till he had naild it to the Cross.
(*EG* [i] 524, ll. 50–54)

Insofar as "we are with *Adam*, gone forth from the image of the Cross," Los comes to recognize that "the own-will . . . crucifieth" Christ within man: "O Rahab I behold thee I was once like thee a Son / Of Pride and I also have piercd the Lamb of God in pride and wrath" (*FZ* 380, Night 8, ll. 354–55). Such recognition is attained through the "Heavenly Image" that works through man's "humanity formatively . . . immense, uncircumscribed." As "we are created upon the Cross as to our soul," Blake's Jesus declares, "if God dieth not for Man and giveth not himself / Eternally for Man Man could not exist" (*Jer* 256, pl. 96, ll. 25–26). Blake understood that man is dependent on Christ's cross-birth and that the "soul cannot see God, save only in its new-born image": "the dear Saviour . . . took on the likeness of men: / Becoming obedient to death, even the death of the Cross" (*Milton* 118, pl. 22, ll. 57–58). Likewise, "Albion mildest Son of Eden"

is himself become
A piteous example of oblivion. To teach the Sons
Of Eden, that however great and glorious; however loving
And merciful the Individuality; however high
Our palaces and cities, and however fruitful are our fields
In Selfhood, we are nothing: but fade away in mornings breath.
Our mildness is nothing . . .
. . none but the Lamb of God can heal
This dread disease: none but Jesus! O Lord descend and save!
(*Jer* 187, pl. 40, ll. 8–16)

Christ "himself is the Forgiveness of Sin." This view of the eternal in the temporal is also expressed by "the Sons of Eden":

Glory Glory Glory to the holy Lamb of God
Who now beginneth to put off the dark Satanic body
Now we behold redemption Now we know that life Eternal
Depends alone upon the Universal hand and not in us
Is aught but death In individual weakness sorrow and pain.
(*FZ* 376, Night 8, ll. 195–99)

The "Sonne alone . . . declareth unto us the Word and Will of God in our selves." Los understands this and says to Enitharmon,

I see thee like a shadow withering
As on the outside of Existence behold! take comfort!

> Turn inwardly thine Eyes and there behold the Lamb of God.
> (*FZ* 369, Night 7, ll. 412–15)

It is through the union of "God's will and man's will" as "one substance and essence" that the Saviour says at the beginning of *Jerusalem,*

> Awake! awake O sleeper of the land of shadows, wake! expand!
> I am in you and you in me, mutual in love divine:
> . . . .
> I am not a God afar off, I am a brother and a friend;
> Within your bosom I reside, and you reside in me:
> Lo! We are One.
> (146, pl. 4, ll. 6–7, 18–21)

In short, "God becomes as we are, that we may be as he is" (*NNR* 3). The present tense is vital. Through the cross–birth, the entrance of the eternal in the temporal, the "God-man" is Incarnated in the eternal now. The "Bride the Lambs Wife loveth thee: / Thou art one with her and knoweth not of self in thy supreme joy" (*Jer* 155, pl. 12, ll. 41–42).

Man's dependence on the cross-birth speaks of the necessity of Christ's humanity, which finds its beginning and end in the cross. Man should not "climb above the Cross" as he should not aspire "above" that which is revealed in the humanity of the "God-man." All who "come unto God, they come to him in Christ" (*MM* 40.60). Urizen has fallen "into Hell, to the Devil" when he announces in *The Four Zoas,* "I will walk forth thro these wide fields of endless Eternity / A God and not a Man a Conqueror in triumphant glory / And all the Sons of Everlasting shall bow down at my feet" (360, Night 7b, ll. 8–10). Seeing "the monstrous forms that breed among" his "silent waves," the fallen Tharmas declares, "Is this to be A God far rather would I be A Man" (*FZ* 334, Night 4, ll. 145–46). As seen, when Gods are "separated from man or humanity, who is Jesus the Saviour . . . they are destroyers" (*DC* 536). Los speaks of this and the restoration of the temperature in Christ:

> If Gods combine against Man Setting their Dominion above
> The Human form Divine. Thrown down from their high Station
> In the Eternal heavens of the Human Imagination: buried beneath
> In dark Oblivion with incessant pangs . . .
> . . . .
> They must renew their brightness and their disorganizd functions
> Again reorganize till they resume the image of the human
> Cooperating in the bliss of Man obeying his Will
> Servants to the infinite and Eternal of the Human form.
> (*FZ* 395, Night 9, ll. 366–74)

The "Son is many thousand times Greater than the Father." Luvah encapsulates the importance of the cross-birth: "Attempting to become more than Man We become less" (*FZ* 403, Night 9, l. 708). God "*is from Eternity in thy Soul*," as Los understands, speaking for the four Zoas: "in the Brain of Man we live, and in his circling Nerves. / . . . this bright world of all our joy is in the Human Brain" (*FZ* 306, Night 1, ll. 293–94). As "Christ himself is the Forgiveness of Sins" in man, Blake writes that "Forgiveness of Sin is only at the Judgment Seat of Jesus the Saviour where the Accuser is cast out." The "Accuser is cast out" because he would deny the unity of Christ and man: "he torments the Just and makes them do . . . what he knows is opposite to their own Identity" (*VLJ* 565).

THE LAST JUDGMENT

The "new birth" of or in Christ brings with it Judgment. The "seven heads of the beast are the seven properties of nature, which are departed from the temperature, and have attained seven wills" (*MM* 76.26). They are also "*hidden seals*," the seven seals of Revelation, "and *there was none in heaven . . . nor in this world, that was able to break open these seven Seals*," save Christ (*TLM* 3.43, 56). This again shows the necessity of the Incarnation, which breaks open the seals "by the Light of the Heart of God, in the *Center* of the human soul" (*TLM* 3.58). That is, they are opened or "manifested through the humanity of Christ" (*TLM* 3.43). The "*Glassy Sea before the Throne of the Ancient [of Days,]* who is God the Father . . . is the seventh seal, but *opened*" through Christ: "it is brought to *Essence*, by the Word" (*TLM* 3.44). That is, in the seventh property "all things are brought into their end, viz. into the first day of the beginning of all essences." The "seventh day was from eternity without and beyond all time . . . in it the eternal wisdom of God is manifest . . . in which the Deity worketh" (*MM* 16.27). This brings Boehme's visionary scheme full circle to God's first movements out of the *Ungrund*. Through Christ Man is brought into a relationship with the Nothing, into a love-play in which "the creature . . . stands at the end of nature with its life" (*MM* 24.27). Whatever does not reach "the holy element and the eternal fire-world, that, is devoid of an eternal life" and "is consumed and eaten up" (*MM* 8.14). Our "Souls are immortal" (*TP* 27.1) and "at the Last Judgment Day . . . the right Adamical body of the five senses shall come again to the soul; but the grossness or dross of the earthly body hath no more place" (*MM* 72.18).

God "appointed the final Judgment in the *spiritus mundi*, to separate the evil and the good, and to gather in all things, every one into its own Principle" (*EOG[E]* 6.22): "all things shall be proved through the fire. What kind of property every one hath in this time assumed to himself, and impressed on his body (viz. with the desire of the Fiat), that shall be tried in the fire" (*MM* 24.6). This refers again to the free will that is at work in Lucifer and Adam. God has not "ordained a certain number and company to damnation, and the rest to salvation" (*MM* 40.49). Just as man should not "climb above the Cross," "nothing falls into judgment that remains in its order unto which it was created" (*EOG[E]* 9.54). Thus the separation or distinction between time and eternity. That which lives in the eternal light is not realized at some point in the future. It lives there in the eternal now. As Berdyaev understood, "the end of time cannot be within time."[1] Again, the "seventh day was from eternity without and beyond all time." The "soul standeth in three Principles . . . And if this were not, then it could not be said, the soul went into heaven or hell, if they were not in it" (*MM* 18.24). The "*true heaven* is everywhere, even in that very place where thou standest and goest" (*Aur* 19.26). Through this the Last Judgment is everpresent and in the Resurrection man "shall enter again into the first created divine image" (*EOG[E]* 5.33).

Boehme's vision of "the seven heads of the beast," which are "the seven properties . . . departed from the temperature," is echoed in Blake's of "the Great Red Dragon with Seven heads" that would "Create the Seven Headed Kingdoms": "its Brain incloses a reflexion / Of Eden all perverted" (*VLJ* 558; *Jer* 248, pl. 89, ll. 14–15). The restoration of the temperature by the opening of the seven seals is reflected in the ninth Night of *The Four Zoas*, where the Last Judgment reverses the movements that brought about the fallen Creation, drawing in all that God "has brought forth through his Word" in seven days, culminating in the "first day" of the seventh. The breaking open of the seven seals "by the Light of the Heart of God" is seen in Blake's "Saviour . . . The Human Imagination . . . Coming to Judgment . . . and throwing off the Temporal that the Eternal might be Establishd" (*VLJ* 555). Following Boehme's view that the "earthly body" is one of "grossness or dross," he understood that Man cannot "live in Paradise and Liberty . . . till after the Last Judgment." This speaks of the necessity of the Judgment of the cross-birth: the mortal body "cannot be removed but by a Last judgment" (*VLJ* 564). At the end of *Jerusalem*, when the "Time was Finished," the lightning stroke of the cross-birth awakens Albion to the "right Adamical body of the five senses":

> The Breath Divine went forth over the morning hills Albion arose
> In anger: the wrath of God breaking bright flaming on all sides around
> His awful limbs: into the Heavens he walked clothed in flames
> Loud thundring, with broad flashes of flaming lightning and pillars
> Of fire.
>
> (254–55, pl. 94, l. 18; pl. 95, ll. 5–9)

In *The Four Zoas* Blake presents in similar terms the awakening of

> the trembling millions into flames of mental fire
> Bathing their limbs in the bright visions of Eternity
>
> . . . .
> . . . the just man stands erect and looking up to heavn
> Trembling and strucken by the Universal stroke the trees unroot.
> (387, Night 9, ll. 43–44, 50–51)

As Adam's desire first "drew forth the Tree of Temptation" the "tree of Mystery went up in folding flames" (*FZ* 388, Night 9, l. 70). When Urizen arises

> he shook his aged mantles off
> Into the fires Then glorious bright Exulting in his joy
> He sounding rose into the heavens in naked majesty.
> (*FZ* 391, Night 9, ll. 190–92)

His entrance into the light of the second principle is made possible by the separative activity of Boehme's eternal fire of Judgment. At the beginning of the ninth Night of *The Four Zoas,*

> Los and Enitharmon builded Jerusalem weeping
> Over the Sepulcher and over the Crucified body
> Which to their Phantom Eyes appear'd still in the Sepulcher
> But Jesus stood beside them in the Spirit Separating
> Their Spirit from their body.
> (386, Night 9, ll. 1–5)

Judgment is an eternal rather than temporal event in which the mortal is "consumed" and the "hellish" consigned eternally to the darkness. Blake's vision of the Last Judgment is one in which

> Satan is seen falling headlong wound round by the tail of the serpent whose bulk naild to the Cross round which he wreathes is falling into the Abyss . . . Death is Chaind to the Cross and Time falls together with death dragged down. (*VLJ* 556)

The Judgment separates "the evil and the good . . . every one into its own Principle": "The Graves beneath are opend and the Dead awake and obey the call of the Trumpet those on the Right hand awake in joy those on the Left in Horror" (*VLJ* 558). The "call" is that of the "Voice of Christ."

As the separation of the principles distinguishes "What kind of property everyone hath in this time assumed to himself," Los speaks to the "Labourers of the Vintage" of the seventh day in which "the eternal wisdom of God is manifest" eternally:

> The Great Vintage and Harvest is now upon Earth
> . . . .
> All the Wisdom which was hidden in caves and dens, from ancient
> Time; is now sought out from Animal and Vegetable and Mineral
> The Awakener is come . . . the Vision of God is fulfilled
> The Ancient Man upon the Rock of Albion Awakes,
> . . . .
> Therefore you must bind the Sheaves not by Nations or Families
> You shall bind them in Three Classes; according to their Classes
> So shall you bind them. Separating What has been Mixed
> . . . .
> . . . every one remains in his own energy.
> (*Milton* 121–22, pl. 25, ll. 17–28, 43)

In "Eternity one Thing never Changes into another Thing Each Identity is Eternal" (*VLJ* 556). The soul is responsible for its own fate, and the "Last Judgment . . . is seen by the [*Imaginative Eye*] of Every one according to the situation he holds"; "to different People it appears differently" (*VLJ* 554, 555). The "Living Creatures" speak of this in *Jerusalem*: "let every Man be Judged / By his own Works" (*Jer* 205, pl. 55, ll. 57–58). In the Judgment of *The Four Zoas* the dead appear with what they have "impressed" upon themselves in life: "every one of the dead appears as he had livd before / And all the marks remain" (392, Night 9, ll. 245–46). This movement occurs "without and beyond time," as Urizen comes to see:

> Go O dark futurity I will cast thee forth from these
> Heavens of my brain nor will I look upon futurity more
> I cast futurity away and turn my back upon that void
> Which I have made for lo futurity is in this moment.
> (*FZ* 390, Night 9, ll. 180–83)

As "nothing falls into Judgment that remains in its order unto which it was created," the "Lions" of Urthona ask in the last lines of *The Four Zoas*:

> How is it we have walkd thro fires and yet are not consumd
> How is it that all things are changd even as in ancient times.
> (407, Night 9, ll. 844–45)

The light of the eternal now is "not consum'd," and the Last Judgment is everpresent: "whenever any Individual Rejects Error and Embraces Truth a Last Judgment passes upon that Individual" (*VLJ* 562). This insight makes possible the personal experience of the Judgment in "Felphams Vale" at the end of *Milton*:

> Terror struck in the Vale I stood at that immortal sound
> My bones trembled. I fell outstretchd upon the path
> A moment, and my Soul returnd into its mortal state
> To Resurrection and Judgment in the Vegetable Body
> And my sweet Shadow of Delight stood trembling by my side.
> (143, pl. 42, ll. 24–28)

Blake's "Eternals" "enter again" with Boehme's properties "into the first created divine image," the Lord's Supper and the articulate harmony of the temperature. They

> embracd the New born Man
> Calling him Brother image of the Eternal Father. they sat down
> At the immortal tables sounding loud their instruments of joy
> Calling the Morning into Beulah.
> (*FZ* 402, Night 9, ll. 643–46)

The "Morning" suggests Boehme's Aurora: "When man converteth . . . and casteth away the vanity, and steppeth into the infant's shirt, then the Morning-Star ariseth in the spirit of Christ" (*MM* 25.5). Blake's Bard understands that the fallen man "need only to *turn*" again to the eternal light of the divine principle:

> Turn away no more:
> Why wilt thou turn away
> The starry floor
> The watry shore
> Is giv'n thee till the break of day.
> (*SoE* 18, "Introduction," ll. 16–20)

Enion similarly declares her Faith:

> I said the time of Love
> Appears upon the rocks and hills in silent shades . . .
> A voice came in the night a midnight cry upon the mountains
> Awake the bridegroom cometh I awoke to sleep no more.
> (*FZ* 384, Night 8, ll. 538–41)

The millenarian midnight cry is heard in Boehme: "the Time is come for us to awake from the Sleep of Antichrist. Christ comes with the fair Lily out of Paradise . . . It is Time for them to trim their Lamps that will go to the marriage" (*TP* 9.17). As "the fair Lily" is Wisdom he also declares "Bring forth the New Jerusalem: It is Day" (*ToI* 1.6.24). At the end of *Jerusalem* Blake exhorts the return to God's first movements:

> Awake! Awake Jerusalem! O lovely Emanation of Albion
> Awake and overspread all Nations as in Ancient Time
> For lo! the Night of Death is past and the Eternal Day
> Appears upon our Hills: Awake Jerusalem, and come away.
> (256, pl. 97, ll. 1–4)

Vala also hears the "Voice of Christ," calling from the "place" of the seventh property:

> Whose voice is this in the voice of the nourishing air
> In the spirit of the morning awaking the Soul from its grassy bed
> Where dost thou dwell for it is thee I seek and but for thee
> I must have slept Eternally nor have felt the dew of thy morning
> Look how the opening dawn advances with vocal harmony
> Look how the beams foreshew the rising of some glorious power
> The sun is thine he goeth forth in his majestic brightness
> O thou creating voice that callest and who shall answer thee
>
> Where dost thou flee O fair one where dost thou seek thy happy place
>
> To yonder brightness there I haste for sure I came from thence
> Or I must have slept eternally nor have felt the dew of morning.
> (*FZ* 396, Night 9, ll. 393–403)

Envisioning the moment in which the seventh seal is opened and the "*Glassy Sea*" "brought to *Essence*, by the Word," Blake writes at the end of *The Four Zoas*:

> The Sun has left his blackness and has found a fresher morning
> And the mild moon rejoices in the clear and cloudless night
> And Man walks forth from midst of the fires the evil is all consumd
> . . . .
> The Expanding Eyes of Man behold the depths of wondrous worlds
> One Earth one sea . . .
> . . . .
> He walks upon the Eternal Mountains raising his heavenly voice
> Conversing with the Animal forms of wisdom night and day
> That risen from the Sea of fire renewd walk oer the Earth.
> (406, Night 9, ll. 825–37)

The Last Judgment makes possible the "converse in the spirit . . . with spirits," as Boehme himself understood:

Dear Sirs and brethren, let us give the honour to Christ . . . Let one show forth his gifts to another in a brotherly will. For there are various kinds of knowledge and exposition; and if only they proceed from the mind of Christ, they are all rooted in one ground.

We should not on account of dissimilar gifts persecute one another, but rather rejoice with each other in love that God's wisdom is so inexhaustible; and think of the future, how it will be well with us when all this knowledge shall be manifested from one and in one soul, so that we shall all recognize God's gifts and have our joy in one another, every one rejoicing in the gift of another, as the fair flowers in their various colours and virtues rejoice in one mother side by side upon the earth. So likewise will be our resurrection and reappearance. (*EOG[E]* 13.20–21)

Conclusion

Boehme did influence Blake. The extent of his influence, however, can only be known by entering imaginatively into the spirit through which both worked. The influence is there because that which worked through Boehme also worked through Blake and not least because Boehme gave the creative spirit individual, personal form. His visionary scheme is not a simple or direct description of the movements of divinity, or of what divinity is or is not, but a medium for approaching it, a similitude. That which is embodied or expressed in the movements of his system was at work between him and Blake. As significant correspondences with the poet have been seen in each aspect or step of Boehme's scheme, from the activities of the *meonic* realm, of will, desire, and imagination, of time and eternity, through those of the seven properties and three principles, to the Fall and Creation, Incarnation, and Judgment, from beginning to end, the "form or frame" of Boehme's system may itself be seen to have been a structure of support and guidance. For both the relationship between man and God is continually moving and the imagination the fullest way of exploring this. Thus the close and necessary correspondence between the creative and the spiritual, and between Blake and Boehme. Boehme's significance is not simply a matter of the provision of the "Contents" of ideas, symbols, or themes, of mere borrowing and adaptation. Something of the character, the feel, emotional force, and aesthetics—in which the sensory and sensual merge—of Boehme "appeard" in Blake's writings.

A nourishing tradition is part of the necessary "stubborn structure," of the living vision that Blake sought in "I must Create a System or be enslav'd by another Man's." Boehme's inspiration is form giving. This view looks to the future. Exploring the fertile *meonic* mirror of Wisdom, the realm of possibility and potentiality through imagination, Blake and Boehme exhort new discoveries and new forms for the life of the spirit. Both worked against the circumscription of reality. For both reality is inexhaustible and often lies at depths beyond surface appearance, and any predominant form of thought and understanding is only partial. There "is no Limit of Translucence" (*Jer* 189, pl. 42, l. 35). "The word … which began with the beginning of the world, is yet still a creating" (*MM* 10:56).

Notes

INTRODUCTION

1. Robin Waterfield, introduction to *Jacob Boehme: Essential Readings* (Northamptonshire: Crucible, 1989), 27.

2. Warren Stevenson, *Romanticism and the Androgynous Sublime* (Madison, N.J.: Fairleigh Dickinson University Press, 1996), 16.

3. William Law, *Selected Mystical Writings of William Law: Edited with Notes and Twenty-Four Studies In the Mystical Theology of William Law and Jacob Boehme*, edited by Stephen Hobhouse (London: C. W. Daniel, 1938), 173.

CHAPTER 1. BACKGROUND

1. As established by scholars such as Will-Erich Peuckert in *Das Leben Jakob Böhme* (Jena: Eugen Diederichs, 1924) and John Joseph Stoudt in *Sunrise to Eternity: A Study of Jacob Boehme's Life and Thought* (Philadelphia: University of Pennsylvania Press, 1957), Boehme's role as a humble cobbler has been overstressed, as has his lack of learning. A degree of myth arose around Boehme as a result of the uncritical adoration and fanciful embellishments of his early biographers. In particular, the biography by his friend and disciple Abraham von Frankenberg established the misleading view of Boehme's life. This biography was written in 1637 and appears in many editions of Boehme's writings. It was printed in the English translation of the *Forty Questions Concerning the Soul* in 1665 and was the source for many other biographies, including the one that appears in the Law edition of Boehme's works.

2. From a letter to W. T. Horton, quoted by Joseph Hone, *W. B. Yeats: 1865–1939* (London: Macmillan, 1943; reprint, Harmondsworth: Pelican Books, 1971), 156.

3. From Paul Tillich's preface to *Sunrise to Eternity*, by Stoudt, 7.

4. G. W. F. Hegel, *Lectures on the History of Philosophy*, translated by Elizabeth S. Haldane and Frances H. Simpson (London: Kegan Paul, Trench, Trübner and Co., 1896), 3:188.

5. Howard H. Brinton, *The Mystic Will: Based on a Study of the Philosophy of Jacob Boehme* (London: George Allen and Unwin, 1931), 75, quoting Friedrich Schlegel, *Vorlesungen aus den Jahren 1804–1806* (n.p., n.d.), and *Geschichte der alten und neuen Literatur* (n.p., n.d.).

6. Robert F. Brown, *The Later Philosophy of Schelling: The Influence of Boehme on the Works of 1809–1815* (Lewisburg, Pa.: Bucknell University Press, 1977), 274, quoting Friedrich Schelling, *Friedrich Wilhelm Joseph von Schellings sämmtliche Werke* (Stuttgart: J. G. Cota'scher Verlag, 1856–61), 8.13:123–24.

7. Law, *Selected Mystical Writings*, 199.

8. Samuel Taylor Coleridge, *Marginalia*, edited by George Whalley, vol. 12, bk. 1 of *The Collected Works of Samuel Taylor Coleridge* (London: Routledge and Kegan Paul, 1983), 558. Coleridge owned and annotated a copy of the Law edition of Boehme's works—a gift from De Quincey in February 1808. He made extensive notes, particularly to the *Aurora* and *The Three Principles*.

9. Samuel Taylor Coleridge, *The Philosophical Lectures of Samuel Taylor Coleridge*, edited by Kathleen Coburn (London: Pilot Press, 1949), 329.

10. Coleridge, *Marginalia*, vol. 12, bk. 1, 558.

11. Samuel Taylor Coleridge, *Biographia Literaria: Or Biographical Sketches of My Literary Life and Opinions*, edited by James Engell and W. Jackson Bate, vol. 7, bk. 1 of *The Collected Works*, 146–52.

12. Evelyn Underhill, *The Mystics of the Church* (London: James Clarke, n.d.), 214.

13. William Law, *The Way to Divine Knowledge*, vol. 7 of *The Works of The Reverend William Law, M.A.*, 9 vols. (London, 1753–56; reprint, 1892–93), 185.

14. Margaret Lewis Bailey, *Milton and Jakob Boehme: A Study of German Mysticism in Seventeenth-Century England* (1914; reprint, New York: Haskell House, 1964), p61–62, quoting Durand Hotham, trans., *An Introduction to the Teutonick Philosophy* (London, 1650).

15. Richard Baxter, *The Autobiography of Richard Baxter*, abridged by J. M. Lloyd Thomas, edited by N. H. Keeble (London: Dent, 1931), 74.

16. William Ralph Inge, *Christian Mysticism* (London: Methuen, 1899), 278, quoting John Wesley and William Warburton. The source of each work is not given.

17. Brinton, *The Mystic Will*, 62 n., quoting Herman Vetterling, *The Illuminate of Görlitz or Jacob Böhme's Life and Philosophy* (Leipzig: Markert and Peters, 1923), 17.

18. Mona Wilson, *The Life of William Blake* (1927; reprint, London: Granada, Paladin Books, 1978), 57.

19. Henry Crabb Robinson, *Diaries, Reminiscences, and Correspondences of Henry Crabb Robinson*, edited by Thomas Sadler, 3 vols. (London: Macmillan, 1869), 2:305.

20. Ampersands have been extended to "and" throughout.

21. All references to and quotations from Blake's work are from David V. Erdman, ed., *The Complete Poetry and Prose of William Blake*, rev. ed. (New York: Doubleday, Anchor Press, 1982). See the list of abbreviations for the abbreviations of individual works. Text citations give, where appropriate, page, plate, and line numbers. Text citations for *The Four Zoas* give page, Night, and line numbers.

22. The contributions to Blake's relationship to Boehme have been "by degrees," from E. J. Ellis and W. B. Yeats, eds., *The Works of William Blake: Poetic, Symbolic,*

and Critical (London: Quatrich, 1893); J. L. Davis, "Blake and Boehme" (Ph.D. diss., University of Cincinnati, 1933); Milton O. Percival, *William Blake's Circle of Destiny* (New York: Columbia University Press, 1938; reprint, New York: Octagon Books, 1977); through Bruce C. Souders, "The Reappearance of Jacob Boehme in the Work of William Law, William Blake and William Butler Yeats" (master's thesis, Columbia University, 1953); G. E. Bentley Jr., "William Blake and the Alchemical Philosophers" (B. Litt. thesis, University of Oxford, 1954); Kathleen Raine, *Blake and Tradition,* 2 vols. (Princeton: Princeton University Press, 1968); Morton D. Paley, *Energy and the Imagination: A Study of the Development of Blake's Thought* (London: Oxford University Press, 1970); to N. V. P. Franklin, "'His Most Hideous Pilgrimage': The Presence of Jacob Boehme's Christian Theosophy in William Blake's *The Four Zoas*" (master's thesis, University College of Swansea, 1979); David Punter, *Blake, Hegel and Dialectic* (Amsterdam: Rudolphi, 1982); and Bryan Aubrey, *Watchmen of Eternity: Blake's Debt to Jacob Boehme* (Lanham, Md.: University Press of America, 1986).

23. Brown, *The Later Philosophy of Schelling,* 273, quoting Schelling, *Werke,* 4.10:189–90.

24. In his lecture "Justifying One's Valuation of Blake," delivered at Bristol University in 1971 and printed in *William Blake: Essays in Honour of Sir Geoffrey Keynes,* edited by Morton D. Paley and Michael Phillips (Oxford: Clarendon Press, 1973), 80, F. R. Leavis declared: "Let me say bluntly that I am not grateful to Yeats for inaugurating the kind of research of which Miss Kathleen Raine is the recognized high-priestess in our time. Blind to Blake's genius, it generates blindness, and perpetuates a cult that, whatever it serves, doesn't serve Blake or humanity. The notion that by a devout study of Blake's symbolism a key can be found that will open to us a supreme esoteric wisdom is absurd; and to emphasize in that spirit the part played in his life's work by Swedenborg, Boehme, Paracelsus, Orphic tradition, Gnosticism, and a 'perennial philosophy' is to deny what makes him important."

25. Edward Larrissy, *William Blake* (Oxford: Basil Blackwell, 1985), 33.

26. Joseph P. Natoli, *Twentieth-Century Blake Criticism: Northrop Frye to the Present* (New York: Garland, 1982), 176.

27. References to and quotations from Boehme's works are, for the most part, from the English translations by John Sparrow, John Elliston, and Humphrey Blunden, in particular those which make up *The Works of Jacob Boehme, the Teutonic Philosopher, with figures illustrating the principles, left by the Reverend William Law, M.A.,* edited by George Ward and Thomas Langcake, 4 vols. (London, 1764–68). Quotations from *Signatura Rerum* are from *The Signature of All Things and Other Writings,* translated by John Ellistone (Cambridge: James Clarke, 1969); and those from *The Three Principles of the Divine Essence* are from *Concerning the Three Principles of the Divine Essence,* translated by John Sparrow (London, 1648; reprint, Chicago: Yogi Publication Society, 1909). Quotations from *Mysterium Magnum* are on the whole from *Mysterium Magnum or An Exposition of the First Book of Moses Called Genesis,* translated by John Sparrow, edited by C. J. Barker, 2 vols. (London: John M. Watkins, 1965). Use of the Law edition of *Mysterium Magnum* is indicated by *[L]* following the abbreviation of the title. Quotations from

Aurora are from *The Aurora*, translated by John Sparrow, edited by C. J. Barker and D. S. Hehener (London: John M. Watkins, 1960). Additional quotations appear in places from other English translations, namely *De Electione Gratiae and Quaestiones Theosophicae*, translated by John Rolleston Earle (London: Constable, 1930), *[E]* indicating where Earle's translation of *Of the Election of Grace* has been quoted; *Six Theosophic Points and Other Writings*, translated by John Rolleston Earle (New York: Knopf, 1920; reprint, Ann Arbor:University of Michigan Press, 1958); *The Way to Christ*, translated by Peter Erb (New York: Paulist Press, 1978); and *The Key and Other Writings*, translated by P. Malekin and L. Malmberg (Durham: New Century Press, 1988). See the list of abbreviations. Text citations give chapter and paragraph and, where appropriate, part numbers.

28. G. E. Bentley Jr., *Blake Records* (Oxford: Clarendon Press, 1969), 41, quoting Samuel Palmer. No source given.

29. Bentley Jr., *Blake Records*, 41, quoting Frederick Tatham to Francis Harvey, 8 June 1864.

30. See Rufus M. Jones, *Spiritual Reformers in the Sixteenth and Seventeenth Century* (1914; reprint, London: Macmillan, 1928), 213–20 for Sparrow's and Ellistone's views and their role in the dissemination of Behmenism in England.

31. See Margaret Lewis Bailey, *Milton and Jakob Boehme*, 185–91.

32. As Christopher Walton records in his curious but invaluable *Notes and Materials for an Adequate Biography of the Celebrated and Divine Theosopher William Law* (London, 1854), 223, the only translation that is not by Sparrow, Ellistone, or Blunden is Francis Lee's *Of the Supersensual Life*, which forms part of *The Way to Christ*.

33. Crabb Robinson, *Diaries*, 2:305.

34. Morton D. Paley, *The Continuing City: William Blake's Jerusalem* (Oxford: Clarendon Press, 1983), 85. See Matthew Arnold, "The Function of Criticism in the Present Time," in *Essays, Literary and Critical* (1906; reprint, London: J. M. Dent and Sons, 1938), 5.

35. T. S. Eliot, "Blake," in *The Sacred Wood: Essays on Poetry and Criticism* (1920; reprint, London: Methuen, 1948), 157–58.

36. John Howard, *Blake's "Milton": A Study in Selfhood* (Rutherford, N.J.: Fairleigh Dickinson University Press, 1976), 260.

37. Crabb Robinson, *Diaries*, 2:323.

38. Bentley Jr., *Blake Records*, 251, quoting Samuel Taylor Coleridge, in a letter to H. F. Cary, 6 February 1818.

39. Nicolas Berdyaev, *Freedom and the Spirit*, translated by Oliver Fielding Clarke (London: Geoffrey Bles, 1955), 19.

40. Crabb Robinson, *Diaries*, 2:323.

41. Lavater was familiar with Boehme and regarded him as "an inexhaustible gold mine of Germanity and poetry," quoted in Brinton, *The Mystic Will*, 74. No source given.

42. As John Beer, among others has suggested in *Blake's Visionary Universe* (Manchester: Manchester University Press, 1968), 24, much of the poem in the letter to Flaxman may be chronological. That Blake refers to Milton's influence "in

childhood," then to Shakespeare's in "riper year," and that he writes after the naming of Boehme and Paracelsus that "The American War began . . . Then the French Revolution commencd" would appear to support this view. Beer proposes that as "The American War" broke out in 1776 (it in fact began in 1775), Blake might have read all the figures cited before he was eighteen. David Erdman gives further weight to this view in *Prophet Against Empire: A Poet's Interpretation of the History of His Own Times*, rev. ed. (Princeton: Princeton University Press, 1969), 11–12, noting that the four volumes of the Law edition of Boehme's works were published in 1764, 1772, and 1781, that is, in the years preceding and during the American War of Independence. Accordingly, referring to the possible chronological order of the poem, Erdman points toward the significant role that Boehme and Paracelsus might well have played in Blake's early years. He writes of the "awful change": "The change was mighty and perhaps sudden but not unexpected. In the Heavens it was presaged by Paracelsus and Boehme. One gathers that Blake's reading in these murky seers corresponded to a growing awareness of social conflict 'in Hell beneath' . . . The large place assigned by Boehme to evil in the cosmos as necessary to the manifestation of God's goodness; the emphasis of Paracelsus on reversal and change, on the interaction of the opposites forming the alchemical unity of generation: Blake would not incorporate these things into his own world-view until much later, but even now they must have lent a larger and at times fearful significance to his formal studies of 'the exact rules of proportion' and the 'Most Exact grounds and Rules of SYMMETRY.'" That Blake cited Boehme and Paracelsus as guiding spirits when he was forty-three not only suggests the impact each made upon him as a young man, but also highlights the continuance of their presence in his life and work.

CHAPTER 2. BOEHME, BLAKE, AND TRADITION

1. Harold Bloom, *Blake's Apocalypse: A Study in Poetic Argument* (London: Victor Gollancz, 1963), 190. See also 429.

2. Gershom Scholem, *Kabbalah* (New York: Quadrangle/The New York Times Book Company, 1974), 200.

3. Gershom Scholem, *Major Trends in Jewish Mysticism* (Jerusalem: Schocken Publishing House, 1941), 237.

4. A. E. Waite, *The Holy Kabbalah* (Secaucus N.J.: Citadel Press, University Books, n.d.), 225.

5. Scholem, *Kabbalah*, 200.

6. Stoudt, *Sunrise to Eternity*, 39 n.

7. Stoudt, *Sunrise to Eternity*, 95. Boehme might well have been familiar with the works of his contemporary Johann Arndt (1555–1621), particularly through his popular *True Christianity*, which bore the influence of Thomas à Kempis, Tauler, and the *Theologia Germanica*.

8. See Stoudt, *Sunrise to Eternity*, 96. Stoudt notes that Walther became acquainted with Boehme in 1617, during the seven years after the circulation of the

Aurora, when Boehme observed the ban on his writing. Stoudt suggests that "the *Aurora* shows little if any allusion to Jewish mysticism; moreover, Boehme knew merely the contents of the Cabala, the name came later. And Walther gave Boehme the androgynous Adam Cadmon of the Cabala and the *En-Sof* or *Ungrund*, neither of which ideas is in the *Aurora*. Walther may also have brought occult materials to Boehme, for . . . Boehme mentions the *Fourth Book of Ezra*, a popular Cabalist work."

9. Frances A. Yates, *The Rosicrucian Enlightenment* (London: Routledge and Kegan Paul, 1972), xi. As Yates notes (17), Rudolph II's court became a Mecca for such notables as Giordano Bruno, Johannes Kepler, John Dee, and Edward Kelly. Following Alexander Koyré's *The Philosophy of Jacob Boehme* (Paris, 1929), 48 n. 51, she suggests (99), that Boehme might well have been familiar with the activities of this short-lived movement, not least because Walther became physician to the Prince of Anhalt, who was involved in the "Rosicrucian Enlightenment" at Heidelberg, while Boehme himself spent time in Prague.

10. See Jones, *Spiritual Reformers*, chaps. 4, 5, 8, and pp. 154–55, 190–91.

11. Stoudt suggests in *Sunrise to Eternity*, 50–51, that through Moller, Boehme "was brought face to face with Christian mysticism at its medieval best," and that "he organised the 'Conventicle of God's Real Servants,' a group in the true German mystical tradition to which Boehme belonged."

12. Bentley, "William Blake and the Alchemical Philosophers," 47.

13. Hans Popper, "Jacob Boehme's Doctrine of a Natural Language ('*Natursprache*'): With special reference to its influence on Novalis and Others" (Ph.D. diss., Stanford University, 1971), 49.

14. Aubrey, *Watchmen of Eternity*, 5–6.

15. Raine, *Blake and Tradition*, 1:12.

16. A. Keith Walker, *William Law: His Life and Thought* (London: SPCK, 1973), 106, suggests that "John Byrom read Boehme before Law and was content to turn the works of Law suffused with Boehme's influence into verse."

17. Brinton, *The Mystic Will*, 72 n.

18. Walton, *Notes and Materials*, 3.

19. Bailey, *Milton and Jakob Boehme*, 115.

20. Jones, *Spiritual Reformers*, 234.

21. William White, *Emanuel Swedenborg: His Life and Writings*, 2 vols. (London: Simpkin and Marshall, 1867), 1:227. For Lavater, Oetinger, and Okeley see 2:455–59, 2:333, 1:227 respectively.

22. This statement is made in a letter to Dr. Beyer, February 1767, printed in *Documents Concerning the Life and Character of Emanuel Swedenborg*, collected by Dr. J. F. I. Tafel and edited in English by Rev. I. H. Smithson (Manchester: Joseph Haywood, 1841), 168. In an earlier letter to Beyer , dated 25 September 1766, which is printed in the same volume, Swedenborg wrote "Of the writings of Behmen I cannot judge, as I have never read them" (168). As this assertion was subsequently repeated, it would appear that Swedenborg's associate was not at first, at least, convinced.

23. A. E. Waite, *The Holy Kabbalah,* 225, suggests that, like Boehme, Swedenborg seemed to have "discovered" Kabbalism "at first hand." See also Signe Toksvig, *Emanuel Swedenborg: Scientist and Mystic* (London: Faber and Faber, 1949), 289–90.

24. J. H. Overton, *William Law: Nonjuror and Mystic—A Sketch of His Life, Character and Opinions* (London: Longmans and Green, 1881), 423.

25. Erdman, *Prophet Against Empire,* 11–12.

26. Noted by J. F. C. Harrison, *The Second Coming: Popular Millenarianism, 1780–1850* (London: Routledge and Kegan Paul, 1979), 72. Like Blake, Sharp came to dissociate himself from the New Church.

27. See Harvey F. Bellin and Darrel Ruhl, eds., *Blake and Swedenborg: Opposition is True Friendship—An Anthology* (New York: Swedenborg Foundation, 1985).

28. Baxter, *Autobiography,* 74.

29. See Walton, *Notes and Materials,* 149 for a list of Pordage's works. Walton notes that most of his writings were not published in English. *A Compendious View* . . . is a reprint of *A Treatise of Eternal Nature with Her seven Essential Forms . . . by J. P. M. D.* (London, 1681), which is an account of Boehme's philosophy by Pordage, bound with *Theologia Mystica.*

30. See Walton, *Notes and Materials,* 148 for details of Lead's writings.

31. For details of Lee's relationship with and interpretations of Lead, see his letters in Walton, *Notes and Materials,* 188–258.

32. J. H. Overton, *William Law,* 181, 408, 410. It is through Law's copying of these manuscripts that Lee's translation of *Of the Supersensual Life* came to be included in the Law edition.

33. Baxter, *Autobiography,* 74.

34. As Brinton, *The Mystic Will,* 68 n notes, Lodowick Muggleton, for instance, suggested in *Looking Glass for George Fox the Quaker* (n.p., n.d.), 10, that "Jacob Behmont's Books were the chief books that the Quakers bought for there is the Principle or Foundation of their Religion."

35. In *One Blow at Babel in those of the pepole [sic] called Behmenites . . .* (London, 1662) for instance, the Quaker pamphleteer John Anderdon criticised the Behmenists for their continued use of the sacraments and their insufficient understanding of Boehme's theology. While differing with the Quakers over the matter of the sacraments, William Law expressed similar reservations in his view of certain Philadelphians. See Overton, *William Law* 407–8.

36. Bailey, *Milton and Jakob Boehme,* 101.

37. Jones, *Spiritual Reformers,* 221.

38. Robert Barclay, *The Inner Life of the Religious Societies of the Commonwealth* (London: Hodder and Stoughton, 1876), 409–10.

39. Jones, *Spiritual Reformers,* 220.

40. Jones, *Spiritual Reformers,* 221. As Jones acknowledges, Barclay, *The Inner Life,* 213–15, suggests Behmenist echoes in Fox, comparing an extract from Fox's *Journal* to a piece from Boehme's *The Second Book Concerning the Three Principles of the Divine Essence,* concluding that "not only was Fox conversant with Boeh-

men's writings, but appears in his journal to presuppose a knowledge of Boehmen's method of stating spiritual experience."

41. A. Keith Walker, *William Law*, 106.

42. Jones, *Spiritual Reformers*, 224.

43. Harry Emerson Wildes, *Voice of the Lord: A Biography of George Fox* (Philadelphia: University of Pennsylvania Press; London: Oxford University Press, 1965), 35 n.

44. Bailey, *Milton and Jakob Boehme*, 101.

45. Stephen Hobhouse, *William Law and Eighteenth-Century Quakerism: including some unpublished letters and fragments of William Law and John Byrom* (London: George Allen and Unwin, 1927), 185–202. Hobhouse notes that despite initial misgivings, William Law came to have a high regard for Fox and the Quakers, and accords his change of attitude to them to "his growing absorption in the teachings of Boehme, whose doctrine of the inner light was not far removed from that proclaimed by George Fox and his followers" (246). Remarking that "Law's fundamental teachings . . . were so near to the Quaker view of Christianity" (243), Hobhouse suggests that, in turn, Law's works were well received by the Quakers, who continued to include admirers of Boehme among them.

46. Gerrard Winstanley, *Truth lifting up its head above Scandals*, in *The Works of Gerrard Winstanley*, edited by George H. Sabine (New York: Russell and Russell, 1965), 116.

47. George H. Sabine, introduction to *The Works of Gerrard Winstanley*, 22.

48. A. L. Morton, *The World of the Ranters: Religious Radicalism in the English Revolution* (London: Lawrence and Wishart, 1970), 49.

49. Christopher Hill, *The World Turned Upside Down: Radical Ideas during the English Revolution* (London: Temple Smith, 1972), 301–2, quoting T. Hall, *Vindiciae Literarum* (np., nd.).

50. Christopher Hill, *The World Turned Upside Down*, 302.

51. Christopher Hill, *Writing and Revolution in Seventeenth-Century England*, vol. 1 of *The Collected Essays of Christopher Hill* (Brighton: Harvester Press, 1985), 46.

52. Harrison, *The Second Coming*, 21.

53. Walton, *Notes and Materials*, 597. See Harrison, *The Second Coming*, 22.

54. Walton, *Notes and Materials*, 595–96. See also Harrison, *The Second Coming*, 21–22, and Désiré Hirst, *Hidden Riches: Traditional Symbolism from the Renaissance to Blake* (London: Eyre and Spottiswoode, 1964), 238–46.

55. A. L. Morton, *The Everlasting Gospel: A Study in the Sources of William Blake* (London: Lawrence and Wishart, 1958), 35.

56. A. L. Morton, *The Everlasting Gospel*, 36, 33.

57. A. L. Morton, *The World of the Ranters*, 139, notes that many of the sects had applied a political interpretation to the doctrine of the Two Seeds, regarding the poor and oppressed as having descended from the divine seed, and the rich and powerful from the diabolical.

58. See Hill, *The World Turned Upside Down*, 118 n.; and A. L. Morton, *The Everlasting Gospel*, 40.

59. See Hill, *The World Turned Upside Down*, 180–81.
60. Walton, *Notes and Materials*, 142.
61. Harrison, *The Second Coming*, 61–62.
62. Harrison, *The Second Coming*, 17–18, quoting W. B. Harrison, *A Letter* [on] *the Divine Mission of the late Joanna Southcott* (Leeds, 1842), 94.

CHAPTER 3. COMMUNION, THE PROPHETIC, AND THE LIVING BIBLE

1. Due to the great number of parentheses and square brackets within the text of both Blake's and Boehme's works, I have used braces to enclose my interpolations (with the exception of the word *sic* in quotations from their works.
2. Morton D. Paley, *The Continuing City*, 50.

CHAPTER 4. OBSCURITY, DIFFICULTY, AND AWAKENING

1. Peter Malekin, introduction to *The Key and Other Writings*, translated by P. Malekin and L. Malmberg (Durham: New Century Press, 1988), 2.
2. Aubrey, *Watchmen of Eternity*, 16.
3. Num. 24:13.
4. C. G. Jung, *Psychology and Alchemy*, vol. 12 of *The Collected Works*, translated by R. F. C. Hull, edited by Herbert Read, Michael Fordham, Gerhard Adler, and William McGuire (London: Routledge and Kegan Paul, 1953, 15–16.
5. Evelyn Underhill, *Mysticism: A Study in the Nature and Development of Man's Spiritual Consciousness* (London: Methuen, 1911), 81.
6. Walton, *Notes and Materials*, 45.
7. Morton D. Paley, *Energy and the Imagination*, 59, 257.

CHAPTER 5. EXPRESSION, CREATION, AND MANIFESTATION

1. Aubrey, *Watchmen of Eternity*, 47.
2. Caroline F. E. Spurgeon, *Mysticism in English Literature* (Cambridge: Cambridge University Press, 1913), 135.
3. Émile Boutroux, *Historical Studies in Philosophy*, translated by Fred Rothwell (1912; reprint, Port Washington, N.Y.: Kennicat Press, 1970), 180.
4. Christine Gallant, *Blake and the Assimilation of Chaos* (Princeton: Princeton University Press, 1978), 9.
5. Hans Lassen Martensen, *Jacob Boehme: His Life and Teaching*, translated by T. Rhys Evans (London, 1885), 38.
6. W. B. Yeats, *Essays and Introductions* (London: Macmillan, 1961), 163.
7. Bailey, *Milton and Jakob Boehme*, 179.
8. Brinton, *The Mystic Will*, 201–2.

CHAPTER 6. THEOGONY: FROM NOTHING TO SOMETHING

1. Popper, "Jacob Boehme's Doctrine of a Natural Language," 56–58.

2. The *Ungrund* bears certain similarities to the apprehension of divine ineffability that characterizes the mystical *via negativa*, and in particular to the apophatic strain of German mysticism. In *Little Book of Eternal Truth and Little Book of Truth*, translated by J. M. Clark (London: Faber and Faber, 1953), 191–92, Henry Suso speaks of "that which is nothing as compared with all things that one can imagine or express in words. By common agreement, men call this Nothing 'God' . . . {but} if anyone calls Him 'Godhead,' or 'Being' or whatever name one gives Him, they are not appropriate to Him in the sense in which these names are applied to the creatures." Meister Eckhart's thought is particularly significant for this strain of understanding: "God is nameless because no one can say anything or understand anything about him . . . So if I say: 'God is good,' that is not true. . . . And if I say: 'God is wise,' that is not true. . . . If I say 'God is a being,' it is not true; he is a being transcending being and a transcending nothingness," *The Essential Sermons, Commentaries, Treatises, and Defense*, translated by Edmund Colledge and Bernard McGinn (New York: Paulist Press, 1981), 206–7.

3. Émile Boutroux, *Historical Studies on Philosophy*, 183, writes of the *Ungrund:* "In the beginning was being which presupposes nothing anterior to itself; in which, consequently, nothing is essence, or nature, or finite, determinate form: for everything that exists as a determinate thing demands a cause and a reason. We, for our part, can conceive of this being only as the eternal no-thing, the infinite, the abyss, the mystery. Boehme uses the word *Ungrund* to designate this first source of things, meaning thereby that, beneath God, there is nothing to serve him as a foundation, and also that in the first being the ground or reason of things is not yet manifested." It may be misleading to talk of the *Ungrund* in terms of being. Paul Tillich, *Theologian of the Boundaries*, edited by Mark Kline Taylor (London: Collins, 1987), 154, addresses the problem of being and nonbeing: "Parmenides realized that in speaking of nonbeing one gives it some kind of being which contradicts its character as the negation of being. Therefore, he excluded it from rational thought. But in doing so he rendered the realm of becoming unintelligible and evoked the atomistic solution which identifies nonbeing with empty space, thus giving it some kind of being. What kind of being must we attribute to nonbeing? This question has never ceased to fascinate and exasperate the philosophical mind."

4. Nicolas Berdyaev, *The Beginning and the End* (London: Geoffrey Bles, 1952), 109, makes great claims for Boehme's view of the freedom of the *Ungrund*: "Freedom . . . is God himself and it was in the beginning of all things. It would appear that Boehme was the first in the history of human thought to locate freedom in the primary foundation of being, at a greater and more original depth than any being, deeper and more primary than God himself. And this was pregnant with vast consequences in the history of thought. Such an understanding of the primordial na-

ture of freedom would have filled both Greek philosophers and medieval scholastics with horror and alarm." Berdyaev also states, "Everything leads us to the conclusion that being is not the ultimate depth, that there is a principle which precedes the emergence of being and that freedom is bound up with that principle. Freedom is not ontic but meonic. Being is a secondary product and it is always the case that in it freedom is already limited, and even disappears all together" (111).

5. Brinton, *The Mystic Will*, 207.

6. Berdyaev, *The Beginning and the End*, 161.

7. Tillich, *Theologian of the Boundaries*, 155, 147. Tillich adds that this "concept ... underlies most mythologies and is indicated in the chaos, the *tohu-va-bohu*, the night, the emptiness, which precedes creation. It appears in metaphysical speculations as *Ungrund* (Böhme), will (Schopenhauer), will to power (Nietzsche), the unconscious (Hartmann, Freud), *élan vital* (Bergson), strife (Scheler, Jung).... Each ... points symbolically to that which cannot be named. If it could be named properly, it would be a formed being beside other beings" (147).

8. As Aubrey notes, *Watchmen of Eternity*, 18, 22, Boehme's *Ungrund* may be compared to the Kabbalistic *Ein Sof*, the "Infinite" in which "all . . . union and wholeness / are secreted in the secrecy / that cannot be grasped and cannot be known, / ... The only one who knows, yet without knowing, / is the highest desire, concealed of all concealed, Nothingness," *Zohar: The Book of Enlightenment*, translated by Daniel Chanan Matt (Ramsay, N.J.: Paulist Press, 1983), 147. This is the Kabbalistic "Primordial Nothingness," which has "more being than any other being in the world, but since it is simple and all other things are complex compared with its simplicity, in comparison it is called Nothing," David son of Abraham he-Lavan in *Masoret ha-Berit*, quoted by Daniel Chanan Matt in his introduction to the *Zohar*, 34.

9. Stoudt, *Sunrise to Eternity*, 196–97.

10. Jones, *Spiritual Reformers*, 175.

11. Jones, *Spiritual Reformers*, 175.

12. Brinton, *The Mystic Will*, 90, quoting Paracelsus, *Philosophy to the Athenians* (n.p., n.d.), 1.1:2.

13. Jones, *Spiritual Reformers*, 175.

14. Tillich, *Theologian of the Boundaries*, 173: "Potentiality and actuality appear in classical theology in the famous formula that God is *actus purus*, the pure form in which everything potential is actual, and which is the eternal self-intuition of the divine fullness (*pleroma*). In this formula the dynamic side in the dynamics-form polarity is swallowed up by the form side. Pure actuality, that is, actuality free from any element of potentiality, is a fixed result: it is not alive.... The nature of life is actualization, not actuality. The God who is *actus purus* is not the living God.... This situation has induced some thinkers ... to emphasize the dynamics in God to depreciate the stabilization of dynamics in pure actuality. They try to distinguish between two elements in God, and they assert that, in so far as God is a living God, these two elements must remain in tension."

15. Brinton, *The Mystic Will*, 109, 23–24, 26.

16. 2 Pet. 3:8.

17. Rev. 5:6, 1:20.

18. This correspondence is apparent in alchemy, which linked the planets to the seven metals, as Boehme does, and which often regarded the *Magnum Opus* as a seven-fold operation. Paracelsus stated, "it is most necessary to know the steps of transmutation, how many there are. There are not more than seven. . . . If any one ascends that ladder, he will arrive at so wonderful a place that he will see and experience many secrets in the transmutation of natural objects," "Concerning the Nature of Things," in *The Hermetic and Alchemical Writings of Aureolus Philippus Theophrastus Bombast of Hehenheim, Called Paracelsus the Great*, edited by A. E. Waite, 2 vols. (London, 1894), 1:151. Kabbalism similarly speaks of seven palaces or mansions that may be understood as "seven stages of union," A. E. Waite, *The Holy Kabbalah*, 247, 175–77; and of seven "Comrades" who watch over and govern the earth, *Zohar*, 168–69, evoking Zech. 4:10: "these seven; they *are* the eyes of the LORD, which run to and fro through the whole earth."

19. Evelyn Underhill, *Mysticism*, 154.

20. Franklin, "'His Most Hideous Pilgrimage,'" 113.

21. Engels wrote of the quality: " 'Qual' is a philosophical play upon words. Qual literally means torture, a pain which drives to action of some kind; at the same time the mystic Böhme puts into the German word something of the meaning of the Latin *qualitas*; his 'Qual' was the activating principle arising from, and promoting in its turn, the spontaneous development of the thing, relation, or person subject to it, in contradistinction to a pain inflicted from without." From a note to *Socialism: Utopian and Scientific*, quoted in Karl Marx and Friedrich Engels, *On Religion* (Moscow: Progress Publishers, 1957), 255.

22. Emanuel Swedenborg, *A Compendium of the Theological Writings of Emanuel Swedenborg*, edited by Samuel M. Warren (1875; reprint, New York: Swedenborg Foundation, 1979), 270.

23. Emanuel Swedenborg, *A Treatise concerning Heaven and Hell, and of the Wonderful Things therein*, translated by William Cookworthy and Thomas Hartley (London, 1784), 389–90.

24. Paley, *Energy and the Imagination*, 13.

25. Swedenborg, *Compendium*, 687.

26. See Raine, *Blake and Tradition*, 2:23–26, and Aubrey, *Watchmen of Eternity*, 125, 138.

27. See Aubrey, *Watchmen of Eternity*, 107, 117.

28. Thomas R. Frosch, *The Awakening of Albion: The Renovation of the Body in the Poetry of William Blake* (Ithaca: Cornell University Press, 1974), 145.

CHAPTER 7. THE FIRST FOUR PROPERTIES

1. See Franklin, "'His Most Hideous Pilgrimage,'" 154–55, and Aubrey, *Watchmen of Eternity*, 65–67.

2. Aubrey, *Watchmen of Eternity*, 67–69, 114.

3. As Brinton, *The Mystic Will*, 106, writes, "Things develop and grow, inspired by irrational wills and do not move along fixed logical lines. Will, as substratum of nature, manifests itself in all things—stones, vegetables, animals, men . . . blind will is force, either attraction, repulsion or rotation. It becomes conscious life in actualizing an idea."

4. Franklin, "'His Most Hideous Pilgrimage,'" 153–55.

5. Aubrey, *Watchmen of Eternity*, 71–72, 116.

6. See Raine, *Blake and Tradition*, 1:25

7. See Aubrey, "The Influence of Jacob Boehme On the Work of William Blake" (Ph.D. diss., Durham University, 1981), 200.

CHAPTER 8. THE FIFTH AND SIXTH PROPERTIES

1. Aubrey, "The Influence of Jacob Boehme," 237–28.

2. Brinton, *The Mystic Will*, 153.

3. Frosch, *The Awakening of Albion*, 145.

4. Paley, *Energy and the Imagination*, 59.

5. Aubrey, *Watchmen of Eternity*, 147–48.

CHAPTER 9. THE SEVENTH PROPERTY AND THE CYCLES OF THE SEVEN

1. Martensen, *Jacob Boehme*, 75.

2. Raine, *Blake and Tradition*, 2:172–73.

3. Frosch, *The Awakening of Albion*, 181–82: "Man falls in love with his own creation and abandons the labors of Eden in favor of the already accomplished; a single Eternity, or creative act, is universalized." The emanation "is only 'for a time' and needs constantly to be renewed. Jerusalem is available to Albion only in so far as she is continuously changing, and thus Blake depicts her as a flickering form, never final, never one thing only—now city, now woman, now light—but always definite in the moment . . . For Blake . . . the integrated emanation only exists in a first appearance. To try to keep her in that form is to transmute her into the enduring idol Vala . . . to seize upon one image, appearance, act, or system as the gratification of all desire is to grant primacy to an object and to bind all future desires to the pattern of the first." William Law suggested that "Regeneration is not to be considered as a Thing done, but as a State that is progressive, or as a Thing, that is continually doing," Law, *Christian Regeneration*, vol. 4 of *The Works of The Reverend William Law*, 170.

CHAPTER 10. THE FIRST AND SECOND PRINCIPLES

1. Aubrey, *Watchmen of Eternity*, 112–14.

2. Percival, *William Blake's Circle of Destiny*, 36–37.

3. Franklin, "'His Most Hideous Pilgrimage,'" 171–80.

CHAPTER 11. THE THIRD PRINCIPLE

1. Paley, *Energy and the Imagination*, 110.
2. Aubrey, *Watchmen of Eternity*, 110.
3. Gen. 2:18.

CHAPTER 12. INCARNATION AND JUDGMENT

1. Berdyaev, *The Beginning and the End*, 232.

Bibliography

JACOB BOEHME

Collected Works

Ward, George, and Thomas Langcake, eds. *The Works of Jacob Behmen, the Teutonic Philosopher, with figures illustrating his principles, left by the Reverend William Law, M.A.* Translated by John Sparrow, John Ellistone, and Humphrey Blunden. 4 vols. London, 1764–81. This edition contains:

I. *"A Dialogue between Zelotes, Alphabetus, Rusticus, and Theophilus"*
"An Address to the Earnest Lovers of Wisdom"
"The Life of Jacob Behmen"
Aurora
The Three Principles of the Divine Essence

II. *The Threefold Life of Man*
Forty Questions Concerning the Soul … Answered
The Treatise of the Incarnation
The Clavis: or, An Explanation of Some Principle Points and Expressions in His Writings

III. *Mysterium Magnum: or, An Explanation of the First Book of Moses Called Genesis*
Four Tables of Divine Revelation

IV. Signatura Rerum
Of the Election of Grace
The Way to Christ
A Discourse Between a Soul Hungry and Thirsty after the Foundation of Life, the Sweet Love of Jesus Christ and a Soul Enlightened
A Treatise of the Four Complexions
A Treatise of Christ's Testaments, Baptism, and the Supper

Single Editions and Selections

The Aurora. Translated by John Sparrow. London, 1656. Reprint, edited by C. J. Barker and D. S. Hehner. London: John M. Watkins, 1960.

Concerning the Three Principles of the Divine Essence. Translated by John Sparrow. London, 1648. Reprint, Chicago: Yogi Publication Society, 1909.

The Confessions of Jacob Boehme. Edited by W. Scott Palmer. London: Methuen, 1920.

De Electione Gratiae and Quaestiones Theosophicae. Translated by John Rolleston Earle. London: Constable, 1930.

The Epistles of Jacob Behmen. Translated by John Ellistone. London, 1649.

The Forty Questions of the Soul and The Clavis. Translated by John Sparrow. London, 1647. Reprint, edited by C. J. Barker and D. S. Hehner. London: John M. Watkins, 1911.

The High and Deep Searching out of the Threefold Life of Man through or according to the Three *Principles.* Translated by John Sparrow. London, 1650. Reprint, edited by C. J. Barker. London: John M. Watkins, 1909.

Jacob Boehme: Essential Readings. Edited by Robin Waterfield. Northamptonshire: Crucible, 1989.

The Key and Other Writings. Translated by P. Malekin and L. Malmberg. Durham: New Century Press, 1988.

Mysterium Magnum or An Exposition of the First Book of Moses Called Genesis. Translated by John Sparrow. London, 1654. Reprint, edited by C. J. Barker. 2 vols. London: John M. Watkins, 1965.

Of the Incarnation of Jesus Christ. Translated by John Rolleston Earle. Edited by S. R. Webster. London: Constable, 1934.

The Remainder of books written by Jacob Boehme. Translated by John Sparrow. London, 1662.

Signatura Rerum, or The Signature of All Things. Translated by John Ellistone. London, 1651. Reprint, in *The Signature of All Things and Other Writings.* Cambridge: James Clarke, 1969.

Six Theosophic Points and Other Writings. Translated by John Rolleston Earle. New York: Knopf, 1920. Reprint, Ann Arbor: University of Michigan Press, 1958.

Thoughts on the Spiritual Life by Jacob Behmen. Translated by Charlotte Ada Rainy. Edinburgh: Oliphant, Anderson and Ferrier, 1896.

The Way to Christ. Translated by Peter Erb. New York: Paulist Press, 1978.

Criticism, Biography, and Comparative Studies

Alleman, George Mervin. "A Critique of Some Philosophical Aspects of the Mysticism of Jacob Boehme." Ph.D. diss., University of Pennsylvania, 1932.

Anderdon, John. *One Blow at Babel in those of the pepole* [*sic*] *called Behmenites Whose foundation is not upon that of the Prophets and Apostles . . . but upon their own carnal conceptions, begotten in their imaginations upon J. Behmen's writings.* London, 1662.

Aubrey, Bryan. "The Influence of Jacob Boehme On the Work of William Blake." Ph.D. diss., Durham University, 1981.

———. *Watchmen of Eternity: Blake's Debt to Jacob Boehme.* Lanham, Md.: University Press of America, 1986.

Bailey, Margaret Lewis. *Milton and Jakob Boehme: A Study of German Mysticism in Seventeenth-Century England.* 1914. Reprint, New York: Haskell House, 1964. Quoting Durand Hotham, trans. *Introduction to the Teutonick Philosophy.* London, 1650.

Barker, C. J. *Pre-requisites for the Study of Jacob Böhme.* London: John M. Watkins, 1920.

Boutroux, Émile. *Historical Studies in Philosophy.* Translated by Fred Rothwell. 1912. Reprint, Port Washington, N,Y.: Kennicat Press, 1970.

Brinton, Howard H. *The Mystic Will: Based on a Study of the Philosophy of Jacob Boehme.* London: George Allen and Unwin, 1931. Quoting Lodowick Muggleton. *Looking Glass for George Fox the Quaker.* Np., n.d.; Paracelsus. *Philosophy to the Athenians.* N.p., n.d.; Friedrich Schlegel. *Vorlesungen aus den Jahren 1804–1806.* N.p., n.d., and *Geschichte der alten und neuen Literatur.* N.p., n.d.; Herman Vetterling, *The Illuminate of Görlitz or Jakob Böhme's Life and Philosophy.* Leipzig: Markert and Peters, 1923.

Brown, Robert F. *The Later Philosophy of Schelling: The Influence of Boehme on the Works of 1809–1815.* Lewisburg, Pa.: Bucknell University Press, 1977. Quoting Friedrich Schelling. *Friedrich Wilhelm Joseph von Schellings Sämmtlliche Werke.* Stuttgart and Augsburg: J. G. Cotta'scher Verlag, 1856–61.

Davis, J. L. "Blake and Boehme." Ph.D. Diss., University of Cincinnati, 1933.

Franklin, N. V. P. "'His Most Hideous Pilgrimage': The Presence of Jacob Boehme's Christian Theosophy in William Blake's *The Four Zoas.*" Master's thesis, University College of Swansea, 1979.

Gibbons, B. J. *Gender in Mystical and Occult Thought: Behmenism and Its Development in England.* Cambridge: Cambridge University Press, 1996.

Haldane, Elizabeth S. *Jacob Böhme and His Relation to Hegel.* Boston: Ginn and Co., 1897.

Hartmann, Franz. *The Life and Doctrines of Jacob Boehme. The God Taught Philosopher. An Introduction to the Study of His Works.* London: Kegan Paul, 1891.

Hegel, G. W. F. *Lectures on the History of Philosophy.* Translated by Elizabeth S. Haldane and Frances H. Simpson. Vol. 3. London: Kegan Paul, Trench, Trübner and Co., 1896.

Jones, Rufus M. *Spiritual Reformers in the Sixteenth and Seventeenth Centuries.* London: Macmillan, 1914.

Martensen, Hans Lassen. *Jacob Boehme: His Life and Teaching.* Translated by T. Rhys Evans. London, 1885.

Miller, Arlene A. "Jacob Boehme: From Orthodoxy to Enlightenment." Ph.D. diss., Stanford University, 1971.

Muses, C. A. *Illumination on Jacob Boehme: The Works of Dionysius Andreas Freher.* New York: King's Crown Press, 1951.

Okely, Francis. *Memoir of the Life, Death, Burial and Wonderful Writings of Jacob Behmen.* Northampton, 1780.

Penny, A. J. *Studies in Jacob Böhme.* London: John M. Watkins, 1912.

Popper, Hans. "Jacob Boehme's Doctrine of a Natural Language ('*Natursprache*'): With special reference to its influence on Novalis and Others." Ph.D. diss., University of Bristol, 1958.

Pordage, John. *A Compendious View of the Grounds of the Teutonic Philosophy. With Consideration by way of Enquiry into the Subject matter and Scope of the writings of Jacob Behmen . . . Also several extracts from his writings.* London, 1770. This is a reprint of *A Treatise of Eternal Nature with Her seven Essential Forms.* London, 1681.

Shepheard, Harold B. *In Jacob Behmen's School.* London: Dent, 1926.

Souders, Bruce C. "The Reappearance of Jacob Boehme in the Work of William Law, William Blake and W. B. Yeats." Master's thesis, Columbia University, 1953.

Stoudt, John Joseph. *Sunrise to Eternity: A Study of Jacob Boehme's Life and Thought.* Philadelphia: University of Pennsylvania Press, 1957.

Swainson, W. P. *Jacob Boehme: The Teutonic Philosopher.* 1905. Reprint, London: Rider, 1921.

Taylor, Edward. *Jacob Boehme's Theosophick Philosophy Unfolded.* London, 1691.

Walsh, David. *The Mysticism of Innerworldly Fulfillment: A Study of Jacob Boehme.* Gainsville: University Press of Florida, 1983.

Weeks, Andrew. *Boehme: An Intellectual Biography of the Seventeenth Century Philosophical Mystic.* Albany, N.Y.: SUNY Press, 1991.

WILLIAM BLAKE

Works

Bindman, David, ed. *The Complete Graphic Works of William Blake.* London: Thames and Hudson, 1978.

Ellis, E. J., and W. B. Yeats, eds. *The Works of William Blake: Poetic, Symbolic, and Critical.* 3 vols. London: Quatrich, 1893.

Erdman, David V., ed. *The Complete Poetry and Prose of William Blake.* Rev. ed. New York: Doubleday, Anchor Press, 1982.

———. *The Illuminated Blake.* London: Oxford University Press, 1974.

Keynes, Geoffrey, ed. *Complete Writings with variant readings.* Oxford: Oxford University Press, 1966.

Bibliographies and Concordance

Bentley, G. E. Jr. *Blake Books: Annotated Catalogues of William Blake's Writings.* Oxford: Clarendon Press, 1977.

Bentley, G. E. Jr., and Martin K. Nurmi. *A Blake Bibliography: Annotated Lists of Works, Studies and Blakeana.* Minneapolis: University of Minnesota Press, 1964.

Erdman, David V. *A Concordance to the Writings of William Blake.* 2 vols. Ithaca : Cornell University Press, 1967.

Criticism and Biography

Adams, Hazard. *Blake and Yeats: The Contrary Vision.* Ithaca: Cornell University Press, 1954.

Allis, Una. "William Blake's Concept of Vision." Ph.D. diss., University of Manchester, 1981.

Altizer, Thomas J. J. *The New Apocalypse: The Radical Christian Vision of William Blake.* East Lansing: Michigan State University Press, 1967.

Beer, John. *Blake's Humanism.* Manchester: University of Manchester Press, 1968.

———. *Blake's Visionary Universe.* Manchester: Manchester University Press, 1969.

Bellin, Harvey F., and Darrell Ruhl, eds. *Blake and Swedenborg: Opposition Is True Friendship—An Anthology.* New York: Swedenborg Foundation, 1985.

Bentley, G. E. Jr. *Blake Records.* Oxford: Clarendon Press, 1969.

———. "William Blake and the Alchemical Philosophers." B. Litt. thesis, University of Oxford, 1954.

Berger, P. *William Blake: Poet and Mystic.* London: Chapman and Hall, 1914.

Bindman, David. *Blake as an Artist.* New York: E. P. Dutton, 1977.

Bloom, Harold. *Blake's Apocalypse: A Study in Poetic Argument.* London: Victor Gollancz, 1963.

Bottrall, Margaret. *The Divine Image: A Study of Blake's Interpretation of Christianity.* Rome: Edizioni Di Storia E Letteratura, 1950.

Bronowski, J. *William Blake: A Man Without a Mask.* London: Secker and Warburg, 1944.

Cox, Stephen. *Love and Logic: The Evolution of Blake's Thought.* Ann Arbor: University of Michigan Press, 1992.

Crehan, Stewart. *Blake in Context.* Dublin: Gill and Macmillan Humanities Press, 1984.

Damon, S. Foster. *A Blake Dictionary: The Ideas and Symbols of William Blake.* London: Thames and Hudson, 1973. Reprint, 1979.

———. *William Blake: His Philosophy and Symbols.* London: Constable, 1924.

Damrosch, Leopold, Jr. *Symbol and Truth in Blake's Myth.* Princeton: Princeton University Press, 1980.

Davies, D. G. *The Theology of William Blake.* Oxford: Clarendon Press, 1948.

De Luca, Vincent Arthur. *Words of Eternity: Blake and the Poetics of the Sublime.* Princeton: Princeton University Press, 1991.

Erdman, David V. *Prophet Against Empire: A Poet's Interpretation of the History of His Own Times.* Rev. ed. Princeton: Princeton University Press, 1969.

Erdman, David V., and John E. Grant, eds. *Blake's Visionary Forms Dramatic.* Princeton: Princeton University Press, 1970.

Fisher, Peter F. *The Valley of Vision: Blake as Prophet and Revolutionary.* Toronto: University of Toronto Press, 1961.

Frosch, Thomas R. *The Awakening of Albion: The Renovation of the Body in the Poetry of William Blake.* Ithaca: Cornell University Press, 1974.

Frye, Northrop. *Fearful Symmetry: A Study of William Blake.* Princeton: Princeton University Press, 1947.

Gallant, Christine. *Blake and the Assimilation of Chaos.* Princeton: Princeton University Press, 1978.

Gilchrist, Alexander. *Life of William Blake.* 1863. Reprint, edited by Ruthven Todd. London: Dent Everyman Library, 1942.

Gillham, D. G. *Blake's Contrary States: The "Songs of Innocence and of Experience" as Dramatic Poems.* Cambridge: Cambridge University Press, 1966.

Hagstrum, Jean H. *William Blake, Poet and Painter: An Introduction to the Illuminated Verse.* Chicago: University of Chicago Press, 1964.

Hamblen, Emily S. *On the Minor Prophecies of William Blake.* New York: Haskell House, 1968.

Harper, G. M. *The Neoplatonism of William Blake.* London: Oxford University Press, 1961.

Hilton, Nelson. *Literal Imagination: Blake's Vision of Words.* Berkeley and Los Angeles: University of California Press, 1983.

Hirst, Désirée. *Hidden Riches: Traditional Symbolism from the Renaissance to Blake.* London: Eyre and Spottiswoode, 1964.

Howard, John. *Blake's "Milton": A Study in Selfhood.* Rutherford, N.J.: Fairleigh Dickinson University Press, 1976.

Larrissy, Edward. *William Blake.* Oxford: Basil Blackwell, 1985.

Mee, Jon. *Dangerous Enthusiasm: William Blake and the Culture of Radicalism in the 1790s.* Oxford: Clarendon Press, 1992.

Morton, A. L. *The Everlasting Gospel: A Study in the Sources of William Blake.* London: Lawrence and Wishart, 1958.

Natoli, Joseph P. *Twentieth-Century Blake Criticism: Northrop Frye to the Present.* New York: Garland, 1982.

Nurmi, Martin K. *Blake's "The Marriage of Heaven and Hell": A Critical Study.* Kent: Kent State University Press, 1957.

Paley, Morton D. *The Continuing City: William Blake's Jerusalem.* Oxford: Clarendon Press, 1983.

———. *Energy and the Imagination: A Study in the Development of Blake's Thought.* London: Oxford University Press, 1970.

Paley, Morton D., and Michael Phillips, eds. *William Blake: Essays in Honour of Sir Geoffrey Keynes.* Oxford: Clarendon Press, 1973.

Percival, Milton O. *William Blake's Circle of Destiny.* 1938. Reprint, New York: Octagon Books, 1977.

Punter, David. *Blake, Hegel and Dialectic.* Amsterdam: Rudolphi, 1982.

Raine, Kathleen. *Blake and the New Age.* London: George Allen and Unwin, 1979.

———. *Blake and Tradition.* 2 vols. Princeton: Princeton University Press, 1968.

———. *From Blake to "A Vision."* Dublin: Dolmen Press, 1979.

———. *William Blake.* London: Thames and Hudson, 1970.

Rosenfeld, Alvin H., ed. *William Blake: Essays for S. Foster Damon.* Providence: Brown University Press, 1969.

Saurat, Denis. *Blake and Modern Thought.* London: Constable, 1929.

Schorer, Mark. *William Blake: The Politics of Vision.* New York, 1946. Reprint, Gloucester, Mass.: Peter Smith, 1975.

Singer, June K. *The Unholy Bible: A Psychological Interpretation of William Blake.* New York: Putnam's, 1970.

Singh, Charu Sheel. *The Chariot of Fire: A Study of William Blake in the Light of Hindu Thought* Salzburg: University of Salzburg, 1981.

Stevenson, Warren. *Divine Analogy: A Study of the Creative Motif in Blake and Coleridge.* Salzburg: Salzburg University, 1972.

———. *Romanticism and the Androgynous Sublime.* Madison, N.J.: Fairleigh Dickinson University Press, 1996.

Thompson, E. P. *Witness Against the Beast: William Blake and the Moral Law.* Cambridge: Cambridge University Press, 1993.

Trigilio, Tony. *"Strange Prophecies Anew": Rereading Apocalypse in Blake, H. D. and Ginsberg.* Madison, N.J.: Fairleigh Dickinson University Press, 2000.

Wellburn, A. J. "The Gnostic Imagination of William Blake: A Comparative and Typological Investigation into the Unity and Structure of Blake's Mythology." Ph.D. diss., Selwyn College, 1980.

White, Helen. *The Mysticism of William Blake.* Madison: University of Wisconsin, 1927.

Wilson, Mona. *The Life of William Blake.* 1927. Reprint, London: Granada, Paladin Books, 1978.

Witcutt, W. P. *Blake: A Psychological Study.* London: Hollis and Carter, 1946.

OTHER WORKS

Abrams, M. H. *Natural Supernaturalism: Tradition and Revolution in Romantic Literature.* London: Oxford University Press, 1971.

Altizer, Thomas J. J. *The Gospel of Christian Atheism.* London: Collins, 1967.

Angelus Silesius. *The Cherubinic Wanderer.* Translated by Mana Shrady. New York: Paulist Press, 1986.

Arnold, Matthew. *Essays, Literary and Critical.* 1906. Reprint, London: J. M. Dent and Sons, 1938.

Ashe, Geoffrey. *Camelot and the Vision of Albion.* London: Heinemann, 1971.

Ashmole, Elias, ed. *Theatrum Chemicum Britannicum: Containing Severall Poeticall Pieces of Our Famous English Philosophers, Who Have Written the Hermetique Mysteries in Their Owne Ancient Language.* London, 1652.

Atwood, Mary Anne. *A Suggestive Enquiry into Hermetic Mystery with a Dissertation on the More Celebrated of the Alchemical Philosophers.* London: John Watkins, 1918.

Augustine, Saint. *The Confessions.* Translated by E. B. Pusey. London: Dent Everyman Library, 1907.

Barclay, Robert. *The Inner Life of the Religious Societies of the Commonwealth.* London: Hodder and Stoughton, 1876.

Baxter, Richard. *The Autobiography of Richard Baxter.* Abridged by J. M. Lloyd Thomas. Edited by N. H. Keeble. London: Dent, 1931.

Beer, John, ed. *Coleridge's Variety: Bicentenary Studies.* London: Macmillan, 1974.

Berdyaev, Nicolas. *The Beginning and the End.* London: Geoffrey Bles, 1952.

———. *The Destiny of Man.* London: Geoffrey Bles, 1937.

———. *Freedom and the Spirit.* Translated by Oliver Fielding Clarke. London: Geoffrey Bles, 1955.

———. *The Meaning of the Creative Act.* Translated by Donald A. Lowrie. London: Victor Gollancz, 1955.

———. *Solitude and Society.* Translated by George Rearey. London: Geoffrey Bles, 1938.

Bullett, Gerald. *The English Mystics.* London: Michael Joseph, 1950.

Bultman, D. Rudolph. *History and Eschatology.* Edinburgh: Edinburgh University Press, 1957.

Byrom, John. *Miscellaneous Poems.* 2 vols. Manchester, 1773.

Churton, Tobias. *The Gnostics.* London: Weidenfeld and Nicolson, 1987.

The Cloud of Unknowing. Edited by James Walsh. London: SPCK, 1981.

Cohn, Norman. *The Pursuit of the Millennium: Revolutionary Millenarians and Mystical Anarchists of The Middle Ages.* London: Secker and Warburg, 1957.

Coleridge, Samuel Taylor. *Biographia Literaria: or Biographical Sketches of My Literary Life and Opinions.* Edited by James Engell and W. Jackson Bate. 2 bks. Vol. 7 of *The Collected Works of Samuel Taylor Coleridge.* London: Routledge and Kegan Paul, 1983.

———. *Marginalia.* Edited by George Whalley. 2 bks. Vol. 12 of *The Collected Works of Samuel Taylor Coleridge.* London: Routledge and Kegan Paul, 1983.

———. *The Philosophical Lectures of Samuel Taylor Coleridge.* Edited by Kathleen Coburn. London: Pilot Press, 1949.

Cooke, Michael G. *The Romantic Will.* New Haven: Yale University Press, 1976.

Cox, Michael. *Mysticism: The Direct Experience of God.* Northamptonshire: Aquarian Press, 1983.

Davie, Donald. *A Gathered Church: The Literature of the English Dissenting Interest—1770–1930.* London: Routledge and Kegan Paul, 1978.

Dobbs, Betty Jo Teeter. *The Foundation of Newton's Alchemy in "The Hunting of the Greene Lyon."* Cambridge: Cambridge University Press, 1975.

Duché, Jacob. *Discouses on Various Subjects.* 2 vols. London, 1779.

Eckhart, Meister. *The Essential Sermons, Commentaries, Treatises, and Defense.* Translated by Edmund Colledge and Bernard McGinn. New York: Paulist Press, 1981.

Eliot, T. S. *The Sacred Wood: Essays on Poetry and Criticism.* 1920. Reprint, London: Methuen, 1948.

Emerson, Ralph Waldo. *Representative Men: Seven Lectures.* Vol. 4 of *The Complete Works of Ralph Waldo Emerson.* Boston: Houghton Mifflin Company, 1903.

Fawcett, Thomas. *The Symbolic Language of Religion: An Introductory Study.* London: SCM Press, 1970.

Fox, George. *The Journal of George Fox.* Edited by N. Penney. 2 vols. Cambridge: Cambridge University Press, 1911.

Frye, Northrop. *The Stubborn Structure of the Language: Essays on Criticism and Society.* London: Methuen, 1970.

Grant, Patrick. *A Dazzling Darkness: An Anthology of Western Mysticism.* London: Collins, Faust Paperbacks, 1985.

———. *Literature of Mysticism in Western Tradition.* London: Macmillan, 1983.

Happold, F. C. *Mysticism: A Study and an Anthology.* Harmondsworth: Penguin Books, 1963.

Harrison, J. F. C. *The Second Coming: Popular Millenarianism, 1780–1850.* London: Routledge and Kegan Paul, 1979. Quoting W. B. Harrison, *A Letter* [on] *the Divine Mission of the late Joanna Southcott* (Leeds, 1842).

Hartmann, Franz. *The Life and the Doctrines of Philippus Theophrastus, Bombast of Hohenheim,Known by the Name of Paracelsus.* New York: Theosophical Publishing Company, 1918.

Hill, Christopher. *The Experience of Defeat: Milton and Some Contemporaries.* London: Faber and Faber, 1984.

———. *The World Turned Upside Down: Radical Ideas during The English Revolution.* London: Temple Smith, 1972. Quoting T. Hall, *Vindiciae Literarum.* Np., nd.

———. *Writing and Revolution in Seventeenth-Century England.* Vol. 1 of *The Collected Essays of Christopher Hill.* Brighton: Harvester Press, 1985.

Hitchcock, Ethan Allen. *Remarks upon Alchemy and the Alchemists.* Boston: Crosby and Nichols, 1857.

Hobhouse, Stephen. *William Law and Eighteenth-Century Quakerism—including some unpublished letters and fragments of William Law and John Byrom.* London: George Allen and Unwin, 1927.

Hone, Joseph. *W. B. Yeats: 1865–1939.* London: Macmillan, 1943. Reprint, Harmondsworth: Pelican Books, 1971.

Hoyles, John. *The Edge of Augustinism: The Aesthetics of Thomas Ken, John Byrom and William Law.*The Hague: Martinus Nijhoff, 1972.

Huxley, Aldous. *The Perennial Philosophy.* London: Chatto and Windus, 1946.

Inge, William Ralph. *Christian Mysticism.* London: Methuen, 1899.

James, William. *The Varieties of Religious Experience.* London: Longmans and Green, 1902.

Jonas, Hans. *The Gnostic Religion: The Message of the Alien God and the Beginning of Christianity.*Boston: Beacon Press, 1958.

Jones, Rufus M. *Studies in Mystical Religion.* London: Macmillan, 1909.

Julian of Norwich. *Revelations of Divine Love.* Translated by Clifton Wolters. Harmondsworth: Penguin Books, 1966.

Jung, C. G. *Alchemical Studies.* Vol. 13 of *The Collected Works of C. G. Jung.* Translated by R. F. C. Hull. Edited by Herbert Read, Michael Fordham, Gerhard Adler, and William McGuire. London: Routledge and Kegan Paul, 1967.

———. *Psychology and Alchemy.* Rev. ed. Vol. 12 of *The Collected Works of C. G. Jung.* Translated by R. F. C. Hull. Edited by Herbert Read, Michael Fordham, Gerhard Adler, and William McGuire. London: Routledge and Kegan Paul, 1980.

Kahn, Charles H., ed. *The Art and Thought of Heraclitus: An edition of the fragments with translation and commentary.* Cambridge: Cambridge University Press, 1979.

Law, William. *Selected Mystical Writings of William Law: Edited with Notes and Twenty-Four Studies In the Mystical Theology of William Law and Jacob Boehme by Stephen Hobhouse.* London: C.W. Daniel, 1938.

———. *The Works of the Reverend William Law, M.A.* 9 vols. London, 1753–56. Reprint, Canterbury, 1892–93.

Lawrence. D. H. *Apocalypse.* London: Granada, 1981.

Lineham, Peter James. "The English Swedenborgians, 1770–1840: A Study of the Social Dimensions of Religious Sectarianism." Ph.D. diss., University of Sussex, 1978.

Marx, Karl, and Friedrich Engels. *On Religion.* Moscow: Progress Publishers, 1957.

Milton, John. *The Poems of John Milton.* Edited by John Carey and Alastair Fowler. London: Longmans and Green, 1968.

Morton, A. L. *The World of the Ranters: Religious Radicalism in the English Revolution.* London: Lawrence and Wishart, 1970.

Overton, J. H. *William Law: Nonjuror and Mystic—A Sketch of His Life, Character and Opinions.* London: Longmans and Green, 1881.

Pachter, Henry M. *Paracelsus: Magic into Science.* New York: Henry Schuman, 1951.

Pagel, W. *Paracelsus: An Introduction to Philosophical Medicine in the Era of the Renaissance.* Basel and New York: S. Karger, 1958.

Paglia, Camille. *Sexual Personae: Art and Decadence from Nefertiti to Emily Dickinson.* New Haven: Yale University Press, 1990.

Paracelsus. *The Hermetic and Alchemical Writings of Aureolus Philippus Theophrastus Bombast of Hohenheim, called Paracelsus the Great.* Edited by A. E. Waite. 2 vols. London: James Eliot, 1894.

———. *Paracelsus: Selected Writings.* Translated by Norbert Guterman. Edited by Jolande Jacobi. Princeton: Princeton University Press, 1988.

Parrinder, Geoffrey. *Mysticism in the World's Religions.* London: Sheldon Press, 1976.

Pistorius, P. V. *Plotinus and Neoplatonism: An Introductory Study.* Cambridge: Bowes and Bowes, 1952.

Plato. *The Last Days of Socrates: Euthyphro, The Apology, Crito and Phaedo.* Translated by Hugh Tredennick. Harmondsworth: Penguin Books, 1959.

———. *The Republic.* Translated by Desmond Lee. Harmondsworth: Penguin Books, 1974.

———. *The Timaeus and the Critias or Atlanticus.* Translated by Thomas Taylor. Washington, D.C.: Pantheon Books, 1944.

Plotinus. *The Enneads.* Translated by Stephen MacKenna. Edited by John Dillon. Rev. ed. Harmondsworth: Penguin Books, 1991.

Price, Martin. *To the Palace of Wisdom: Studies in Order and Energy from Dryden to Blake.* London and Amsterdam: Southern University Press, 1964.

Read, John. *The Alchemist in Life, Literature and Art.* London: Nelson and Sons, 1947.

———. *Prelude to Chemistry: An Outline of Alchemy, Its Literature and Relationships.* London: G. Bell, 1936.

Reeves, Marjorie, and Warwick Gould. *Joachim of Fiore and the Myth of the Everlasting Evangel in the Nineteenth Century.* Oxford: Clarendon Press, 1987.

Robinson, Henry Crabb. *Diaries, Reminiscences, and Correspondences of Henry Crabb Robinson.*Edited by Thomas Sadler. 3 vols. London: Macmillan, 1869.

Rolle, Richard. *The Fire of Love.* Translated by Clifton Wolters. Harmondsworth: Penguin Books, 1972.

Roston, Murray. *Prophet and Poet: The Bible and the Growth of Romanticism.* Evanston: Northwestern University Press, 1965.

Rudolph, Kurt. *Gnosis:The Nature and History of an Ancient Religion.* Translated by Robert McLachlan Wilson, P. W. Coxon, and K. H. Khan. Edinburgh: T & T Clark, 1983.

Ruusbroec, John. *The Spiritual Espousals and Other Works.* Translated by James A. Wiseman. New York: Paulist Press, 1985.

Saurat, Denis. *Literature and the Occult Tradition.* Translated by Dorothy Bolton. London: G. Bell, 1930.

Schelling, F. W. J. *Philosophical Inquiries into the Nature of Human Freedom.* Translated by James Gutman. Chicago: Open Court Publishing Company, 1936.

Scholem, Gershom. *Kabbalah.* New York: Quadrangle/New York Times Book Company, 1974.

———. *Major Trends in Jewish Mysticism.* Jerusalem: Schocken Publishing House, 1941.

Spalding, John Howard. *Introduction to Swedenborg's Religious Thought.* New York: Swedenborg Foundation, 1956.

Spurgeon, Caroline F. E. *Mysticism in English Literature.* Cambridge: Cambridge University Press, 1913.

Stace, W. T. *Mysticism and Philosophy.* London: Macmillan, 1961.

Suso, Henry. *Little Book of Eternal Wisdom and Little Book of Truth.* Translated by J. M. Clark. London: Faber and Faber, 1953.

Swedenborg, Emanuel. *A Compendium of the Theological Writings of Emanuel Swedenborg.* Edited by Samuel M. Warren. 1875. Reprint, New York: Swedenborg Foundation, 1979.

———. *A Treatise concerning Heaven and Hell, and of the Wonderful Things therein,* Translated by William Cookworthy and Thomas Hartley. London, 1784.

———. *The Wisdom of Angels, concerning Divine Love and Divine Wisdom.* Translated by N. Tucker. 1788. Reprint, London, 1816.

Tafel, Dr. J. F. I. *Documents Concerning the Life and Character of Emanuel Swedenborg.* Edited by Rev. I. H. Smith. Manchester: Joseph Hayward, 1841.

Tauler, John. *The Following of Christ.* Translated by J. R. Morell. London: T. Fisher Unwin, 1886.

Tawney, R. H. *Religion and the Rise of Capitalism: A Historical Study.* London: John Murray, 1926.

Taylor, F. Sherwood. *The Alchemists.* London: William Heinemann, 1952.

The Theologia Germanica of Martin Luther. Translated by Beng and Hoffman. London: Paulist Press, 1980.

Tillich, Paul. *Theologian of the Boundaries.* Edited by Mark Kline Taylor. London: Collins, 1987.

Toksvig, Signe. *Emanuel Swedenborg: Scientist and Mystic.* London: Faber and Faber, 1949.

Traherne, Thomas. *Centuries.* Oxford: Clarendon Press, 1960. Reprint, London: Mowbray, 1985.

Underhill, Evelyn. *Mysticism: A Study in the Nature and Development of Man's SpiritualConsciousness.* London: Methuen, 1911.

———. *The Mystics of the Church.* London: James Clarke, n.d..

———. *The Mystic Way: A Psychological Study in Christian Origins.* London: Dent, 1913.

Vaughan, Thomas. *The Works of Thomas Vaughan: Eugenius Philalethes.* Edited by A. E. Waite. 1919. Reprint, New York: University Books, 1968.

Waite, A. E. *The Holy Kabbalah.* Secaucus, N.J.: Citadel Press, University Books, n.d.

———. *Lives of the Alchemistical Philosophers: Based on Material Collected in 1815 and Supplemented by recent researches.* London: George Redway, 1888.

Walker, A. Keith. *William Law: His Life and Thought.* London: SPCK, 1973.

Walker, D. P. *The Ancient Theology: Studies in Christian Platonism from the Fifteenth to the Eighteenth Century.* London: Duckworth, 1972.

———. *The Decline of Hell: Seventeenth-Century Discussion of Eternal Torment.* London: Routledge and Kegan Paul, 1964.

Walton, Christopher. *Notes and Materials for an Adequate Biography of the Celebrated and Divine Theosopher William Law.* London, 1854.

White, William. *Emanuel Swedenborg: His Life and Writings.* 2 vols. London: Simpkin and Marshall, 1867.

Wildes, Harry Emerson. *Voice of the Lord: A Biography of George Fox.* Philadelphia: University of Pennsylvania Press; London: Oxford University Press, 1965.

Winstanley, Gerrard. *The Works of Gerrard Winstanley.* Edited by George H. Sabine. New York: Russell and Russell, 1965.

Yates, Frances A. *The Rosicrucian Enlightenment.* London: Routledge and Kegan Paul, 1972.

Yeats, W. B. *Essays and Introductions.* London: Macmillan, 1961.

Zaehner, R. C. *Dialectical Christianity and Christian Materialism.* London: Oxford University Press, 1971.

Zohar: The Book of Enlightenment. Translated and edited by Daniel Chanan Matt. Ramsey, N.J.: Paulist Press, 1983.

Index